Tourism and the Environment

Issues in tourism series
Edited by Brian Goodall, *University of Reading* and
Gregory Ashworth, *University of Groningen,*
The Netherlands.

The Advisory Board includes K.H. Din, *University of
Kedangsaan,* Malaysia; C.R. Goeldner, *University of
Colorado,* USA; J. Jafari, *University of Wisconsin,* USA;
and D.G. Pearce, *University of Canterbury,* New Zealand.

The growing significance of tourism as an economic activity is
reflected in the increased recognition it has been given at national
and local levels. There has been a rapid development of specialist
educational and training facilities for academics and professionals,
including widespread research activity, and the discipline could
now be said to have 'come of age'. The books in this series provide
rigorous, focused discussions of key topics in current international
debates on tourism. They tackle the social, economic and environmental consequences of the rapid developments, taking account
of what has happened so far and looking ahead to future prospects. The series caters for all those wanting to understand what is
happening at the forefront of the field and how it will filter
through to general tourism practice.

Other titles in the series

Tourism Research
Critiques and Challenges
Edited by Douglas Pearce and Richard Butler

Change in Tourism
Peoples, Places, Processes
Edited by Douglas Pearce and Richard Butler

Tourism and Heritage Attractions
Richard Prentice

Tourism and the Environment

A sustainable relationship?

Colin Hunter and Howard Green

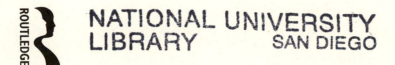

London and New York

First published 1995
by Routledge
11 New Fetter Lane, London EC4P 4EE

Simultaneously published in the USA and Canada
by Routledge
29 West 35th Street, New York, NY 10001

© 1995 Colin Hunter and Howard Green

Typeset in Times by
J&L Composition Ltd, Filey, North Yorkshire.

Printed and bound in Great Britain by
TJ Press (Padstow) Ltd, Padstow, Cornwall.

British Library Cataloguing in Publication Data
A catalogue record for this book is available from the British Library

Library of Congress Cataloguing in Publication Data
A catalogue record for this book has been requested

ISBN 0–415–08524–1

Contents

List of figures and tables   vii
Preface   ix

1 Introduction   1
Colin Hunter and Howard Green
The nature of tourism   1
Tourism and environmental resources   6

2 The environmental impacts of tourism   10
Colin Hunter and Howard Green
Introduction   10
The environmental resource base for tourism   10
The nature of tourism impacts   12
Impacts on the natural environment   13
Impacts on the built environment   27
Impacts on the cultural environment   33
An overview of tourism impacts and the impact literature   40
Impact amelioration measures   47

3 Key concepts for tourism and the environment   52
Colin Hunter
Introduction   52
The general concept of sustainable development   52
Sustainable development and tourism carrying capacity   63
Sustainable tourism development   69
Alternative tourism   78
Issues in the implementation of sustainable tourism
    development   86

4 Planning for sustainable tourism development   93
Howard Green
Introduction   93
Planning and tourism   94
Land use planning   96
National plans and policies   98
Land use planning at the local level   99
Land use planning: international comparison   119

5 Environmental impact assessment and tourism development   122
Colin Hunter
Introduction   122
Background to EIA   123
Basic features of an EIA system   130
EIA methods and techniques   136
Tourism and community involvement through EIA   157
Issues in the use of EIA   164

6 Conclusions   169
Colin Hunter

Bibliography   183
Index   203

Figures and tables

FIGURES

3.1 A schematic representation of Butler's model of the evolution of tourism development at a destination area   64

3.2 Overview of the main policy instruments in tourism management   88

5.1 An extract from a quantified and graded environmental impact matrix   145

5.2 An extract from an impact network associated with dredging for a marina development   147

TABLES

1.1 A classification of the main types of activity representing aspects of tourist demand   3

1.2 The development of international tourism arrivals and receipts world-wide   4

1.3 Changes in international tourist arrivals to selected countries between 1985 and 1990   5

2.1 Some major potential impacts of tourism on the natural environment   14

2.2 Some major potential impacts of tourism on the built environment   28

2.3 Some major potential impacts of tourism on the cultural environment   35

3.1 A summary of the goals and legal principles of sustainable development, as proposed by the World Commission on Environment and Development (1987)   56

3.2   Examples of practical measures for businesses to
      minimise the environmental impacts of tourism
      beyond the destination area   79
3.3   Attributes of mass and alternative tourism   81
3.4   The potential advantages and disadvantages of
      different approaches to the environmental
      management of tourism   87
4.1   A model land use planning structure   97
4.2   The importance of tourism in Malaysian Structure
      Plans   103
5.1   Basic features of an EIA system   131
5.2   Extracts from a checklist of the potential
      environmental impacts of a marina/resort complex   140
5.3   Extracts from a scaling checklist of the general
      impacts of tourism in the Patara Valley, Turkey   141
5.4a Impact matrix for the construction phase of a
      tourist railway development in Norfolk, England   143
5.4b Impact matrix for the operational phase of a tourist
      railway development in Norfolk, England   143
5.5   Extracts from a matrix showing the general impacts
      of tourism in the Patara Valley, Turkey   144
5.6   Examples of impact magnitude prediction
      techniques used in EIA   155

Preface

The last two or three decades have witnessed a growing interest in the relationship between tourism development and environmental quality; an interest driven by a number of factors including the rapid growth in tourism activity around the world and an enhanced awareness of the, frequently negative, impacts of mass tourism on environmental resources. The search for ways to better integrate the needs of tourism with the protection of environmental resources has been given further recent impetus by the emergence of sustainable development as a management concept. Consequently, there now exists a substantial volume of literature on the meaning, implications and implementation of sustainable tourism development, encompassing both new forms of alternative tourism and the management of existing mass tourism centres.

This book is an attempt to provide a timely, research-based overview and analysis of the relationship between tourism development and environmental quality, taking sustainable tourism development as its central theme. As well as reviewing much of the relevant tourism and environmental management literature, the text draws on several years of research and consultancy work by the authors, and on discussions held at a number of international tourism conferences. It is the hope of the authors that the book will appeal to a wide audience including academics, professionals involved in the tourism industry, and decision-makers at local and central levels of government.

Following a review of the impacts of tourism on the quality of the natural, built and cultural resources which support tourism, the general concept of sustainable development is examined as a prelude to a detailed treatment of the principles and implications of sustainable tourism development. Appropriate policy directions for sustainable tourism development are indicated, with new forms of alternative tourism analysed within this context. The book then proceeds to consider the potential of land use planning and Environmental Impact Assessment (EIA) systems as instruments in the translation of principles of sustainable tourism development into practice. The authors recognise that much of the discussion in the book of land use planning and EIA centres around the potential, rather than the actual, role and utilisation of these management tools. This reflects the unfortunate dearth of detailed case study material currently available in the tourism literature, and is indicative of the relatively late recognition, by many policy-makers and others with an interest in tourism, of the environmental implications and practical management of tourism developments.

Finally, we would like to thank Brian Goodall for his valuable comments on the manuscript, and the editorial and production staff at Routledge for their help and patience. Naturally, we accept full responsibility for the text ourselves.

Chapter 1

Introduction

Colin Hunter and Howard Green

This book is about the relationship between tourism and environmental quality. More specifically, it seeks to examine the impacts of tourists and the tourism industry on environmental resources, and some key concepts and techniques for the better environmental management of tourism. The search for ways to integrate the demands of tourism development with environmental protection is critical, and of growing relevance to all those with an interest in tourism. This contention is based upon a number of inter-related factors, including:

- the direct and indirect reliance of tourism on a wide range of environmental resources;
- a heightened awareness of environmental issues and problems over the last three decades amongst the general public, politicians, decision-makers, etc.; and,
- the very rapid growth of tourism activity around the world since the Second World War combined with an increasing awareness of the frequently negative impacts of tourism on environmental quality.

Before going on to expand on these factors later in this chapter, it is important to begin with a statement of the interpretations of 'tourist' and the 'tourism industry' used throughout this book.

THE NATURE OF TOURISM

There is no universally accepted definition of tourism. This is not surprising, since what constitutes a 'tourist' and the 'tourism industry' are still matters of debate. Detailed reviews of the evolution of the interpretation of these words are provided elsewhere (e.g. Smith 1989; Gilbert 1990). For the purposes of this book, broad interpretations are employed. Frequently, the tourist is regarded as belonging to a wider sub-set comprising visitors (non-residents) and travellers. Throughout this book, the term 'tourist' is used to describe any visitor of relevance to the study of travel and tourism. Thus, following the classification of Chadwick (1987), the word 'tourist' is used to describe any person who travels for the primary purpose of:

- business (e.g. consultations, conventions and inspections);
- other personal business (e.g. shopping, medical or legal appointment or an educational study trip);
- visiting friends or relatives (primary activities might include socialising, dining out or home entertainment, for example); and,
- pleasure (e.g. sport, recreation, sightseeing and dining out).

As long as such a traveller is visiting (for less than one year) an unfamiliar community (the host community) from that in which the person normally resides, then that person may be regarded as being a tourist. The view of the tourist adopted in this book encompasses day visitors (excursionists) as well as those who visit a host community for one or more nights. The tourist trip may be international (either continental or inter-continental) or domestic (either regional or inter-regional). Other travellers, not within the scope of tourism, include commuters, crews of airlines and ships who do not stop over and visit another community, migrants, temporary workers, military personnel, refugees and students travelling between home and their place of education (Chadwick 1987; Smith 1989). In other words, those outwith the scope of tourism can be excluded because their travel is very short, usually does not involve the use of tourism businesses and is not affected by tourism promotions (Smith 1989). Relatedly, the tourist demands a range of (one or more) activities in the destination area which other travellers do not require specifically from that area. Gilbert (1990) provides a classification of the main types of activities which the tourist may demand of a destination area. These are summarised in Table 1.1.

Frequent mention is made in the tourism literature of the tourism industry. The idea of tourism as a single industry has come in for criticism, with some authors suggesting that tourism cannot properly be described as an industry because it does not

Table 1.1 A classification of the main types of activity representing aspects of tourist demand

Demand	Main types of activity
Communing with nature	demand for open areas, parks, commons, rambling, walking, etc.
Attractions	visiting zoos, safari parks, waxworks, theme parks, etc.
Heritage	visiting castles, stately homes, museums, ancient monuments, religious sites, galleries and battlefields.
Sport activity	taking part in or watching various forms of indoor or outdoor sport including those of a specifically rural or urban nature. These would include; ten-pin bowling, fishing, sailing, golf, shooting, swimming, surfboarding, motor racing, football, cricket, etc.
Entertainment	other than sport, this would include visits to the cinema, theatre, bars, concerts, discos, restaurants, etc.
Relaxation	sunbathing, resting, reading, etc.
Health	taking healthcare treatment, saunas, massage, therapy. Includes moral health such as religion and pilgrimages, etc.
Shopping	browsing, souvenir or antique hunting, special-purchase trips for new outfits, gifts, new high-cost equipment, etc.
Business activities	meetings, conferences, exhibitions, etc.

Source: modified from Gilbert (1990)

produce a single, distinct product (e.g. Jefferson and Lickorish 1988). Certainly, tourism as an industry is difficult to define. Gilbert (1990), suggests that this difficulty of definition arises from the very broad nature of both tourism as a concept and of the service inputs involved in satisfying tourist demands and needs. Tourism embraces various other trades and industries, including the airline, rail, cruise, accommodation and food service industries. It also involves tour wholesalers, retailers and a variety of attractions, as well as a wide range of other private and public services and facilities. Some of these service inputs are crucial to tourism, while others are peripheral or supportive. Moreover, many services required for tourism, such as those associated with catering and transport, are also used by non-tourists. Gilbert (1990) also argues that tourism requires a range of essentially non-industrial resources which provide an input to the tourism product. Such 'free' resources include climate, scenery, beaches, wildlife and the culture of the host community.

Tourism is, therefore, a nebulous phenomenon, characterised by an amalgam of fragmented trades, organisations and activities. However, tourism can be viewed as an industry in itself. In the words of Gilbert:

> tourism while having no clear boundary delineations or concise conceptual clarification does, due to the overall size and impact of spatial and temporal movements of people with varying service needs for shelter, sustenance, entertainment and travel, produce the basis of an industry.
>
> (Gilbert 1990: 17)

The phrase 'tourism industry' is employed throughout this book in a broad sense to represent the amalgam of services and resources used by tourists.

Tourism has become one of the world's biggest industries, and is a major, if dynamic, component of the world economy. Already, in terms of direct and indirect employment generation, tourism is the largest industry in the world, and could become the largest single sector of world trade early in the next century (Lascurain 1991; Morrison and Selman 1991). For many countries, tourism has become an important means of promoting economic development and a major source of foreign currency. The growth in the importance of tourism to the world economy is illustrated in Table1.2. According to Latham (1990), the best estimates for

Table 1.2 The development of international tourism arrivals and receipts world-wide

Year	Tourist arrivals 1,000s	Tourism receipts* mill. $US
1950	25,282	2,100
1960	69,296	6,867
1970	159,690	17,900
1980	284,841	102,372
1990	429,250	249,300

*excluding international fare receipts.
Source: WTO (1991)

the late 1980s suggest that, world-wide, the annual expenditure on domestic and international tourism combined amounted to some US $2,000 billion (with domestic tourism accounting for approximately 90 per cent of this total). This represents some 12 per cent of world GDP, or more than twice what is spent annually on defence world-wide.

The phenomenal growth in standardised and rigidly purchased (mass) tourism since the Second World War can be attributed to a number of factors, including increased paid leave from employment and increased disposable income in Developed Countries, the arrival of the commercial jet aircraft in 1958, promotional fares, cheap oil and the entry of multi-national companies to the tourism industry (Poon 1989). Most international tourists originate from Developed Countries, with Germany, the USA, the UK and Japan being particularly noteworthy. In terms of international tourist arrivals, Europe is the dominant host region, followed by the Americas, East Asia and the Pacific, Africa, the Middle East and South Asia. However, international tourism is dynamic and some world regions have grown faster than others in recent decades, in terms of international tourist arrivals. Most notably, East Asia and the Pacific has increased its market share significantly, largely at the expense of the Americas where growth has been slower (Latham 1990). Considerable national variations do, however, exist within statistics for world regions. The relative position of many countries is changing rapidly, as indicated by

Table 1.3 Changes in international tourist arrivals to selected countries between 1985 and 1990

Country	Arrivals in 1985 1,000s	Rank in 1985	Arrivals in 1990 1,000s	Rank in 1990
Turkey	2,230	26	4,799	22
Malaysia	2,933	20	7,477	16
Thailand	2,438	25	5,299	20
Korea	1,426	36	2,959	29
Indonesia	749	49	2,178	35
Botswana	327	60	844	55
Malta	518	58	872	53
Dominican R.	660	53	1,533	42
Cyprus	770	47	1,561	41

Source: WTO (1992)

the data in Table 1.3. The fastest rates of growth in international tourism are often found in Developing Countries. The international tourist market is also dynamic in the sense that recent years have seen a growth in interest in forms of tourism which provide alternatives to mass tourism. Such alternative tourism is discussed in detail in Chapter 3.

TOURISM AND ENVIRONMENTAL RESOURCES

Given the huge growth in, and scale of, tourism activity around the world, and the likelihood that international tourism will continue to grow for the foreseeable future (Latham 1990), the impact of tourism on environmental quality should be of interest and relevance to academics, decision-makers and tourism operators alike. The ever more apparent concern amongst the general public about environmental issues and problems, such as pollution and habitat destruction, is reason enough for those involved with tourism to show an interest in the relationship between tourism development and the use of environmental resources. This is because tourism utilises environmental resources and may be prone to changing attitudes towards environmental quality amongst both tourists and the communities which host them.

The reliance of tourism on environmental resources is not difficult to appreciate. Frequently, tourism has grown in areas able to offer distinct and attractive environmental characteristics. Romeril (1985), for example, states that natural assets and attractions, such as 'sun, sea and sand', have usually been the major reason for a destination's popularity. Similarly, Morrison and Selman (1991) suggest that tourism tends to develop in areas which are able to provide natural amenities, together with human assets such as exotic cultures and historic sites. Indeed, there is no tourist activity which does not rely on environmental resources in some way. All of the activities in Table 1.1, for example, involve the use of natural or human resources. The natural and built environments not only provide features which attract tourists directly, but also support tourism by serving other functions. For example, natural resources are used to supply tourists with heat, power, food, laundry facilities, sanitation facilities and drinking water. Similarly, the natural environment is called upon to absorb the wastes generated by tourists, including refuse, sewage and other effluents. Natural or built resources are not, however, either infinitely renewable or endlessly resilient to the pressures exerted on them by tourism. In other words, the pressures exerted on the environment by some tourism developments may be of such magnitude that tourism activity becomes unsustainable, and declines over the long term. Much of Chapter 2 is devoted to a review of the often deleterious effects of tourism on the environment, a topic which has received considerable attention in the tourism literature of the past two decades.

With the heightened awareness of environmental issues comes the possibility that tourists will become more discerning in their choice of destination area, and that host communities will become less amenable to the possibility of environmental degradation, even if tourism brings substantial economic and social benefits. It seems likely that pressure will grow to find ways of integrating tourism-generated economic development with the sympathetic management and use of environmental resources. The need to give greater consideration to the relationship between tourism development and environmental protection has been recognised in the tourism literature.

Liu *et al.* (1987), for example, studied the perceptions of residents to the impacts of tourism in Hawaii (a tourism-dominated island resort), North Wales (a modest tourism centre) and Istanbul (a diversified urban area with a rapidly growing tourism sector). The residents of Hawaii and North Wales ranked the protection of the environment as the highest priority, above cultural benefits, social costs and even economic benefits. It was concluded from this study that the protection of the environment is essential for the continued success of any tourism destination, since a positive attitude to tourism is required from the local community. With reference to the attitude of tourists, a number of researchers have concluded that tourists are becoming more discerning, seeking activities, arrangements and experiences which depend, crucially, on a high-quality physical and cultural environment (Romeril 1985; Tyler 1989; Grahn 1991). Indeed, Krippendorf (1987) argues that only an ecologically-minded tourism industry will safeguard its prospects for growth through the 1990s and into the next century.

Given the increasingly expressed view that tourism needs to become more environmentally-conscious, this book seeks to contribute to the growing debate on tourism development and the protection of environmental resources in the following ways.

Chapter 2, in adopting a broad interpretation of environmental resources of use to the tourism industry, provides a review of the impacts of tourism on the environment. This review is based upon recent studies from the tourism literature. Difficulties in assessing the environmental impacts of tourism are included, as are suggested impact amelioration measures. The review in this chapter also encompasses the broad range of opinion to be found in the literature concerning the relationship between tourism and environmental quality, and includes emerging policy prescriptions for the harmonisation of tourism development needs with concerns for the protection of environmental resources.

Chapter 3 builds upon the growing concern for tourism development to become more environmentally-conscious by considering the concept of sustainable tourism development. Following a description of the general concept of sustainable development, the principles underlying sustainable tourism development are considered in some detail, as are the policy implications of such a strategy. Within this context, the growing interest in 'alternative' forms of tourism is also examined, again based upon recent views expressed in the tourism literature. Finally, Chapter 3 considers some of the barriers to the realisation of sustainable tourism development.

The need for principles and policies of sustainable tourism development to be translated into appropriate action 'on the ground' provides the rational basis for Chapters 4 and 5. Chapter 4 provides an overview of the potential contribution of planning, particularly land use planning, to the objectives of sustainable tourism development. This provides the basis for an examination of the specific use of Environmental Impact Assessment (EIA) in the appraisal of tourism development projects, given in Chapter 5. Despite the relative lack of detailed case studies of the use of EIA in relation to tourism projects, Chapter 5 attempts to describe EIA within the context of tourism research, providing specific examples of relevance to the tourism industry, and highlighting areas of mutual concern in both the general EIA literature and the tourism literature. For example, the opportunity for greater local community involvement in decision-making over tourism developments is considered within the context of an emerging concern, in the general EIA literature, over the role of local communities in the 'scoping' of project impacts.

The final chapter attempts to bring together the various theoretical and practical aspects of sustainable tourism development considered in this book, providing a summary of the key issues of concern to those with an interest in the relationship between tourism development and environmental protection. Areas where future research effort might be concentrated are also considered.

Chapter 2

The environmental impacts of tourism

Colin Hunter and Howard Green

INTRODUCTION

Over the last two decades, the impacts of tourism on the environment, especially those encountered through mass tourism, have received much research attention. Following a description of the environmental resource base for tourism and some of the difficulties encountered in assessing the impacts of tourism, this chapter provides a review of tourism impacts based largely on retrospective, post-development studies from the tourism literature. Measures designed to ameliorate the detrimental effects that tourism can have on environmental quality are also discussed.

Before embarking on the tourism impact review, it is worth noting that research attention has focused on impacts at the tourist destination, with studies usually limited to a defined and often relatively small geographical area. Moreover, impact studies have frequently been approached from the viewpoint of a single academic discipline, including ecological, geographical, sociological and economic perspectives. The study of tourism impacts is, as yet, relatively immature and it is perhaps not surprising, therefore, that a true multi-disciplinary approach to their description, categorisation and assessment has yet to fully emerge. This lack of coherence also reflects the complexity of the subject area, a topic which is returned to below.

THE ENVIRONMENTAL RESOURCE BASE FOR TOURISM

Although relatively fragmented and unstructured, recent research on tourism impacts does provide a typology for the 'classification' of environmental resources of importance to the tourism industry. Such a classification is important if the maintenance or enhancement of environmental quality is to become a major component of tourism impact assessments, allowing a more systematic and comprehensive appraisal of tourism projects, programmes and policies. Both the literature on tourism impacts and the broader environmental management literature suggest that a holistic approach to the definition of environment is necessary to appreciate the complete range of impacts, and their interactions, which may result from tourism development. However, despite the need for a broad appreciation of what constitutes the environmental resource base for tourism, a reductionist approach to the classification of environment is frequently adopted, whereby the environment is divided into a number of components. Such a conceptual division of environmental resources, if used with an awareness of its inherent artificiality, is convenient and can aid in the discussion and understanding of tourism impacts, at least initially.

There are a number of possibilities in the classification of environmental components or the categorisation of environmental impacts. Frequently, the environment is considered under three main headings: physical (or abiotic), biological (living) and socio-economic (including cultural) (e.g. Romeril 1989). The headings may also be expressed as natural, built (or human-made) and cultural (e.g. OECD 1981a). Other variations of typology and meaning under three main headings have also been employed. For the purposes of this book, the natural, built and cultural divisions have been adopted. This categorisation closely relates to the typology utilised to describe the environmental assets that attract tourists, and provides a simple framework for the discussion of tourism impacts. Also, impacts of tourism on local economies are outwith the scope of this text, and so the narrower term 'cultural' is preferred to 'socio-economic'.

The natural environment includes such features as air, water, flora, fauna, soil, natural landscape (including geological features) and climate. The built environment encompasses urban fabric and furniture, buildings and monuments, infrastructure, human-made parks and open spaces and other elements of 'townscape'. The cultural environment includes the values, beliefs, behaviour, morals, arts, laws and history of communities. The cultural environment will include 'high' culture such as opera and ballet, and popular culture including elements of native expression such as folk music and craft work. Taken together, these aspects of the environment make up the 'sense of place', and can be viewed as the basic environmental resources which attract tourists.

THE NATURE OF TOURISM IMPACTS

Tourism impacts can arise through the construction and operation of tourist facilities or services and from the activities of tourists themselves. They may be short-term or long-term, positive or negative, local, regional, national and even global, and direct, indirect or induced. This diversity in the range and type of impact partly reflects the characteristics of the tourism industry, and makes the comprehensive appraisal of the environmental consequences of tourism development problematical. Briassoulis (1991) provides a summary of the major difficulties involved in the assessment of tourism impacts:

- tourism is an amalgam of inter-linked activities and it is often difficult to distinguish impacts arising from individual activities;
- tourism activities may be pursued both by tourists and by the host population and occur together with other economic activities, again presenting problems for those attempting to separate impacts arising from tourism alone;
- environmental change occurs naturally, making tourism-induced change more difficult to quantify;
- a lack of detailed knowledge of environmental conditions prior to the advent of tourism in an area frequently limits the viability of post-development investigations;
- in addition to direct environmental impacts, tourism may have indirect impacts and induce further development and associated impacts, which may be difficult to identify and not amenable to straightforward assessment;
- some tourism impacts will only manifest themselves over the long term, making the establishment of causality links more difficult; and,
- components of the environment are inter-linked, and so a tourism activity which impacts on one aspect of the environment may produce an indirect impact on another.

In addition, the impacts of tourism development are not restricted to destination areas, but will spread over a wider area depending on the strength of the linkages (economic, social, transport, environmental, etc.) between the host area and its surroundings, making the task of comprehensive impact assessment even more difficult as the scale of analysis widens (Briassoulis 1991).

The difficulties outlined above are reflected in the limited (both geographically and in terms of the environmental components considered) nature of the majority of tourism impact studies in the literature. Pearce (1989) considers a number of other, if related, factors to be responsible for the incompleteness of tourism impact studies. These include lack of resources, inadequate assessment methodologies, a failure to appreciate the processes of tourism development and the lack of an inter-disciplinary research ethos. With these limitations in mind, the following sections consider some of the major reported impacts of tourism on the environment.

IMPACTS ON THE NATURAL ENVIRONMENT

Table 2.1 provides a summary of some of the major potential impacts of tourism developments on the natural environment, and the specific, although inter-related, aspects of the environment which may be altered. Examples from the literature concerning such impacts on the natural environment are considered below. Although impacts are discussed to some extent in isolation, in reality an environmental impact will rarely, if ever, stand alone, isolated from other impacts. This should become apparent as the section progresses.

Floral and faunal species composition

The ecological balance of an area, which takes perhaps thousands of years to evolve to a mature, self-regulating, stable system, can be disrupted and even destroyed by a variety of tourism-related activities in a relatively short period of time. These range from the obvious impacts associated with the wholesale removal of vegetation and related wildlife, to more subtle effects on animal behaviour. Any activity which changes floral and faunal species composition is a potential threat to an area's ecological balance. It may also threaten the local human culture which has evolved as part of this ecosystem and, therefore, depends on it for continued survival.

Table 2.1 Some major potential impacts of tourism on the natural environment

Impact aspect	Potential consequences
Floral and faunal species composition	• disruption of breeding habits • killing of animals through hunting • killing of animals in order to supply goods for the souvenir trade • inward or outward migration of animals • trampling and damage of vegetation by feet and vehicles • destruction of vegetation through the gathering of wood or plants • change in extent and/or nature of vegetation cover through clearance or planting to accommodate tourist facilities • creation of a wildlife reserve/sanctuary or habitat restoration
Pollution	• water pollution through discharges of sewage, spillages of oil/petrol • air pollution from vehicle emissions, combustion of fuels for heating and lighting • noise pollution from tourist transportation and activities
Erosion	• compaction of soils causing increased surface run-off and erosion • change in risk of occurrence of land slips/slides • change in risk of avalanche occurrence • damage to geological features (e.g. tors, caves) • damage to river banks
Natural resources	• depletion of ground and surface water supplies • depletion of fossil fuels to generate energy for tourist activity • change in risk of occurrence of fire • depletion of mineral resources for building materials • over-exploitation of biological resources (e.g. overfishing) • change in hydrological patterns • change in land used for primary production
Visual impact	• facilities (e.g. buildings, chairlift, car park) • litter • sewage, algal blooms

Source: modified from Green and Hunter (1992)

A well-known example of the large-scale destruction of an ecosystem through vegetation removal to accommodate tourist facilities is the case of the European Alps. Here, hundreds of square kilometres of forest have been removed and replaced by ski pistes, cable cars, pylons, buildings and access roads, making the slopes less able to absorb and retain water, causing increased susceptibility to soil erosion, floods, landslides and avalanches (Tyler 1989). In Switzerland, the evacuation of tourists is a regular occurrence in certain areas at certain times due to the avalanche risk brought about by deforestation (Smith and Jenner 1989). Similar wholesale destruction of forest ecosystems has occurred elsewhere in areas used primarily for winter skiing (Borgula 1987). A series of mudslides and floods in north and south Tyrol, Austria, occurred over a three week period in July 1987, killing more than sixty people, leaving 7,000 people homeless and fifty towns, villages and holiday centres wrecked (Romeril 1989). Severe ecological consequences have also been reported in other popular tourist destinations, such as the Mediterranean Basin, as a result of deforestation (Grenon and Batisse 1989). The direct loss of, sometimes rare and ecologically valuable, floral and faunal species from an area through removal for tourism development has been reported in, for example, Cyprus (Andronikou 1987), the reefs and coral formations of areas in the Caribbean (Holder 1988), and Majorca in Spain (Morgan 1991).

Vegetation cover may also be lost or damaged through trampling by walkers or crushing by tourist vehicles. Loss of vegetation cover in this way is frequently accompanied by soil compaction and a loss of soil structure, leading to increased surface water run-off, soil erosion and a decline in species diversity. Vehicular crushing of vegetation has been identified as a problem in some of Kenya's national parks and wildlife reserves, for example (Sindiyo and Pertet 1984; EIU 1991), while Thiele (1987) reports restrictions on access to the Bavarian National Park in Germany due to unacceptable environmental degradation by tourists and other recreators, including damage to flora and fauna, trampling and soil erosion. In heavily used skiing areas, compaction of the surface snow layer by skis and snow vehicles may prolong the spring thaw reducing the growth period for the plants beneath, thereby disrupting local ecological balance (Hamele 1988). This provides a good example of indirect impacts which may be difficult to foresee and which reflect the often intricate inter-dependencies of plants, animals and their physical environment.

The adverse impacts of tourists' feet are not restricted to terrestrial ecosystems. Hamele (1988), mentions the damage to coral reefs resulting from the contact of divers' flippers and the choking effect of disturbed sediment. Milne (1990), considering tourism in the Pacific Island States, reports that a large proportion of the coral and small fish life around the margins of boat jetties and hotel beaches has been killed due to excessive walking on coral reef beds by tourists at low tide. The action of motor boats, surf boards and yachts may also damage aquatic ecosystems, such as reed beds, while marinas built to house these craft can completely destroy, or degrade beyond repair, important mangrove and other lagoonal habitats (Jackson 1984).

Tourism may also result in the selective removal, collection or killing of (often rare) plants and animals. Dupuy (1987), for example, argues that the natural environment of some African countries is gradually being destroyed through pressures from wildlife tourism. The disappearance of wild plant and animal species in countries like Senegal for the manufacture and marketing of trophies, gifts and souvenirs is highlighted. This has occurred even where the animals are 'protected', and is reported as resulting in ecological imbalances. The collection and killing of marine animals for the souvenir trade has also been noted, for example in the Mediterranean and Pacific Islands (Milne 1990), with marked impacts on local ecology. De Groot (1983) observed the collection of shells, rocks and plants on the unique Galapagos Islands by poorly controlled groups of tourists from private yachts and small tourist boats, often venturing beyond marked tourist routes. Also observed in this study was the increased disturbance of plant and animal life close to tourist trails, leading to fears that animals would ultimately avoid certain areas. Animals may well migrate out of an area used by tourists if harassed (Sindiyo and Pertet 1984). Alternatively, the over-reliance on tourists as a source of food may prove to be disadvantageous to the animals in the long run.

At certain times of year, tourists may have a profound impact on animal breeding success, and the protection of breeding grounds from the impacts of tourism and tourists has become a matter of great contention in some areas in recent years. The beaches of some resort centres along the Mediterranean coasts of

Greece and Turkey, for example, are used by rare turtle populations as breeding grounds, whereby clutches of eggs are laid in
chambers dug out of the sand. In certain resorts, conservationists
have taken to distributing multi-lingual leaflets warning tourists
not to lay towels on the sand (which can reduce the temperature
of the eggs incubating beneath), not to use beach umbrellas
(which can spike whole clutches) and not to build bonfires at
night (which can disorientate hatchlings trying to reach the sea)
(Greth 1989; Morrison and Selman 1991). This example demonstrates both the strength of feeling that can be generated against
tourism impacts, and the profound consequences of apparently
innocent and relatively passive tourist activities. Similar fears over
tourist disruption to important breeding grounds have been
expressed by, for example, Erize (1987) with reference to cruises
in the Antarctic, and Walker (1991) when considering the sympathetic management of Heron Island in the Great Barrier Reef
of Australia, for sea-bird and sea-turtle breeding grounds.

At other, non-breeding, times of the year, animals may also be
under stress which can be exacerbated by the presence of tourists.
Some of the animals (including birds) in mountain forests, for
example, can be severely disturbed by the activities of skiiers and
walkers. In trying to escape the tourists, the rapid use of their
energy resources can lead to starvation if disturbance is frequent,
especially during harsh winter months (Hamele 1988).
Disturbance by tourists, amongst others, was thought to be
responsible for an 80 per cent decline in the giant petrel population of Ardley Island in the the South Shetland Islands of
Antarctica (Harris 1991). Insensitivity by tourists towards nesting
penguins was also noted in this study, whereby these animals were
deliberately disturbed for wildlife photography. General disturbance by tourists has seriously affected cheetah populations in the
Serengeti National Park, Tanzania, despite the relatively small
number of tourists involved (Smith and Jenner 1989).

In certain areas, the sheer rarity of the plant and animal
communities can be threatened by tourism even before tourists
arrive. Such is the case for the island of Saint Martin in the West
Indies, where plans to construct a land/sea link to facilitate
tourism developments threatened the unique plant communities
of the island through colonization by incoming alien species
(Monnier 1987). Similarly, the unique flora of the Tiede National
Park in Tenerife, Canary Islands, is at risk from alien seeds carried

unintentionally on the shoes and bodies of Park visitors (Romeril 1989). Frequently, it is islands such as Saint Martin and the Galapagos which are the most fragile in terms of the tourism threat, and which consequently receive much attention in the impact literature.

On a more positive note, there are many studies in the literature which emphasise the actual or potential benefits of tourism to the wildlife of an area. Tourism may result in the creation, or continued existence, of a wildlife park or reserve, for example. Similarly, habitat restoration appears to be becoming more frequently associated with tourism projects. Luxmoore (1989) concludes that wildlife tourism and controlled hunting are amongst the less intensive forms of wildlife exploitation, and are generally of greater benefit to wildlife conservation than more intensive forms of wildlife exploitation and production. Sindiyo and Pertet (1984) state that many national parks and wildlife reserves in Kenya have benefited greatly from tourist expenditure and associated publicity, while others owe their very existence to the tourism industry. In discussing the network of protected natural areas in the Sahel, spanning several African countries, Green et al. (1989) argue that tourism provides the national governments of the Sahel states with an economic rationale for the continued protection of the natural areas. With regard to a very different situation, O'Donnell (1991) similarly stresses the positive role of rural or agri-tourism in preserving the rural environment and culture of Ireland. Briereton (1991) recognises the development and upgrading of national parks and natural attractions that has occurred through tourism in parts of the Caribbean. Finally, Martinez-Taberner et al. (1990) in describing the major criteria required for the restoration of a coastal marsh ecosystem in Majorca, Spain, conclude that such projects are necessary in order to retain the appeal of the area for tourists.

Pollution

Pollution involves the anthropogenic introduction of substances or energy into the environment. Pollution may cause hazards to human health, harm to living resources and ecological systems, damage to structures or amenity, and interfere with the legitimate use of the environment. Since tourism (as a legitimate use of the environment) relies partly on amenity value, one might reasonably assume that the tourism industry has a history of concern over the potential threat posed by pollution to the success of destination areas. This has, however, generally not been the case. Moreover, the tourism industry itself has been, and still is, a major contributor to environmental pollution in many parts of the world. As such, the industry is in the ignominious position of contributing directly to its possible downfall over the long term in certain areas.

One of the best-known consequences of rapid tourism development is the overload of local sewage treatment and disposal infrastructure. Water pollution from untreated or partially treated sewage effluent can have profound implications for local aquatic life and also for the health of tourists and locals who use contaminated waters for drinking, bathing and as a source of food. Sewage pollution can alter the ecological balance of an area, often resulting in a marked decline in species diversity, by reducing dissolved oxygen in water and sediments, by increasing water turbidity, by smothering sea, lake or river beds and by promoting the accelerated eutrophication (nutrient enrichment) of water bodies.

Frequently, it is difficult to disaggregate water pollution (indeed, any form of pollution) resulting from tourism from other sources within a given area. However, there are many examples where tourism makes a significant contribution to local total pollution loads, sometimes to the apparent detriment of the tourism industry. Becheri (1991), for example, considers the effect of algal blooms, resulting from accelerated eutrophication, on the Italian bathing resort of Rimini, on the Adriatic coast. Although the area was already suffering from environmental problems associated with over-development, the blooms acted as a catalyst on these negative impacts and tourist bookings fell by over 25 per cent in 1989 compared to the previous year. An accelerated decline was also noted in many other areas of the mid- and northern Adriatic coast (Bywater 1991). Elsewhere, sewage-related tourism problems are also well known. For example, localised marine pollution has been implicated in the degradation of mangrove seagrass and coral reef ecosystems in Fiji (Lal 1984). Similar effects have been observed in Jamaica, where sewage effluent has encouraged the growth of seaweeds damaging the attractiveness of beaches and killing the coral reefs which protect the shorelines from erosion (Henry 1988). Sewage pollution is recognised as a major adverse impact of mass tourism in areas as diverse as Cyprus (Andronikou 1987), the Norfolk Broads of England (Owens and Owens 1991), the lakes of the Shinshu mountain region of Honshu Island in Japan (Watanabe 1990) and the mountain streams of the French Pyrenees (Smith and Jenner 1989). Westlake and White (1992) contend that the pollution of Venice's lagoon has detracted from the city as a place to live throughout the whole year.

Untreated or partially treated sewage may contain a range of micro-organisms, principally bacteria and viruses, which are pathogenic to humans. Those bathing in sewage-contaminated waters or eating sewage-contaminated foods (especially shellfish) may be at risk from diseases such as gastro-enteritis, hepatitis, polio, typhoid and dysentery. Tyler (1989), highlights the health hazard to tourists and locals from sewage entering the Mediter-ranean, thereby undermining the attraction of a beach holiday as public awareness of potential hazards increases. Health surveys conducted in the coastal resorts of Bodrum and Cesme, Turkey, found foreign tourists and children to be particularly prone to sewage-related diseases contracted by bathing during the high season (Kocasoy 1989). Pawson *et al.* (1984) describe the faecal contamination of drinking water supplies by tourists as a major cause of gastro-intestinal disorders in villages of Nepal's Everest region. Results of surveys of bathing water quality in English coastal resorts demonstrate a significantly greater incidence of sewage-related disease amongst swimmers as compared to non-swimmers. Such impacts and subsequent concerns may translate directly into loss of tourist activity in affected resorts (Smith and Jenner 1989).

Other forms of water pollution may accompany tourism devel-opments. The release, dumping or spillage of oil, petrol, inorganic and organic wastes from tourist boats has been noted in a number of studies. For example: Stark (1990), with reference to the coastal environment of Hawii; Holder (1988), on the general impacts of coastal tourism throughout the Caribbean; de Groot (1983), with reference to the activities of tourists and tour boat operators in the Galapagos Islands; Harris (1991), in relation to the discharge of oil-contaminated bilge water by tourist ships in parts of the South Shetland Islands of Antarctica; and Milne (1990), in relation to oil seepages from boats carrying tourists to off-shore attractions in the Pacific Islands. Less obviously, Tananone (1991) reports the contamination of groundwater supplies in Thailand associated with the application of large quantities of pesticides and fertilizers to golf courses. In Japan, the government has had to regulate the building of golf courses because of pollution-related public health concerns.

Air pollution can accompany tourism developments in a number of ways, for example during the construction of buildings and other tourist facilities and associated infrastructure, from the burning of fossil fuels to provide heating and power, from the exhausts of private tourist vehicles, and in the transport of tourists to destinations by air, road, rail, etc. Whereas the impacts of water pollution are generally restricted to a relatively small and well-defined area, the impact of tourism on atmospheric quality takes on a wider, and even global, perspective through, for example, global air travel. Similarly, tourism-related demand for electricity will often result in the increased burning of fossil fuels and the release of pollutants such as carbon dioxide and oxides of sulphur and nitrogen in areas far removed from popular destinations. Carbon dioxide is an important contributory gas to global warming and the so-called 'greenhouse effect', while oxides of sulphur and nitrogen are the causative agents of dry and wet acid deposition.

These wider regional and global issues have been recognised in the literature. Wheatcroft (1991), for example, considers the relationships between environmental quality, airlines and tourism at the global scale, and suggests that both the airlines and the tourism industry must be seen to be concerned for the natural environment by taking measures to reduce emissions to the atmosphere. These sentiments are echoed by Copeland (1992), who argues that aviation contributes some 2 per cent of global carbon dioxide emissions from fossil fuels, and that airlines should become more involved in the tourism and environment debate, especially with regard to long-haul tourism to Developing Countries. Hamele (1988) argues that aircraft, tourists' private cars and heating systems in tourism developments all contribute to air pollution resulting in acid precipitation, forest blight and soil degradation. Briand *et al.* (1989) demand action to prevent further tourism-related damage to the vulnerable landscapes of the European Alps, which are suffering from forest blight. Smith and Jenner (1989) report a loss in tourism income to the Black Forest area of Europe due to reduced appeal as a result of damage caused by acid precipitation. These authors also cite the example of the St Gothard Pass in Switzerland, where weekend traffic alone deposits 30 tonnes of nitrogen oxides, 75 kg of lead and 25 tonnes of hydrocarbons into the local atmosphere, resulting in tree damage. Acid deposition also causes the degradation of fresh-water quality, with a range of impacts on aquatic flora and fauna, and on human health. Hamele (1988) also notes that air pollution in many health resorts has reached levels usually only encountered in large cities.

At a local level, dust generated by various forms of construction for the tourism industry is a common problem for both locals and tourists (see, for example, Morgan 1991, referring to problems generated by tourism in Majorca). Air pollution in the form of excess noise from air and road transport, construction, 'canned' music, etc. is a very common problem for residents, tourists and wildlife alike in many resorts. Harris (1991) notes the disturbance caused to nesting penguins and other species by tourist aircraft in the South Shetland Islands of Antarctica. The noise nuisance of artificial snow generators used extensively in skiing resorts is highlighted by Smith and Jenner (1989). Tourists to the Shark Bay area of Western Australia have ranked noise pollution from hovercraft as a high adverse environmental impact, which also disturbs fish and wildlife (Dowling 1991).

Tourism may not necessarily always create or add to pollution problems. Increasingly, it would appear that infrastructure for the treatment and disposal of waste is being built or upgraded (if, often, rather belatedly) to accommodate tourism developments, with net benefits for local environmental quality. Hadjivassilis (1990), for example, describes the installation of some 200, mainly coastal, small waste-water treatment plants in Cyprus over the past ten years. These have alleviated sewage pollution problems. Tourism may also bring improved pollution prevention legislation to some areas (Liu *et al.* 1987; Becheri 1991).

Erosion

As well as soil erosion resulting from trampling, vegetation removal, vehicular compaction, etc., described above, tourist activity can also result in damage to natural geological features and river banks. The latter issue is considered by Brooke (1990) in a study which highlights the often complex inter-dependencies between various components of an ecosystem. The Norfolk

Broads is one of England's most popular holiday destinations, especially for motor cruises along the network of inland fresh-water canals which characterise the area. According to Brooke, in recent years it has no longer been possible to ignore the severe water pollution and bank erosion problems, which are to some extent inter-linked. Accelerated eutrophication arising from water pollution, to which tourism makes an important contribution, has caused a decline in the populations of emergent and submerged plants along most of the Broads' waterways. This, in turn, has decreased the resistance of river and canal banks to erosion from tourists' motor cruisers through boat-wash and inappropriate mooring. Increased erosion has led to a loss of reed-bed flora, and so a cycle of ecological imbalance is complete.

Perversely, erosion of sand from popular resort beaches has proved a problem in some locations due to the siting of buildings and other superstructures too close to the high-water mark (Jackson 1984). The erosion of natural geological features from general 'people pressure' can also present problems, as is the case with Ayres Rock in Australia (Romeril 1989).

Natural resources

In order to construct and maintain tourism developments, the natural resources (biological and physical, renewable or non-renewable) of a destination area may become altered and depleted. Indeed, the use of resources may not be restricted to the immediate vicinity and may involve the importation of con-struction materials, for example, from another region or country, extending the potential environmental sphere of influence of a particular development. Again, as with air pollution, the use of natural resources by the tourism industry may have global environmental implications; for example, the use of tropical hard-wood tree species in building/decoration work, or the use of building insulation materials made with ozone-depleting chloro-fluorocarbons (CFCs). Studies in the literature, however, have concentrated on the use of natural resources within, or very close to, the destination area.

One resource over which conflict between locals and those involved in tourism has occurred, is fresh-water. Frequently, tourists are attracted to warm, relatively dry climates where precipitation and fresh-water supplies are scarce. In the

Mediterranean, for example, hotels can easily consume 400 litres of water per guest per day for washing, showering, swimming pools, watering lawns, etc. Locals may only require a maximum of 70 litres per person per day (Hamele 1988). Evidence from the Caribbean suggests that tourist water use can be over three times higher than the consumption by local residents (Jackson 1984). Furthermore, so called 'environment-friendly' or 'green' forms of tourist recreation, such as golfing, may require large quantities of fresh-water for watering purposes, exerting an unsustainable drain on renewable supplies. Tananone (1991), with reference to the boom in golf courses for tourists in Thailand, reports that each golf course requires around 3,000 cubic metres of water per day.

In Goa and other southern Indian beach resorts, tourism has also taken valuable water supplies away from local communities (Tyler 1989). Similarly, Holder (1988) reports a lack of adequate supplies of high quality drinking water for both tourists and residents in some Caribbean resorts. Milne (1990) highlights an interesting sequence of environmental impacts which occurs in some off-shore island resorts in the Pacific. Since these islands have a very limited supply of fresh-water, salt water has to be used in septic tanks. The salt in the water, however, inhibits the natural breakdown of sewage by micro-organisms, leading to the discharge of poorly treated sewage into surrounding coastal waters, with inevitable damage to marine life.

With reference to the use of artificial snow generators in skiing resorts, Smith and Jenner (1989) report that these machines require millions of litres of fresh-water, making sudden demands on feeder lakes, disrupting their ecology. Tourism development may require the construction of a new water supply reservoir. Topographical limitations may dictate that this be sited in an ecologically sensitive area, or on high quality agricultural land. Below the new water impoundment river flow may be reduced, altering the ecology of the channel and reducing its ability to dilute pollution (Romeril 1989). Changes in local hydrological drainage patterns may also result from tourism-induced urban expansion. Localised flooding may follow the replacement of natural soil surfaces with impermeable tarmac or concrete. On a more positive note, rapid tourism development in Cyprus has promoted the installation of waste-water treatment plants to allow the re-use of water for agricultural irrigation purposes (Hadjvassilis 1990).

Other physical resources have been severely depleted as a result of tourism development. The extraction of sand from beaches and coastal waters for use in concrete is not uncommon, and this can impact upon tidal current patterns and visual or recreational amenity, with implications for tourist satisfaction and wildlife (Smith and Jenner 1989). Threats to the long-term supplies of animal species used for food can also occur to satisy tourist demand over the short term. Problems of tourism-related over-fishing have been noted in some parts of the Caribbean, for example. Jackson (1984) reports that lobster and conch, particularly favoured by tourists, have been especially affected. Shark Bay in Western Australia provides an example of a remote and fragile area suffering from over-fishing problems (Dowling 1991). The over-exploitation of wildlife may upset the local ecological balance sufficiently for there to be serious repercussions for the local human population.

Vegetation can also be affected. In some small Pacific Island States the increase in demand for handicrafts and the development of mass-production techniques has placed a strain on vegetation resources. Most of the wood used for carvings in Cook Island, for example, is now imported (Milne 1990). A small increase in the rate of deforestation to provide fuel-wood for tourists has been noted in Khumbu National Park in Nepal's Everest region (Pawson *et al.* 1984). More generally, Ahmad *et al.* (1990) state that tourists to the Himalayas do not obey regulations when camping, using local firewood for heating and cooking, thereby creating fire hazards. Changes in the distribution of land used for primary production may also follow tourism development, through direct loss following urban expansion or indirectly as a consequence of changes in land values. Loss of agricultural land has been reported in a number of studies (e.g. Jackson 1984; Milne 1990). Tananone (1991) notes that since 1987, Thailand has built some 50 golf courses to cater for (mainly) Japanese tourists. An average of 1.6 square kilometres of land is required to build each course, and golf courses are now the major cause of farm land contraction in Thailand. Conversely, Sindiyo and Pertet (1984) with reference to tourism in Kenya, found that the expansion and intensification of agriculture necessary to sustain tourism resulted in encroachment and pollution problems.

As has been noted above, tourism may encourage and facilitate the conservation of flora and fauna in an area. These are, of course, biological natural resources and it would be wrong to conclude this section without referring the reader back to the section on flora and fauna which demonstrates the capability of tourism to protect such natural resources.

Visual impact

Litter is a seemingly ubiquitous consequence of tourist activity, and one which can seriously detract from the quality of the natural environment and act as a hazard to wildlife. Many mass tourism resort destinations suffer from litter (especially from the increased consumption of canned and boxed take-away foods), giving the landscape an unclean and untidy appearance. Even remote destinations, where tourist use is still light, suffer from this particular problem (see, for example, Harris 1991). Pawson *et al.* (1984) describe litter problems in the Khumbu National Park, Nepal, and report that despite requirements that visitors remove or bury trash, campsites and trails are becoming increasingly littered. In some places, streams have become so polluted with rubbish that trekkers are warned not to use the water.

Visual impairment of the quality of the natural environment may follow as a consequence of water pollution. Sewage can detract from the visual (not to mention olfactory) amenity of waters and beaches. Relatedly, algal blooms can be particularly unsightly, detracting from the appeal of water areas. Venice, for example, the most famous of all Adriatic resorts, has a pollution-generated problem with algal blooms in its lagoon. The algae reproduce up to 35,000 tons a year. As it rots it produces a stench that permeates the city and encourages large infestations of flies. Local estimates are of a subsequent 30 per cent fall in tourist arrivals and Riccione hoteliers alone have put the cost to themselves at £45 million (Smith and Jenner 1989).

Poorly designed, sited and constructed buildings and other tourist facilities are a well-known consequence of much tourism development, frequently detracting from the visual amenity of the natural environment by, for example, blocking views. Tyler (1989), writing of tourism in Developing Countries, comments that all too often this has meant the construction of glass and concrete blocks which are not in keeping with the local environment. Such 'architectural pollution' has been high-lighted around the world, where there has been a failure to integrate resort infrastructure with aesthetically pleasing charac-teristics of the natural environment, whether this be coastal, rural or mountain.

IMPACTS ON THE BUILT ENVIRONMENT

Urban areas with significant cultural, heritage and other attrac-tions may be especially prone to negative tourism impacts. However, environmental benefits can also follow the growth in tourism. Tourism may be used as a catalyst, for example, to revitalise and improve decaying urban areas, bringing investment and environmental upgrading. Despite the capacity of tourism to alter the built environment there has, apparently, been a relative lack of interest and research on tourism in towns and cities (Page 1992). Some of the major impacts which have been identified are given in Table 2.2, and discussed briefly below.

Urban form

Tourism may induce profound changes in the character and form of built areas, either through urban expansion or alterations within existing village, town or city limits. New or upgraded urban fabric may follow tourism development, with the provision of roads and pavements, for example. Alternatively, existing fabric may suffer increased damage and erosion through increased pedestrian and vehicular traffic, leading to higher repair costs. In many towns and cities, the importance of providing high quality street furniture to attract tourists has been recognised. Jones (1985), for example, in discussing the tourism-based revitalisation strategy adopted by the English town of Halifax, stresses the need for high quality furnishings in keeping with townscape character, rather than furnishings provided for the sake of mere expediency. A large-scale tourism project designed to transform the 'acropolis' area of Avignon in France, was successful in improving traffic flows by reinstating old access points, paths and roads (Ronsseray 1989).

However, less desirable effects can also occur. Tourism may encourage changes in land use within urban boundaries; for example, the balance between residential and other land uses.

Frequently, a move away from residential housing use towards hotels and boarding houses can be detected, driven by rising land and building stock prices. In some cases, the private housing sector can become almost completely displaced and excluded from certain areas. This is noted by Milne (1990) in a review of tourism impacts in small Pacific Island States. Less dramatically, Page (1989) reports tensions between residents and tourists in certain parts of London due to the *ad hoc* development of

Table 2.2 Some major potential impacts of tourism on the built environment

Impact aspect	Potential consequences
Urban form	• change in character of built area through urban expansion or redevelopment • change in residential, retail or industrial land uses (e.g. move from private homes to hotels/ boarding houses) • changes to the urban fabric (e.g. roads, pavements, street furniture) • emergence of contrasts between urban areas developed for the tourist population and those for the host population
Infrastructure	• overload of infrastructure (e.g. roads, railways, car parking, electricity grid, communications systems, waste disposal, buildings, water supply) • provision of new infrastructure or upgrading of existing infrastructure • environmental management to adapt areas for tourist use (e.g. sea walls, land reclamation)
Visual impact	• growth of the built-up area • new architectural styles • people and belongings, litter • beautification
Restoration	• re-use of disused buildings • restoration and preservation of historic buildings and sites • restoration of derelict buildings as second homes
Erosion	• damage to built assets from feet and vehicular traffic (including vibration effects)
Pollution	• air pollution from tourists and tourist traffic • air pollution from non-tourist sources causing damage to built assets

Source: modified from Green and Hunter (1992)

hotels, leading to a reduction in available housing stock. Even where environmental benefits have flowed from tourism developments, these may accrue largely to the tourists or those who work in the area, due to the absence of local residential communities (DoE 1990).

Miller (1989), in an overview of European urban tourism, warns of the negative consequences of the overly enthusiastic embracement of tourism. Whilst recognising that under-used or abandoned heritage resources can be reactivated for the greater economic and social benefit of the local community, Miller warns that such reactivation can become a sterile exploitation if it is not done with caution and a respect for limits. It is argued that there is always a limit to a building's or town's capacity to absorb adaptation or manipulation. The relationship between the tourist attraction and the wider environment (including the local community) should be respected, otherwise there is a risk that the host area will ultimately contain only offices and shops, lacking a vibrant local population which has largely been displaced by tourist pressure. This point is also made by Westlake and White (1992), with respect to Venice, where the tourism-induced rise in the cost of houses to buy or rent is excluding much of the indigenous population, with the attendant risk that Venice will become a city museum, only ever fully 'open' during the summer months.

It is not only in the old historic urban centres where tourism may encourage such profound changes. Holder (1988), for example, cites negative changes to the character of villages as a major impact of tourism in the Caribbean. Ahmad *et al.* (1990) report that hill stations in the Himalayas are often converted into slums by a lack of planned growth to meet the needs of tourism.

Infrastructure

In many cases, the net outcome of tourism on the form and character of built areas will depend upon the resulting pressures on existing infrastructure and attitudes to the provision of new infrastructure. The overload of infrastructure is a well-known consequence of tourism development in many urban areas. Romeril (1989), for example, states that overcrowding and traffic congestion are obvious manifestations of tourism in resort centres. Miller (1989) makes direct reference to pedestrian traffic jams in Venice, and the all too often overcrowded museums of Florence which have to turn people away shortly after opening. Reviewing the development of London as a tourist destination, Page (1989) recognises the contribution that tourism can make to urban renewal, environmental improvements and amenities for residents, but qualifies these positive aspects with reference to local residents' opposition to tourism-generated noise and vehicular traffic/pedestrian congestion around major attractions like the Tower of London and St Paul's Cathedral. Tourism also contributes more widely to overcrowding on existing Underground tube services, resulting in a pressing need to upgrade the capacity of this infrastructure. Similarly, Page (1992) reports some antagonism by the local community in Canterbury, England, towards perceived investments in new tourism infrastructure as a result of problems associated with the over-use of the city centre by tourists. These problems include traffic congestion, insufficient coach and car parking facilities, and the over-concentration of tourists at major heritage sites within the city. Other types of infrastructure can also be adversely affected. Jackson (1984), for example, points out that per capita tourist electricity consumption in the Caribbean is much higher than resident consumption, and that electricity blackouts are aggravated by tourist demands. This can be compounded by the construction of new buildings which are wasteful of energy.

Tourism does not inevitably cause or seriously aggravate infrastructure overload. Ashworth and Tunbridge (1990), for example, suggest that tourist use of infrastructure and services in historic cities incurs only marginal costs to existing facilities. In a major study of the environmental impacts of tourism projects in twenty inner city areas of the UK, virtually no problems relating to vehicular traffic, parking provision or pedestrian overcrowding were found. Indeed, many projects resulted in the restoration of derelict land (DoE 1990). It should be noted, however, that the areas considered lacked large residential communities, making problems associated with infrastructure overload less likely. Again on a more positive note, Holder (1988) provides a list of positive infrastructure benefits from tourism in the Caribbean, including: improved telephone, telex and other communication systems; development and upgrading of human-made attractions, recreational and health facilities; improved air and sea ports; and, improved and increased air, sea and road transport. All of these were thought to help the local population through greater

mobility and the pursuit of secondary trade and business relationships. Similarly, Papadopoulos (1988), states that tourist receipts
have often allowed the upgrading of basic infrastructure in areas
of Greece. Henry (1988) provides a summary of tourism-related
infrastructure improvements in Jamaica, including the provision
of basic infrastructure beyond the immediate future needs of local
communities (e.g. a second airport), improved roads, and
improvements in sewerage, water supply and garbage collection.
The small village of Negril is used by Henry as a specific example
where the introduction of tourism has radically improved the
quality of life of the inhabitants through the provision of piped
water, electricity, a telephone system, a modern shopping centre,
small airport, good main road, a clinic, a bank and a fire station.

Henry (1988) also notes the beautification of areas in Jamaica
following the construction of new tourist infrastructure such as
beaches and piers for cruise ships. In fact, it is quite common for
environmental management techniques to be employed in the
beautification and environmental enhancement of previously
poor quality areas as they are adapted for tourist use. McNulty
(1989), for example, considers heritage tourism as a factor in town
regeneration in North America. Examples of environmental
improvement include:

- Jacksonville, Florida where the principal development area is
  now the river front, once a polluted channel;
- San Antonio, Texas where the tourism industry was the key to
  the reclamation of the Paseo del Rio, a former flood control
  sewer and sewage channel;
- Chattanooga, Tennessee where heritage tourism was employed
  as a method of attacking the problem of derelict housing, with
  historic preservation acting as a catalyst for more general
  environmental improvement; and,
- Roanoke, Virginia where a linear heritage park was
  constructed in the river valley.

Bettum (1989) in describing the recent history of development in
the Aker River area of Oslo in Norway, provides an evocative
testament to the potential benefits of urban recreation and
tourism provision. The river has slowly been transformed from
a heavily polluted open sewer into a 10 km long urban park, with
clean water for bathing and fishing, and grassy areas along its
banks suitable for winter sledding and summer sunbathing.

Clearly, environmental improvements, such as those outlined above, can create a very favourable visual impact. The beautifica-tion of derelict or aesthetically unappealing areas can do much to counteract the potential negative visual impacts associated with overcrowding, litter, traffic congestion, urban expansion and the construction of inappropriate buildings which are not in keeping with the local townscape. Relatedly, urban tourism can do much to instil a greater appreciation of vernacular architecture and cultural heritage in visitors and locals alike, through the restora-tion and preservation of important built assets, as described below.

Restoration

Historic sites, monuments and buildings can be great tourist attractions, and tourism itself frequently allows their restoration and preservation for the benefit of the local community, and beyond. Such restoration and preservation for the tourist market has been noted as a significant benefit in many areas around the world, for example the small Pacific Island States (Milne 1990), Mediterranean beach resorts (Romeril 1989), Caribbean resort centres (Holder 1988), inner city areas of the UK (DoE 1990), and Greek resorts (Papadopoulos 1988). Battista (1989) provides a lengthy list of important sites and buildings which have been restored as a means of exploiting the architectural heritage of the Italian city of Genoa.

The potential benefits of tourism on the built environment need not be confined to large historic centres. Appropriate tourism strategies directed at larger centres can have beneficial impacts on surrounding areas. Jones (1985), for example, found that the promotion of the town of Halifax in northern England as a tourist centre also encouraged the re-use of derelict or redundant agri-cultural buildings in surrounding rural areas for tourist-related activities; some, for example were converted into countryside interpretative centres. Similarly, Michael (1991), with reference to the development of agri-tourism in Cyprus, suggests that this form of tourism is a promising avenue for the protection of rural architecture, heritage and culture.

Erosion and pollution

While the restoration and utilisation of important built assets can clearly bring great benefits, such benefits can be lost or reduced where built assets are allowed to suffer degradation from erosion or pollution. The erosion of important structures by tourists' feet can become a major problem, as is the case with the Parthenon in Greece (Romeril 1989) and the historic fabric of the city of Canterbury in England (Page 1992). Air pollution from tourist vehicles can also damage built structures. In Athens, Greece, for example, tourist coaches are no longer permitted close to the top of the Acropolis hill (Smith and Jenner 1989). In extreme cases, tourists have had to be banned from some sites. A recent article in a daily British newspaper reported that the tomb of Tutankhamun in Egypt (some 3,000 years old) has had to be closed to tourists. The 5,000 tourists a day were generating over 100 litres of sweat and this, combined with the dust and bacteria brought in by tourists, was causing unacceptable damage to the tomb (especially the wall paintings) by encouraging the growth of fungus and bacteria (*Guardian*, 24th of September 1992).

Smith and Jenner (1989) focus on the threat of corrosion to ancient monuments from acid precipitation. They point out that around the world buildings have suffered more from acid attack in the past 25 years than in the preceeding 2,400 years. Examples given include:

- the sixteenth-century Sigismund Chapel of Wawel Cathedral in Krakow, Poland, where much of the original roof gold has dissolved and has had to be replaced, and where statues have had to be removed for safe-keeping;
- the caryatids of the Parthenon in Greece which have been taken to a museum and replaced on site by replicas;
- London's St Paul's Cathedral where some 2.5 cm of stone have now dissolved;
- the crumbling Renaissance frescos of Venice; and,
- the threat to the Taj Mahal in India from acid pollution.

Although tourism itself may contribute to acid pollution, in these examples it is unlikely to be the major contributor. Nevertheless, these examples serve to illustrate the threat to tourism from pollution and the frequent reliance of tourism success on environmental quality.

IMPACTS ON THE CULTURAL ENVIRONMENT

Both the tourism-driven regeneration strategies of many European countries and the growing demand for holidays in remoter parts of the world, have helped to raise the awareness of local culture as an important tourism resource. Cultural tourism draws on specific aspects of a destination area, and concern has grown over the impacts of tourism on local cultural environments. In this respect, the discussion of cultural tourism has largely focused on specific areas, including remote regions of Developed Countries such as Lapland, upland Wales and Switzerland (Grahn 1991; ECTARC 1988a; Witt 1991; Marfurt 1983), and Developing Countries like Nepal, Thailand and Bali (Kaur and Singh 1990; Tananone 1991; McKean 1976). Research emphasis on such areas may reflect a narrow view of the nature of indigenous culture and the stereotyping of the 'native' (Cohen 1982). It is only recently that the literature has begun to widen the discussion to include aspects of culture and heritage in urban areas, for example. Yet, clearly, the 'high culture' of major urban centres is a key attraction in city tourism.

Often, social and cultural aspects of the environment of a host area are seen as synonymous in the tourism literature. Alternatively, however, cultural attributes (and impacts) may be regarded as a sub-set of social conditions (e.g. Mathieson and Wall 1982), or the two may be viewed as covering separate sets of environmental attributes (e.g. ECTARC 1988b). The brief overview of tourism impacts which follows adopts the terms 'culture' and 'cultural' in a broad sense to encompass many 'social' impacts (such as the position of women, moral conduct, prostitution and crime) which have been the subject of social/cultural discussion in the tourism literature.

As with tourism impacts on natural and built components of the host environment, impacts on local culture may be beneficial or detrimental. Frequently, the latter have been stressed in the tourism literature. The nature and magnitude of cultural impacts are a function of characteristics of the tourist, the local tourism industry and the host community. The nature, scale and duration of interactions between tourists and the local community are crucial in determining tourism-induced cultural changes. Such factors influence the social and economic distance between tourist and host. Thus, the influence of forms of mass tourism on the cultural environment may be less than anticipated if tourist and host remain largely separated. Mature mass tourism may be associated with the evolution of 'tourist ghettos' (perhaps as tensions between tourists and residents become apparent),

Table 2.3 Some major potential impacts of tourism on the cultural environment

Impact aspect	Potential consequences
History	• loss of artifacts by unscrupulous sales people • enhancement of museums with greater interest in cultural resources (e.g. the development of industrial or other specialised museums) • changes in the cultural landscape (e.g. loss of traditional agriculture or a move away from traditional hut dwellings to houses built using more Western methods)
Traditional arts	• the development of a market for traditional paintings, sculpture and crafts increasing the demand for local crafts people • increased demand for traditional drama, music and dance • renaissance of traditional festivals and other cultural and artistic events • increased awareness of, and demand for, traditional literary forms
Language	• changes in the vocabulary of languages (e.g. the inclusion of Western words and phrases in language) • the growth of minority languages (e.g. the growth of Welsh as an element of cultural tourism)
Religion	• increased importance of religious festivals and pilgrimages • pressures on religious places and shrines as a result of increased visitor numbers • decline in religious practices
Traditions	• changes to the traditional economic order (e.g. a move away from self-sufficiency to dependency) • pressures to adopt Western rather than traditional clothing • dominance of leisure time by Western television • increased variety of food (e.g. introduction of foods for tourists) • changes in eating habits • growth in the availability of international drink products and alcohol
Values and norms	• changes in family structures and values • adoption of servile attitudes towards tourists • increase in prostitution • increase in criminality

reducing the potential for interaction (Gray 1974). Aspects of local culture may therefore be segregated as 'only for the tourists'. Hassan (1975), for example, in a study of organised mass tourism in Singapore, concluded that the (mainly Japanese) tourists made little contribution to cultural change. However, during the early stages of rapid tourism development the potential for cultural change may be great, given significant interactions between tourists and members of the host community.

Table 2.3 summarises some of the major potential impacts of tourism on the cultural environment. Examples of some of the impacts are described in the following sections. Clearly, many cultural impacts will occur simultaneously and are inter-related. Moreover, it is frequently difficult, if not impossible, to disaggregate tourism-related chains of cause and effect from the more general changes brought about by the globalisation of development.

History

The characteristics of a place may be the result of hundreds or even thousands of years of evolution and the unique combination of attributes and characteristics associated with such change. Around the world, the globalisation of development is placing increasing stress on unique cultural systems, with tourism frequently being an important agent of rapid change. Prechil (1983), for example, in a discussion of the impact of resort development in Kenya, notes how evolved self-sufficiency may quickly become dependency as the tourism industry develops. Any move towards a dependency on tourism may manifest itself in a number of ways. For example, the local cultural landscape itself may alter as agricultural practices are modified to meet the needs and desires of tourists. In Developing Countries particularly, traditional agriculture may collapse as people move off the land in search of more lucrative employment in the tourism industry (Srisang 1991).

However, tourism need not be an agent of collapse. Indeed, it can be used as a means of reinforcing cultural history and practices. Grahn (1991), for example, describes the ways in which tourism can help to retain the pattern of traditional small farms and associated activities in Swedish Lapland. Grahn demonstrates how direct involvement in traditional culture can change the attitude of tourists to their cultural heritage, instilling a respect for other ways of life. The tourism-related preservation of historic buildings and sites (see previous section) may provide an associated means of communicating an appreciation of cultural heritage if these structures are used as industrial or folk museums, for example. Such developments have become very popular in England in recent years, and have an important role to play in recording (and making available) changing cultural patterns and attitudes (Buckley and Witt 1989; Johnson and Thomas 1990).

Traditional arts

The growth of tourism can have significant impacts on the pattern and development of traditional arts, and these have received increasing research attention following the work of Graburn (1976) on tourism-related changes to 'Fourth World' art forms. The research, however, has been far from conclusive in a general sense. Some writers (e.g. Bascom 1976; May 1977) suggest that traditional forms are debased with goods being produced for tourist consumption by non-traditional methods. Others have pointed to a renaissance of traditional art forms (including drama and music), driven by a demand from tourists for cultural authenticity (e.g. Deitch 1977; McKean 1977). It is not unlikely that both views are consistent, according to the nature of the tourist/host relationship under specific conditions.

Language and literature

Language and literature are key aspects of local culture. Inevitably, international tourism floods the world with the languages of those nations with a propensity (and/or the means) for travel. Thus, the subtle inclusion of alien vocabulary, perhaps especially of North American origin, may ensue. More positively, tourism can reinforce minority languages and strengthen their key role in developing cultural identity. The Welsh language, for example, is one of the oldest in Europe and is spoken by only 20 per cent of the Welsh population. The growth of tourism has, however, had a generally positive impact on its development and use (ECTARC 1988a). A less encouraging influence has been detected with reference to the use of Gaelic in Sleat on the Isle of Skye, Scotland (Butler 1978). The language may have been declining at the time as a result of the growth in second homes and the increasing use of imported, casual labour, although local residents were generally of the opinion that tourism had little effect on the language.

Religion

Religious traditions provide many of the characteristic elements of culture and may underpin a wider set of cultural attributes than those directly associated with the practice of the religion itself. These wider attributes range from shrines and other religious buildings to aspects of behaviour and clothing. Thus, the impacts of tourism are potentially very broad ranging. Some forms of tourism may have a very strong, inherent religious component which provides the underlying rationale for tourist travel. Kaur and Singh (1990), for example, make particular reference to the impact of secular tourism in areas of traditional religious tourism such as the pilgrimages in Garhwal in the Himalayas. They are concerned that increasing numbers of secular tourists and the greater pressures on infrastructure may have a negative effect on the traditional culture-based tourism of the area, and ultimately may modify the latter permanently. For example, religious sites may be adversely affected by increasing numbers of secular tourists and the paraphernalia (such as signs and snack bars) designed to attract them. Such inappropriate development will reduce the religious experience for the devotee-visitor or for local people.

Other traditions

Several researchers have noted the impacts that tourism can have on traditional patterns of economic order within local commun- ities as people aspire to the lifestyle of tourists. In their discussions of changes in rural Mediterranean areas, both Greenwood (1977) and Pacione (1977), for example, report major effects on tradi- tional peasant economies as employment opportunities in the tourism economy appear attractive to local people. In some cases, employment opportunities may be greater for the younger members of the family, leading to rifts in the traditional family and changing patterns of economic leadership (Wilson 1979). Such fundamental changes were observed by Koea (1977) in Tonga, resulting in an erosion of the traditional extended family, although it is often impossible to disaggregate the influence of tourism development from other factors. Patterns of tourism-related economic dependency can create wide local and regional variations. Extensive areas of the High Himalayas, for example, remain economically 'backward', while in others such as Khumbu Himal the influence of tourism development has been strong, bringing modernisation and a decline in traditional ways of life (Bjonness 1983). Less profound changes may follow tourism development, such as the adoption of Western clothes in preference to traditional styles noted by Prechil (1983) in Kenya as a means of signifying 'upward social mobility'.

Values and norms

The last example given above can be taken to represent an expression of the so-called 'demonstration effect', whereby locals modify their own behaviour and aspirations following the example of the tourist. Potentially, this may be the most potent mechanism of cultural impact as local values and norms change under the influence of tourism. Jafari (1974) refers to such societal changes as 'acculturation', which may be particularly evident in Developing Countries as local inhabitants accept the values of Western societies whilst discarding their own. Any causal links between tourism development and processes of societal change are frequently tenuous and the literature offers little in the way of direct causal influence. Some evidence does, however, exist. Smith (1977), for example, in a study of Eskimo communities exposed to tourism development notes how such a community may develop sub-groups, each responding in a different way to the tourist. The older members of the community tend to retain their traditional characteristics and are happy to show these to the tourists. The younger members, however, aspire to the higher standards of living which the tourists display and may take employment in government and commerce in an attempt to realise these aspirations. Traditional family structures may consequently begin to break down.

It would also appear that moral values can be influenced by tourism, and several researchers have based their studies on issues of criminality, gambling and prostitution. Gasparavic (1989), for example, stresses tourism-related impacts on moral values, arguing that increasing incidences of stealing, begging, drug usage and prostitution are directly attributable to a growth in tourism. Some investigations have reported a direct relationship between the growth of tourism and increases in crime. With reference to Cape Cod, Pizam (1978) found increased rates of drug abuse, vandalism and drunken behaviour, and this accords with anecdotal evidence from some mass tourism destinations in Spain, for example. Local attitudes towards sex may also apparently be altered through tourism with, in some cases, the evolution of a tourist 'sex industry' and the promotion of sexual freedom as a selling point (e.g. Turner and Ash 1975, with reference to the Seychelles). Srisang (1991) outlines several aspects of moral behaviour in Asia for which a growth in tourism may be responsible, particularly prostitution. Several other studies make reference to prostitution and changing attitudes towards sex, but provide little quantitative evidence to support assertions of a tourism influence (e.g. Urbanowicz 1977; Archer 1978; Holder 1988).

Indeed, Papadopoulos (1988) points to an over-emphasis of the link between moral decline and tourism, suggesting that prostitution and gambling, for example, occur everywhere and are not the prerogative of a particular Developed or Developing Country with or without a tourism industry. A similar point is made by Cohen (1982) with reference to Thailand. Frequently associated with issues of moral decline, the impact of tourism on the health of local people is of increasing concern, particularly with reference to HIV and AIDS, and other sexually transmitted diseases. Unfortunately, little research evidence is available to provide an adequate basis on which to develop this theme. Alleyne (1990) in a study of health patterns associated with tourism in the Caribbean, points to areas in which the health of nationals is affected by tourism, but concedes that lack of adequate data limits the scope of the analysis.

AN OVERVIEW OF TOURISM IMPACTS AND THE IMPACT LITERATURE

The consideration above of the many specific impacts that tourism development can have on environmental quality, clearly demonstrates that there can be no simple, definitive view of the relationship between tourism and the environment. Individual impacts, and the net effect of impacts grouped together, may be detrimental, neutral, benign or enhancing, according to a number of factors operating in a given place at a given time. An understanding of the full range of actual or potential impacts of tourism requires the consideration of many inter-related characteristics, such as those of the tourists themselves, the nature of the tourist destination and the functioning of various tourism agents which operate between tourists and their destination areas (OECD 1981b). Much will depend upon the types of tourist activities pursued at the destination area; whether these are essentially active or sedentary, for example. The nature and severity of impacts can also be viewed as a function of the intensity of site use, the transformational potential of the tourism development, the resilience of local ecosystems and the rapidity of development (Cohen 1978).

There is some evidence to suggest that tourism pressures on environmental resources and the consequent loss of environmental quality occur most commonly where development has been rapid and in areas with little or no planning control. Problems arising under these circumstances may be exacerbated where there is a lack of technical or financial means to provide adequate infrastructure, and where tourist demand exerts marked seasonal peaks in activity (OECD 1981a; OECD 1981b).

Given the great diversity of tourist and tourism types, tour company operations and destination area characteristics, it is not surprising that opinion in the tourism literature on the specific and net effects of tourism on environmental quality can appear confused (and confusing) and, not infrequently, flatly contradictory. As with any industry, the site-specific, activity-specific and dynamic nature of impacts makes generalisation virtually impossible and, arguably, a redundant quest. This said, a broad range of opinion can be found in the literature on the general relationship between tourism as an entity and the maintenance of environmental quality. Opinion appears to range from the antagonistic, through sceptical, to the broadly 'balanced', to the mildly favourable, to the enthusiastic. This range of opinion is reflected below, within the context of a growing awareness of the need for more environmentally-conscious tourism policies.

The formulation of environmentally-conscious tourism policy

The view of Tyler (1989) provides an example of the expression of the most negative and distasteful aspects of tourism, and a rationale for those involved in the tourism industry to adopt more environmentally-friendly policies:

> Tourism as it developed in the 60s and 70s is self-destructive. It destroys the very things tourists come for. It is a classic case of killing the goose that lays the golden egg.
>
> (Tyler 1989: 38)

Clearly, the argument is that tourism (unlike the majority of other industries) ultimately relies for its continued well-being on the maintenance of environmental resources. Tyler considers the Developing Countries to be particularly prone to tourism-related environmental damage, given the need for such countries to generate income and the frequently low priority given to environmental issues. Tananone (1991) suggests that tourism has acted to transfer the ecological problems of the industrialised nations to Developing Countries. This view has been echoed in other reviews (see, for example, Srisang 1991). Hills and Rinke (1989) conclude that mass tourism in Developing Countries has often occurred at the expense of the host country's biophysical and cultural environments. Similar litanies of tourism-generated environmental degradation can also be found for long-established tourist centres in Developed Countries (e.g. Andronikou 1987, with reference to Cyprus).

Other authors, however, adopt a different view, emphasising the actual and potential benefits of tourism, especially with regard to the conservation and protection of natural and built environments. Stankovic (1991) stresses that tourism is a protector, as well as a consumer, of the natural environment, which has served to enhance the economic value of some aspects of nature which are of no particular value for other activities. Many conservationists might balk at the implication that an environmental resource cannot just 'be', and must have an economic value related to a specific activity. It could, of course, be argued that natural ecosystems have inherent, non-economic worth, not least because they sustain life on Earth. This type of debate is examined in more detail in the following chapter. However, variants of

Stankovic's argument crop up frequently in the tourism literature and could be viewed as a pragmatic approach enabling the justification of the conservation of environmental resources. Brockleman and Dearden (1990), for example, consider the value of nature-based trekking in Thailand as a means of providing an economic rationale for the protection of the natural environment and its wildlife. Norton and Roper-Lindsay (1992) add another dimension by contending that tourism can not only increase the conservation value of natural habitats, but also aid in the ecological education of a wide number of people, enhancing a sense of environmental stewardship. They therefore argue that it is important for conservationists to view some tourism developments as potentially positive activities. Although qualified with references to the potentially destructive nature of inappropriate development, many authors have expressed very similar sentiments on tourism as an actual or potential force for environmental good (see, for example, Grant (1990), with reference to the fragile eucalyptus-dominated mallee shrublands of Australia; and Olokesusi (1990), with reference to the Yankari Game Reserve in Nigeria).

Increasingly, the attention of researchers and decision-makers appears to be turning to focus on how best the frequently competing (and increasingly so) demands of tourism and conservation can be achieved. These conflicts may be very difficult to resolve. This is the case for the Brotonne nature park in Normandy, France, for example, where the undeniable benefits of rural tourism (particularly with reference to the preservation of buildings and culture) and its economic success have meant that the park is struggling to maintain its identity as a nature reserve (Tiard 1987). However, despite such difficulties, the view that tourism and environmental conservation are not necessarily incompatible is growing and being increasingly expressed for a wide variety of environments (Anon 1989).

Furthermore, there are now many calls for conservationists and the tourism industry to begin to work much more closely together; calls based upon the mutual interest of sectors which should be natural allies (Hazell 1989). Compelling arguments can be used to support this aim. Some examples of the apparent loss of tourism revenues due to environmental degradation have already been cited above. This loss of environmental quality may be tourism-generated, or contributed to by tourism, or imposed on the tourism industry by other sectors and activities. Antunac (1989), argues that the greatest problem facing the tourism industry is the threat of pollution to the natural environment, in both Developed and Developing Countries. A further illustration of this threat can be found in the study of Borys and Prudzienica (1987). They examined the threat to the natural environment in the Jelenia Gora region of Poland from pollution associated with the operation of a chemical fibre plant. They found that tourists increasingly failed to visit the region as perception of the pollution hazard widened. Between 1975 and 1985, package tours decreased by 18 per cent and overnight stays decreased by 36 per cent. Similarly, the loss of fishing as an activity for tourists to Lake Balaton due to pollution from tourism and other industrial developments provides another example of the inter-dependency between a healthy environment and a healthy tourism sector (Tyler 1989). Relatedly, Smith and Jenner (1989) point to the fall in Rhine cruise bookings following the Sandoz pollution disaster, and the slump in Eastern European holiday bookings after the Chernobyl nuclear accident.

The importance of this inter-dependency is not restricted to the natural environment. Smith and Jenner (1989) point out that acid corrosion is having a major impact on the capital investments of the tourism/transport industry itself, through damage to aircraft, coaches, railway lines and rolling stock, hotel window frames, concrete, etc. Conversely, conservationists might do well to heed the findings of the English Tourist Board (1991) in a study of the future of smaller seaside resorts in England. It was found that as a consequence of the recent decline in tourist numbers and, there-fore, revenue, environmental degradation and an undermining of the quality of the townscape environment have occurred in the majority of the resorts considered. The whole character and attractiveness of such seaside towns may now be under threat.

Co-operation between the tourism industry and environmental organisations does, therefore, appear highly desirable. This might even extend to the tackling of global environmental issues. Smith and Jenner (1989) further suggest that the threat to winter skiing may force the tourism industry to add its voice to those calling for action to combat the pollution contributing to global warming. They argue that the 'bottom line' for tourism is that if the industry fails to become involved in the 'green' movement, it will not be able to influence environmental policies that affect it, and will become a target for environmental campaigners. This line is echoed by others. Smith (1990), for example, bemoans the lack of interest shown by the tourism industry in its sensitivity to climatic conditions, and suggests that the industry should be planning now for future climatic change brought about through global warming. Smith argues that climate change may influence the overall volume of tourism, the pattern of tourist activity around the world, the degree of tourist satisfaction and even the degree of safety experienced by tourists in certain environments. For example, Smith points to growing concern in areas such as eastern Canada, the European Alps and the Snowy Mountains of Australia, where certain winter holiday resorts may no longer have a viable length of snow season within 20 or 30 years. Similarly, a change to warmer and drier conditions throughout parts of North America may lead to the closure of large areas of forest and heathland to summer visitors due to the increased risk of fire. Changes in water levels may also have serious consequences. The scenario for the Great Lakes of North America, for example, is for declining water levels over the next few decades. This may have a direct impact on the viability of fixed waterfront facilities such as marinas. Also, the potential for tourism development may decline with the shrinkage and loss of wetland areas, a decline in cold-water game fish species and an increase in near-shore pollution levels as the dilution potential of the Great Lakes decreases. Conversely, Smith argues that rising sea levels are likely to have profound effects on recreation and tourism along all marine shorelines. Beaches may be subject to increased erosion, for example, leading to a total loss of this resource in some areas. Indeed, according to some climatologists, certain low-lying tropical islands, such as the Republic of Maldives in the Indian Ocean and the atoll chain of Tuvala in the South Pacific, may even face extinction before the end of the next century. Finally, with reference to tourist safety, Smith points to the increased risk of hurricanes in many parts of the world, as sea temperatures rise.

It now appears increasingly rare for tourism (especially mass tourism) to be regarded as an unqualified panacea for economic ills. Those involved in the tourism industry and in decision-making public authorities, as well as tourism researchers, appear to have a greater appreciation that tourism, as an exploiter of resources, can be environmentally destructive and, therefore, potentially short lived. The conservation of environmental quality has come to be seen as an economic investment for the industry.

An example of how this philosophy has been translated into policy, is provided by the Caribbean Tourism Research and Development Centre (CTRC), as described by Holder (1988). The CTRC makes the following points, many or all of which will be pertinent to other tourist destinations.

- The environment is tourism's resource; the tourism industry promotes and sells the experience/enjoyment of the environment.
- A proper understanding of tourism and commitment to lasting and healthy tourism is possibly the best method of ensuring the preservation of the Caribbean environment.
- Tourism is critical to the economic survival of the Caribbean.
- Long-term commitment to tourism requires careful planning in order to minimise negative environmental effects (this was absent in the early stages of Caribbean tourism development).
- Costs and benefits of tourism developments in the Caribbean should be thoroughly assessed. Successful remedial action will, however, require a great change in attitude towards tourism itself.
- Because of Caribbean economic realities and increasing dependency on tourism, the region has no option but to devise sophisticated systems of management, education, research and monitoring with respect to its environmental resources.

However, although the formulation of appropriate policies for tourism is a necessary precursor to the harmonious integration of tourism and environmental conservation, policies need to be implemented successfully before anything can be achieved. The study of Pyrovetsi (1989) provides a timely reminder that policy formulation and enhanced awareness of environmental issues do not neccessarily translate into practice without efficient tourism planning frameworks and the tools to implement environmental management. Pyrovetsi considers the implementation of a pilot Integrated Mediterranean Programmes (IMPs) project in Prespa National Park, Greece. Pyrovetsi concludes that despite increased concern over the adverse impacts of tourism on the natural environment, the implementation of this IMP operation had detrimental ecological effects in the area, as the development plan made no attempt to integrate the needs of conservation and tourism. Chapters 4 and 5 examine the potential of land use planning and Environmental Impact Assessment for the better integration of tourism and conservation. The remainder of this chapter is devoted to measures which can be adopted to ameliorate the adverse impacts of tourism in existing destination areas. Remedial action is an important issue, as demonstrated by its recognition in the CTRC policy outline given above.

IMPACT AMELIORATION MEASURES

Butler (1991) provides a review and critique of measures which can be used to decrease the pressure of tourism on the environment. According to Butler, there are four main approaches to impact mitigation, namely, changing the tourist type, changing the resource for resistance, education, and curbing tourist numbers.

Changing the tourist type, means moving away from mass tourism to some form of 'alternative' tourism, involving a different type of 'responsible' tourist willing to pay for basic local food and accommodation, on a small-scale, without the services and facilities demanded by the traditional mass tourist. Alternative tourism is discussed in detail in the following chapter, but Butler criticises this amelioration measure in a number of ways. Firstly, it is argued that there are insufficient alternative tourists to supply all the destinations which seek them. Secondly, a large proportion of the expenditure of such tourists is made outwith the destination area. Thirdly, even the most environmentally-conscious tourist can degrade the environment. Finally, it is suggested that small-scale alternative tourism operations may well grow and change through time into potentially more destructive forms.

Another possibility is to try to change the resource base so that it is better able to withstand tourism pressure. This might involve the laying of reinforced and marked trails through a wildlife park, for example, to discourage tourist exploration and, at the same time, reduce footpath erosion. Making the resource more resistant may also be particularly appropriate in and around fragile heritage resources, such as ancient monuments. Relatedly, the provision of new infrastructure, such as a sewage treatment works, although not changing the resource base directly, can reduce environmental degradation while the number of tourists remains constant (OECD 1981a; OECD 1981b). Butler (1991) recognises that increasing the resistance of the resource base has been successful in some cases, but questions its acceptability to tourists and others in situations where any change to the resource might reduce its inherent attractiveness, or where tourists are unconvinced of the need for protection.

Butler is also sceptical of a management approach based on curbing tourist numbers, whether this is used to reduce numbers where they are already too high, or to limit numbers before they reach some 'carrying capacity' level. The carrying capacity concept is discussed in detail in the following chapter, and is not considered any further here. Butler argues that attempts to reduce tourist numbers are rare, because of the risk to jobs and the standard of living amongst the host population which a reduction in tourist revenue might bring. Butler's scepticism is borne out by the experience of some mountain regions, for example, where proposals to reduce tourist numbers have met with resistance from local populations in response to a possible loss of income (May 1991).

For Butler, the best, and possibly only, prospect of reducing tourism pressures in existing centres over the long term lies with education. The environmental impacts of tourism need to be better understood by developers and others in the industry, governments and other public sector agencies, local populations, and tourists themselves. Possible impediments to the implementation and success of education strategies include:

- an unwillingness by developers to consider factors other than profit margins, especially where controls over development are weak;
- a failure by central and local governments to appreciate that it is not necessarily in their own best interests to facilitate the development of every resource for tourism;
- a lack of co-ordination and consistency of approach both between and within different tiers of government; and,
- the assumption that local populations will always assume the role of guardians of the quality of the local environment.

(Butler 1991)

Butler admits to being deliberately critical and sceptical in the review of impact amelioration measures, but argues that examples of the successful management of tourism from an environmental perspective are very rare. The most successful centres, such as St Moritz and Gstaad in Switzerland, appear to be those where development has been strictly curtailed through strong local consensus and local authority development control. The importance of building and land use controls has been recognised elsewhere (e.g. OECD 1981a, OECD 1981b), and is discussed in Chapter 4.

The wider environmental management literature may, however, provide an alternative measure for impact amelioration in existing tourism centres, which could be implemented relatively quickly and may avoid any direct loss of revenue brought about by reducing or limiting tourist numbers. Environmental auditing has been used as an environmental management tool for a number of years by private industrial (largely manufacturing) companies and other organisations seeking to ensure that the activities and products of an enterprise do not cause unacceptable impacts on the environment during its operational phase. It is primarily concerned with impacts on the natural environment. Through a detailed and regular examination of an organisation's operations, it is possible to identify actions to improve environmental performance. Environmental auditing has been defined as:

A management tool comprising a systematic, documented, periodic and objective evaluation of how well environmental organisation, management and equipment are performing with the aim of helping to safeguard the environment by:
i) facilitating management control of environmental practices;
ii) assessing compliance with company policies, which would include meeting regulatory requirements.

(ICC 1989: 6)

A full discussion of the operation of an environmental auditing system is beyond the scope of this book. However, such a system can bring advantages to an organisation, including: safeguarding the quality of the environment; assisting in compliance with local, regional and national laws and regulations; reducing the risk of litigation and additional regulation; increasing employee awareness of environmental policies and responsibilities; identifying potential cost-savings (e.g. through reduced energy or water consumption, or by waste minimisation); and, by assuring an adequate and up-to-date environmental data-base to aid decision-making in relation to operational modifications or new development proposals (ICC 1989).

Assuming a degree of willingness on the part of tourism enterprises to conduct regular environmental audits of their activities, the widespread adoption of such audits by individual operators might reduce the environmental pressures of tourism as an entity in a destination area. This possibility has been recognised in the tourism literature (e.g. Klemm 1992). Indeed, environmental audits have already been conducted for operations in the tourism sector, including hotels, a range of tourist attractions and transport organisations (ETB *et al.* 1992). However, much needs to be done before one can envisage regular environmental audits being conducted by the range of operators involved in the tourism industry. Not least, continuing education is required on the potential benefits of impact amelioration, whether through environmental audits or other measures.

Impact amelioration needs to be addressed by all operators in the tourism industry; it should not be merely the concern of those functioning within destination areas, because tourism impacts are generated and felt outwith these areas. It has already been pointed out that tourism impact studies have focused almost solely on destination areas. The same can also be said of studies on impact amelioration measures, including the use of environmental audits which often have a limited geographical scope, being restricted to operational concerns at a specific site. In order to fully appreciate the impacts of tourism and the efficacy of amelioration measures, more systematic research, which views tourism as a series of 'cradle-to-grave' activities with associated environmental pressures, would be helpful. In this context, the approach of Thurot (1980) may be useful. Thurot recognises that the nature and magnitude of tourism impacts are not merely functions of internal factors at the destination area (such as the characteristics of the local environment, society and economy), but also of external factors in both tourist-generating areas and transit areas. Thus, for example, conditions in both generating and transit areas may combine to accentuate destination area impacts by concentrating tourist demand both spatially and temporally (Pearce 1989).

It is perhaps worth concluding this chapter with an illustration of how tourist demand can, apparently, be affected by environmental conditions in generating areas, thus demonstrating the complexities inherent in the study of tourism and environmental quality. Smith (1990), in considering the relationship between tourist activity and climate, provides an interesting example of how conditions in a tourist-generating region can influence the level of demand and, therefore, the degree of environmental pressure, experienced elsewhere. Smith plotted the number of UK residents travelling to Portugal for a holiday in the months of July, August and September between 1979 and 1987. The calculated best-fit regression line indicated a strong linear growth in UK tourists during this period. However, the interesting aspect to this study emerged when the annual residuals from the regression line were plotted against a measure of rainfall over Britain in the *previous* summer. A strong and statistically significant relationship was found between these two parameters. Smith argues that this indicates that a poor summer in the UK persuades more residents to holiday in Portugal the following year, thus demonstrating that vacation decisions are influenced by conditions at home, as well as conditions at destination areas.

Chapter 3

Key concepts for tourism and the environment

Colin Hunter

INTRODUCTION

Much of the previous chapter demonstrated a need for tourists and the tourism industry to become more aware of their environmental impacts. The aim of this chapter is to consider key concepts for the harmonious integration of tourism development and the environment. The concept of 'sustainable development' is used as a focus of the chapter. It is a phrase which has entered our vocabulary only relatively recently, but an idea which encompasses earlier recognitions of the need for environmental management, including the environmental management of tourism. Potentially, it provides a basis for the management of tourism which integrates concern for the natural, built and cultural environments with continued economic development, so as to embrace all 'quality of life' issues, at the destination area and beyond. At the start of the chapter, the meaning of sustainable development is examined in a general sense. Towards the end of the chapter, the concept is re-examined in the context of tourism, and the meaning of sustainable tourism development is more fully explored. In between, other concepts and conceptual developments, such as tourism carrying capacity, which have a bearing on sustainable tourism development, are considered.

THE GENERAL CONCEPT OF SUSTAINABLE DEVELOPMENT

'Sustainable development' is a phrase which quickly entered into the common vocabulary with the heightened environmental awareness of the late 1980s. There is no universally accepted definition of sustainable development (indeed, Pearce *et al.* 1989 list over 20 separate definitions). However, the most widely cited definition is found in the World Commission on Environment and Development (1987) report which brought the term into common usage. According to the World Commission, sustainable develop-ment is 'development that meets the needs of the present without compromising the ability of future generations to meet their own needs' (WCED 1987: 43). This, most basic, definition appears simple. However, much controversy and fundamental debate is concealed within this apparently self-evident phrase. Some of these issues are considered below. As should become evident, the concept of sustainable development and, therefore, sustainable tourism development, is far from being clear-cut and value-free.

The above definition contains two important ingredients: human needs and environmental limitations. Firstly, human needs. The World Commission places particular emphasis on the essential needs of the world's poor, to which over-riding priority should be given. Such needs include sufficient food, clean water, shelter and clothing. Added to these, are the normal human aspirations for those things which contribute to a better quality of life (e.g. higher standard of living, greater consumer choice, more security, increased vacation opportunities etc.). Thus, the World Commission regards the major objective of development as the satisfaction of human needs and aspirations. Where basic needs are not being met, the World Commission states that sustainable development clearly requires economic growth. The position of the World Commission is less clear with reference to the fulfilment of aspirations in areas where basic needs are already met. If development implies economic growth, it is by no means certain that sustainable development requires economic growth in Developed Countries. This is one of the contentious issues surrounding the meaning of sustainable development. The World Commission merely states that the opportunity to satisfy aspirations for a better life should be extended to all people, and that perceived needs are socially and culturally determined, so that sustainable development requires the promotion of values that encourage consumption rates that are ecologically possible over the long-term and to which all people can reasonably aspire.

This view certainly does not preclude the continued pursuit of economic growth in Developed Countries. This may explain why many politicians have eagerly embraced the concept of sustainable development, with its apparent acceptance that environmental concern need not mean the abandonment of economic growth as a political goal. The same eagerness can be found in the response of some agencies involved in the promotion of tourism to the concept of sustainable development (see, for example, ETB *et al.* 1992). Munt (1992), considering tourism and sustainable development in Developing Countries, argues that sustainability has been seized upon by the political mainstream as a convenient concept for ensuring 'sustainable' material growth.

For the World Commission, meeting human needs and aspirations means equity or fairness in terms of access to wealth-generating resources and in the distribution of development costs and benefits. Equity of access to resources is crucial to the realisation of sustainable development. This applies both in the sense of current social justice (intra-generational equity) and in terms of fairness between generations (inter-generational equity). The apparent inability of tourism developments in many Developing Countries to deliver fairness of access to benefits to local populations is a frequent criticism in the tourism literature.

The second critical idea embodied within the World Commission's concept of sustainable development, is that of limitation. There is a limit to the natural environment's ability to meet present and future needs. This applies to the need for non-renewable resources, renewable resources and the 'free services' which the natural environment supplies in terms of waste accumulation, climate regulation, clean air and water, food resources, etc. Such limitation is analogous to the concept of a destination area's 'physical carrying capacity' for tourism activity (discussed later on). Thus, calls in the tourism literature for environmental conservation are echoed in the World Commission's belief that sustainable development is development that does not endanger the natural systems that support life on Earth. In the words of the World Commission:

> Different limits hold for the use of energy, materials, water, and land. Many of these will manifest themselves in the form of rising costs and diminishing returns, rather than in the form of any sudden loss of a resource base. The accumulation of knowledge and the development of technology can enhance the carrying capacity of the resource base. But ultimate limits

there are, and sustainability requires that long before these are reached, the world must ensure equitable access to the constrained resource and reorient technological efforts to relieve the pressure.

(WCED 1987: 45)

The idea of limiting development to within environmental carrying capacities applies to the various types of resource. Thus, renewable resources, such as animal and plant species used for food, clothing, building, fuel, medicines etc., need not be depleted for future generations provided the rate of use does not exceed the limits of natural regeneration and growth. This is the concept of 'sustainable yield'. In the previous chapter, examples were given of tourism-related activities, such as collection and killing for the souvenir trade, which exceeded the sustainable yield for individual species. Since species interact, the reduction in numbers of one species through human exploitation may have ecosystem-wide impacts, and the maximum sustainable yield must also take account of these potential system-wide effects. With reference to non-renewable resources such as fossil fuels, metallic and non-metallic minerals, the World Commission argues that sustainable development requires that the rate of depletion of these resources should foreclose as few future options as possible. Basically, a non-renewable resource should not be exhausted before acceptable substitutes or alternatives are available. Emphasis should, therefore, be placed on economy of use, re-use and recycling. Finally, the World Commission argues that the Earth's life support systems (atmosphere, oceans, fresh-waters, soils, rock formations) are too often regarded as infinite or infinitely renewable 'free goods' for human activities like waste disposal. Adverse impacts on these natural elements should be minimised so as to sustain the overall integrity of the Earth's ecosystems.

Even given the short introduction above, it should be clear that sustainable development is a long-term and global endeavour. This is apparent in the goals and legal principles set out for sustainable development by the World Commission (see Table 3.1). It should also be apparent from the more refined definition of sustainable development as:

a process of change in which the exploitation of resources, the direction of investments, the orientation of technological

Table 3.1 A summary of the goals and legal principles of sustainable development, as proposed by the World Commission on Environment and Development (1987)

Goals	*Legal principles*
• a political system that secures effective participation in decision making • an economic system that is able to generate surpluses and technical knowledge on a self-reliant and sustained basis • a social system that provides for solutions for the tensions arising from disharmonious development • a production system that respects the obligation to preserve the ecological base for development • a technological system that can search continuously for new solutions • an international system that fosters sustainable patterns of trade and finance • an administrative system that is flexible and has the capacity for self-correction	• All human beings have the fundamental right to an environment adequate for their health and well-being • states shall conserve and use the environment and natural resources for the benefit of present and future generations • states shall maintain ecosystems and ecological processes essential for the functioning of the biosphere, shall preserve biological diversity, and shall observe the principle of optimum sustainable yield in the use of living natural resources and ecosystems • states shall establish adequate environmental protection standards and monitor changes in and publish relevant data on environmental quality and resource use • states shall make or require prior environmental assessments of proposed activities which may significantly affect the environment or use of a natural resource • states shall inform in a timely manner all persons likely to be significantly affected by a planned activity and to grant them equal access and due process in administrative and judicial proceedings • states shall ensure that conservation is treated as an integral part of the planning and implementation of development activities and provide assistance to other states, especially to developing countries, in support of environmental protection and sustainable development • states shall co-operate in good faith with other states in implementing the preceding rights and obligations

Source: WCED (1987)

development, and institutional change are all in harmony and enhance both current and future potential to meet human needs and aspirations.

(WCED 1987: 46)

As if such a process of change will not be problematical enough, the concept of sustainable development itself is by no means universally accepted or interpreted in the same way. Yet, some interpretation is required before progress can be made on the meaning of sustainable tourism development. To this end, a brief examination of the broader debate between economic development and resource conservation is provided in the following section.

Sustainable development and conservation versus development

Unfortunately, the more one examines the concept of sustainable development, the more illusory its apparent simplicity becomes. The term can be held to represent different viewpoints according to one's stance on the more general debate between economic development and resource conservation. The concept is plastic and can be moulded to 'fit' widely differing approaches to environmental management. There appears little sign of an early emergence of an accepted consensus view on the meaning and policy implications of sustainable development (see, for example, O'Riordan 1989). It is, therefore, perhaps too easy to assume that disparate groups, such as certain tourism developers and conservationists, will converge on a common interpretation of sustainable development so that the co-operation necessary to achieve sustainable tourism development will be forthcoming. The gulf that may exist between certain tourism developers and conservationists, for example, can be illustrated by considering two 'extreme' 'world-views' on the relationship between economic development and resource conservation. These, rather simplified, attitudes are largely taken from the review of Turner (1991).

At one 'extreme', are those who might be described as holding a traditional, resource-exploitative, growth-orientated view of resource management. The environment is viewed as a collection of goods and services of instrumental value to humans. Clearly, this is a strongly utilitarian and anthropocentric stance. Under this paradigm, intra-generational equity considerations are typically not addressed explicitly at all, and it is immaterial who, in a particular society, receives the benefits or bears the costs of development. This attitude would appear to have dominated much tourism development in Developing Countries, to date. Furthermore, future costs and benefits are given less weight than current costs and benefits. This can be justified on the grounds that the pursuit of economic growth now, provides increasing material benefits, increasing consumer choice and need/aspiration satisfaction and, therefore, improved human welfare. Resource scarcities can be mitigated by investment in new technologies to provide technical fixes and substitution mechanisms for environmental problems. Thus, research and development expenditure (paid for by the prerequisite of continuing economic growth) contributes to a stock of human capital, including knowledge, that is inherited by future generations who will then be richer and better able to cope with any environmental cost burdens left by earlier generations.

For those who adhere to this world-view, sustainable development can be seen as equivalent to sustained economic growth, with no particular need for resource conservation. However, in the context of tourism, this attitude might result in a direct and short-term threat to economic activity if the resources which attract tourists are undermined. In terms of the appraisal of development projects, programmes and policies, the typical approach under the resource-exploitative paradigm is to utilise conventional Cost–Benefit Analysis (CBA) as a narrow measure of the economic efficiency of alternatives. While Environmental Impact Assessment (EIA) (see Chapter 5) might be used as part of the appraisal process, to gain a wider appreciation of associated environmental impacts, it is likely that the EIA would be regarded as a small, separate, 'add-on' to the CBA. It is more than likely that the full range of environmental impacts will fail to be fully incorporated into the decision-making process.

At the other 'extreme' of the development/conservation debate, is what can be described as the extreme resource-preservationist, zero-growth world-view. This may also be described as a 'deep ecology' or 'ecocentric' or 'bioethics' paradigm. In this case, nature is not regarded as merely a conglomeration of goods and services of instrumental value to humans, but rather it is seen as having intrinsic or inherent value in itself. In other words, nature does not have to provide any function or service to humans in order to be of value. This view presents difficulties for decision-makers since intrinsic value cannot be quantified and cannot, therefore, appear on the balance-sheet of a particular development project, policy or programme. The effective outcome of this philosophy would be to keep the use of natural assets to an absolute minimum, so as not to deplete intrinsic value more than is absolutely necessary. There is, therefore, a complete abandonment of the traditional CBA approach to the assessment of alternative developments. Even the use of EIA might be seen as irrelevant, since EIA is essentially a tool used within an anthropocentric context which recognises, implicitly, the right of humans to exploit natural resources.

The extreme resource-preservationist view entails only the use of technologies and products which minimise the loss of intrinsic value. Such an 'if in doubt, do nothing' approach to development and technological innovation can be criticised as overly constraining, and would logically imply zero or negative world economic and human population growth. With reference to tourism, this might result in a tourist scene of a rather 'dull shade of green' (Pigram 1990: 6). There is also the risk that the conservation of intrinsic value in nature will be at the expense of social justice and even survival in the Developing Countries where economic development is required to meet basic needs and increase quality of life. However, to the extreme preservationist, the concept of sustainable development might be seen as inherently ambiguous, since economic growth, as currently understood, can be viewed as fundamentally unsustainable. O'Riordan, for example, writes:

> Sustainability is becoming accepted as the mediating term which bridges the gap between developers and environmentalists. Its beguiling simplicity and apparently self-evident meaning have obscured its inherent ambiguity.
>
> (O'Riordan 1989: 93)

For O'Riordan, and others, sustainable development represents a profound challenge to the existing status quo, requiring a break with the traditional growth mentality of politicians and most existing institutions of economic investment and resource allocation. Thus, it is possible to view development which implies economic growth as inherently unsustainable, and, therefore, the concept of sustainable development as inherently ambiguous.

The crucial point to the world-views outlined above, is that sustainable development is not an objective, value-free concept, or even an idea which can be universally adopted by all parties involved in the development/conservation debate. In much of the literature on tourism development and the environment, there appears to be very little appreciation of this point. Munt (1992), however, recognises that the concept of sustainable tourism development is prone to flexibility of interpretation. In examining the unfolding debate over new forms of alternative tourism and sustainable development in Developing Countries, Munt detects a dichotomy of interpretation of sustainable tourism development. It is suggested that the standpoint frequently adopted in indebted Developing Countries emphasises political and economic imperatives, while other interpretations reflect a 'quintessentially Western environmentalism' (Munt 1992: 213). It is further suggested that such divergence may be indicative of a coming crisis in attempts to produce a 'greenprint' for tourism in Developing Countries.

Arguably, the most fruitful interpretation of sustainable development lies between the extremes outlined above. A resource-conservationist, managed growth world-view (Turner 1991) could be regarded as the most pragmatic doctrine of environmental management, including the management of tourism. While there are many potential variants which might be included under this philosophical approach, basically it is a modified or extended growth-orientated view. Although this view retains an anthropocentric bias, allowance is made for the non-utilitarian values of intra-generational and inter-generational equity, as espoused by the World Commission on Environment and Development (WCED 1987). In particular, this world-view entails an environmental stewardship ethic to protect the interests of future generations, so that they inherit a stock of natural resources no less (and preferably larger) than that inherited by the current generation. The passing on of an equivalent stock of natural resources is sometimes referred to as the 'constant natural assets rule' (Pearce *et al.* 1989). This argument rests on the belief that the present generation does not 'own' the natural resource base, and so has no right to deplete the economic and other opportunities afforded by it. The reader should note, however, that debate continues regarding the philosophical basis of the concepts of inter-generational equity and constant natural assets (Turner 1991).

With reference to the above, it is critical to note the importance placed on natural resources. This is because the notion of inter-generational equity can be interpreted in two very different ways. One interpretation of the need to leave the next generation a stock of resource capital no less than that inherited stresses *total* resource assets (including human-made as well as natural assets), while the other interpretation is narrower, being confined to *natural* assets only. Under the first interpretation, a tourism development which destroys or degrades the natural environment may still be seen as contributing to sustainable development if the wealth created and resultant built assets (which are passed on to the next generation) are of greater 'value' than the pre-existing natural environment. (It should be noted that the human-made forests, lakes, wildlife parks etc. which sometimes accompany tourism developments can be regarded as both human-made and natural assets). A requirement of this interpretation is that the natural environment can be 'valued' in monetary terms. This is the subject of heated debate, and the reader is referred to Pearce *et al.* (1989) and Pearce (1991) for details on how such valuation might be achieved.

However, this first interpretation of the inter-generational equity aspect of sustainable development is not in keeping with the spirit of the WCED (1987) report, as outlined in the previous section. There are also compelling utilitarian and moral arguments for the adoption of the narrower interpretation of inter-generational equity based upon the constant natural assets rule. Pearce *et al.* (1989) summarise these as follows.

Non-substitutability – there are many types of natural assets for which there are no human-made substitutes (e.g. the ozone layer and the gene pools of plants and animals). Such assets help to maintain life on Earth and should be preserved.

Uncertainty – since we cannot be certain that human-made substitutes for natural assets will be forthcoming, it is not logical to behave now as if they will. Therefore, a risk-aversion strategy should be adopted at least until our understanding of the functioning of natural life support systems (individually and in total) is adequate.

Irreversibility – while some facets of the natural environment can be re-established up to a point (e.g. a hedgerow), many cannot. No amount of human-made capital can recreate a species, for example. Such a loss is suffered by all subsequent generations. The same applies to some forms of human-made capital, most notably the loss of architectural heritage or ancient monuments or historically unique settlements and cultures.

Equity – since the poor are usually more directly affected by degraded natural environments than the rich (e.g. through direct dependence on vegetation for livestock fodder, fuel-wood and raw materials; wildlife for food; crop residues, animal waste, and organic matter for fertilisers), adherence to the constant natural assets rule is most likely to fulfil the aim of intra-generational equity in places where ecosystem productivity is essential to human livelihoods.

The passing on of an 'intact' natural resource stock does not necessarily mean literally physically intact. Rather, where natural resources are depleted in a given area, these should be replaced elsewhere or compensated for by investment in technological development aimed at resource conservation; e.g. recycling innovation, conservation of renewable resources etc. However, there are areas, such as those containing rare or fragile ecosystems or built heritage, where *preservation* rather than compensating conservation might well be more appropriate. It is important that each area earmarked for development is considered separately on its own merits. Under the broad resource-conservationist view, traditional CBA is modified because the relative importance of environmental impacts is raised in the appraisal of development projects, programmes and policies. In this case, EIA is viewed as a complementary procedure to CBA, providing the necessary information on environmental impacts so that cumulative environmental impacts can be offset by environmental improvements. In other words, EIA provides the data which allows the development to be debited with the costs of creating alternative environmental assets of equal (or greater) value than those lost or degraded through the development. Should an EIA indicate that the cumulative environmental costs of a development are too high and cannot be easily offset, then the proposal can be prevented from progressing based upon rational, 'objective' reasoning.

In summary, the interpretation of sustainable development advocated here, and used as a basis for the discussion of sustainable tourism development, incorporates the idea of the need for constant (or rising) natural assets through time. Clearly, the potential exists, through wildlife or nature tourism, for example, for tourism to make a crucial contribution to global sustainability in this regard. In addition, sustainable development also implies moving towards greater intra-generational equity of access to resources and respect for environmental limits. It is further assumed that there is no inherent ambiguity in the concept of sustainable development and that the conservation, and where necessary preservation, of environmental resources can co-exist alongside economic growth.

The above descriptions deal with alternative views of development versus conservation, and the meaning of sustainable development, at the global scale. Clearly, however, for the concept of sustainable development to be applied in day-to-day decision-making, it also has to be examined on a more local scale. In this respect, the concept of environmental carrying capacity, much utilised in the tourism literature, potentially provides a useful mechanism for translating sustainable development as a global issue into one capable of being applied on the ground. This is the focus of the following section.

SUSTAINABLE DEVELOPMENT AND TOURISM CARRYING CAPACITY

There are a number of models, and model variants, which purport to describe and explain the way in which tourism develops in a given region or destination area (see, for example, Pearce 1989). Sustainable development is essentially about the management of change over time, and the work of Butler (1980) provides a useful, if much debated, model of the evolution of a tourism destination area over time. Butler's tourist-area cycle of evolution is useful because it addresses the idea, inherent in the concept of sustainable development, of an environmental limit, or carrying capacity, to tourist numbers beyond which development at the destination area becomes unsustainable and declines. In other words, 'unless specific steps are taken, tourist destination areas and resources will inevitably become over-used, unattractive, and eventually experience declining use' (Butler 1991: 203). According to Martin and Uysal (1990), for example, the decline of a tourist destination may be attributed to various causes when the actual cause is that the carrying capacity of the area has been exceeded.

Butler's model recognises several stages of evolutionary development, namely, exploration, involvement, development, consolidation, stagnation, decline and (perhaps) rejuvenation. It is argued that a decline in tourist numbers is inevitable, with an inevitable over-reaching of environmental capacity parameters unless remedial measures such as environmental improvements and new marketing strategies are adopted. Thus, following the stagnation phase, tourist numbers may follow a variety of different pathways, depending on the success of new interventions. These are illustrated in Figure 3.1. It has been suggested that decline cannot be reversed or halted through re-marketing alone, without preceding or parallel environmental improvements and management strategies (e.g. Reime and Hawkins 1979). The reader is directed to Butler (1980) for a full account of the model, but for the purposes of this book it is sufficient to briefly outline the origin of the tourist-area cycle concept.

Butler's cyclical view of tourism development at a destination area, is based upon two widely utilised principles; the product

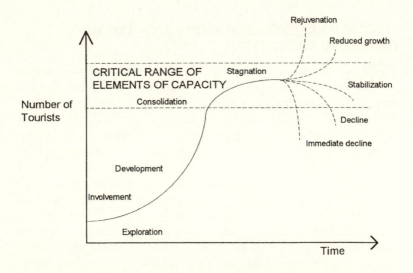

Figure 3.1 A schematic representation of Butler's model of the evolution of tourism development at a destination area
Source: redrawn from Pearce (1989), from Butler (1980)

life-cycle concept, widely used in the business/advertising community, and the growth curves of animal populations. With the former, a product will:

> experience a period of slow growth, followed – if marketed properly – by a take-off period of rapid growth, and subsequently a period of stability. If product improvements are not made, the appeal of the product will thereafter decline and sales will fall, and eventually the product will be taken off the market.
>
> (Butler 1991: 203)

In the context of tourism, being taken off the market might involve a tourist destination reverting to its original function, if possible, or finding another reason for its existence, e.g. by becoming a retirement area. The second principle, that governing the growth of animal populations, is of more direct interest here, because of its recognition of the importance of environmental limits to growth. In this case, it has frequently been observed that the growth in numbers of a particular animal species in a particular location, often proceeds rapidly (following a period of hesitant colonisation) until the population reaches or exceeds the capacity of the environment to support it (e.g. through diminishing food supplies). This can give rise to the classic 'S'-shaped, logistic growth curve, so prevalent in population ecology textbooks. The curve shown in Figure 3.1, up to the stagnation phase, is in fact a logistic curve. Such a curve can be described mathematically by the governing differential equation:

$$\frac{\delta N}{\delta t} = \frac{rN(K-N)}{K}$$

where

N = population size,
t = time,
r = rate of population growth per capita,
K = upper asymptote or environmental carrying capacity.

Thus, Butler's model of change in tourist numbers at a destination area is density dependent, such that a self-limiting or self-crowding negative feedback reduces the rate of growth, linearly, more and more as population (tourist) density increases. In the true logistic curve, population density levels off before reaching the environmental carrying capacity, which represents the maximum sustainable population density. However, in the real world of animal population growths, the density may overshoot the carrying capacity, perhaps due to time-lags in feedback control. Thereafter, the population density may oscillate around the carrying capacity or within a carrying capacity zone, as envisaged by Butler (1980). If oscillation decreases in amplitude with time, or is only relatively small and constant through time, then the population can be said to have reached a 'steady state' or 'dynamic equilibrium' with the environment. Such a pattern could be regarded as sustainable over the long term, and can be taken to represent sustainable tourism development over time, at least in terms of an individual destination area.

Despite the relative lack of empirical testing of Butler's model (and, indeed, other models of tourism development), it has received much attention in the tourism literature, being an inherently attractive concept for those concerned with the environmental impacts of tourism and for those seeking a rationale for interventionist management. However, much of the literature on the tourist-area model has questioned the scope and interpretation of 'carrying capacity'. With animal populations, environmental carrying capacity equates to elements of the natural environment. In a tourism context these might include such attributes as demands on water supplies, fossil fuels for energy generation, land availability and the resilience of flora and fauna to tourist disturbances. However, such a focus on the natural environment is widely regarded as being insufficient in the context of tourism, and there have been many interpretations of the meaning of tourism carrying capacity. Opinion now, however, appears to be consolidating around the interpretations of O'Reilly (1986).

According to O'Reilly there are two facets to tourism carrying capacity. The first deals with the ability of the destination area to absorb the impacts of tourism development, in a variety of ways, before negative impacts become evident. The second relates to the tourists' perceptions of environmental quality, i.e. the risk that tourist numbers will decline because perceived capacities have been exceeded and the destination area ceases to attract (a psychological carrying capacity). Both these facets are evident in the interpretation of carrying capacity provided by Mathieson and Wall (1982), who equate tourism carrying capacity with the maximum number of people who can use a site without unacceptable effects on the physical environment and/or without an unacceptable decline in the quality of experience gained by visitors. Here, the physical environment can be taken to mean natural (biotic and abiotic) features and/or built elements, such as transport links. However, tourism is a complex agglomeration of activities which also affects the local society and economy. The view has grown that any measure of tourism carrying capacity must incorporate social and economic elements. Thus, carrying capacities exist for a number of inter-related features of the destination area. O'Reilly (1986) describes the various carrying capacities as follows.

Physical carrying capacity – the limit of a site beyond which wear and tear will start taking place or environmental problems will arise.
Psychological (or perceptual) carrying capacity – the lowest degree of enjoyment tourists are prepared to accept before they start seeking alternative destinations.
Social carrying capacity – the level of tolerance of the host population for the presence and behaviour of tourists in the destination area, and/or the degree of crowding users (tourists) are prepared to accept by others (other tourists).
Economic carrying capacity – the ability to absorb tourism activities without displacing or disrupting desirable local activities.

Clearly, these individual capacities will be inter-related. For example, tourists may no longer feel comfortable in the destination area (the psychological capacity has been exceeded) because of a deterioration in the quality of the physical environment (excedence of physical capacity) or because of the negative attitudes of locals (excedence of social carrying capacity). Similarly, social carrying capacity might be over-reached due to tourism-induced degradation or over-exploitation of the physical environment, intrusion into aspects of local culture or competition with other economic activities.

Factors which influence capacity thresholds can be divided into two categories: the characteristics of the tourists and the characteristics of the destination area, including its local population. The former category includes factors which determine the nature, magnitude and frequency of interaction between tourists and the destination area and its people (e.g. age, sex, spending power, motivations, attitudes, expectations, ethnic background, behaviour patterns etc.). The latter category will be influenced by features of the natural environment, economic development levels and structures, social structures, political organisation, and the pre-existing level and nature of tourism development. O'Reilly (1986) argues that the inter-relationships between all these factors need to be taken into account to ensure appropriate tourism development. As if this were not problematical enough, attempts to quantify carrying capacity thresholds face a number of other difficulties. These include differences in acceptable levels of crowding, use-dependency in terms of acceptable tourist densities, and the fact that changes in area management may alter carrying capacities through time (Pearce 1989). To this list might be added the frequent lack of background environmental data necessary to calculate threshold limits. Even if one excluded social and economic capacity considerations, the likelihood is that baseline information on existing pollution levels or detailed knowledge of local ecosystems, for example, would be lacking. Considerable expenditure might, therefore, be required in order to determine even one or two carrying capacity limits for individual aspects of the natural environment.

Moreover, tourism develops and changes in any area over time. Similarly, the perceptions of local residents to tourists and tourism are unlikely to remain fixed as development proceeds. Martin and Uysal (1990), for example, in linking the carrying capacity and tourist-area life-cycle concepts, argue that a destination area's carrying capacity will differ according to the life-cycle stage. Thus, in the exploration stage, a lack of facilities might limit tourist density, while social carrying capacity might be very high. However, at the stagnation phase, social factors such as tensions between locals and tourists might provide a limit to expansion, despite under-used physical capacity. Similarly, Duffield and Walker (1984) point out that dimensional changes occur as tourism develops in an area, and that tourism is a dynamic agent of change. At least some aspects of composite carrying capacity cannot, therefore, be regarded as absolute, fixed limits.

For these, and other, reasons the carrying capacity concept has not found wide application as a planning tool in terms of allowing the quantification of development thresholds (WTO 1984; O'Reilly 1986; Pearce 1989). Many authors have expressed scepticism about the practical use of the concept. Romeril (1989), for example, whilst recognising the relevance of the concept to environmental impact studies, bemoans the lack of appropriate research and data. Pearce (1989), following a review of the concept, concludes that it will not be easy to determine quantifiable levels of development that can be readily included in local plans or planning regulations. Duffield and Walker (1984) point out that ultimately defining what is acceptable is a value choice, rather than a technical issue. O'Reilly (1986) argues that capacity cannot be used as a fixed, absolute limit. It is perhaps best to regard the concept as a means of fostering the greater consideration of environmental issues and the quality of experiences available to tourists and the local community, by encouraging tourism planners and managers to set specific goals and objectives (Wall 1982). Similarly, it can be said that:

> While recognizing that tourism carrying capacity is difficult to define, and even more difficult to measure, it, nevertheless, is impossible to ignore. Tourism carrying capacity and the concept of a tourism lifecycle enjoy a synergistic relationship that creates a more viable framework for tourism management.
> (Martin and Uysal 1990: 330)

The tourism carrying capacity concept is important because it may instil a precautionary approach to tourism development and a respect for local environmental limits, in keeping with the resource-conservationist interpretation of sustainable development. Having examined the general concept of sustainable development and the related issue of tourism carrying capacity, it is now possible to examine the theoretical and practical requirements and implications of sustainable tourism development.

SUSTAINABLE TOURISM DEVELOPMENT

Although in recent years a considerable amount has been written on the need to adopt principles and policies of sustainable tourism development, surprisingly little appears to have been written, in depth, on the meaning and implications of sustainable tourism development. Frequently, there appears to be an acceptance of the WCED (1987) principle of inter-generational equity combined with the hope that various alternatives to mass tourism will fulfil this requirement in practice. 'Alternative' tourism is considered later in this chapter, but this can only be examined within the context of a working definition of sustainable tourism development, based on the discussions above. Such an interpretation of sustainable tourism development is given below.

Sustainable tourism development recognises the inter-dependency between the long-term viability of economic invest-ment in tourism projects, programmes and policies and the successful management of the natural, built and human resource bases. Therefore, sustainable tourism development seeks to main-tain and enhance the quality of life, and the quality of the tourist experience, at destination areas through the promotion of economic developments which conserve (and where necessary preserve), local natural, built and cultural resources. Moreover, sustainable tourism development recognises the links which exist between destination areas and the wider environment and, there-fore, seeks to contribute to regional, national and global resource conservation and preservation measures in order to advance intra-and inter-generational equity of access to wealth-generating natural resources.

Aspects of this interpretation of sustainable tourism develop-ment are evident in the tourism literature. One of the most detailed investigations of the meaning of sustainable tourism development is provided by Cronin (1990), who presents the cumulative work of a number of Canadian academics, business people and government officials. In the words of Cronin:

> In the case of the tourism industry, sustainable development has a fairly specific meaning – the industry's challenge is to develop tourism capacity and the quality of its products without adversely affecting the physical and human environment that sustains and nurtures them.
>
> (Cronin 1990: 13)

Cronin further provides a list of criteria that must be met for tourism developments to conform to the principles of sustainable development. These are that development should:

- follow ethical principles that respect the culture and environ-ment of the destination area, the economy and traditional way of life, the indigenous behaviour, and the leadership and political patterns;
- involve the local population, proceed only with their approval and provide for a degree of local control;
- be undertaken with (intra-generational) equity in mind, i.e. with the idea of access to a fair distribution of benefits and

costs among tourism promoters and host peoples and areas, not only now but in the future;

- be planned and managed with regard for the protection of the natural environment for future generations;
- be planned in an integrated manner with other economic sectors; and,
- be assessed on an ongoing basis to evaluate impacts and permit action to counter any negative effects.

Cronin's definition of sustainable tourism development and criteria for its realisation appear to conform explicitly or implicitly to the principles of inter- and intra-generational equity and constant natural assets. As in the interpretation provided at the beginning of this section, the environment is viewed in a holistic sense and encompasses cultural aspects of the destination area, as well as natural and built attributes. The use of integrative planning and environmental impact assessment, mentioned in Cronin's criteria above, are discussed in Chapters 4 and 5, respectively.

Cronin (1990) places considerable emphasis on the intra-generational aspect of sustainable tourism development. It is argued that sustainable tourism development must recognise the contribution that local communities and cultures make to the experience of tourists and that local people must share in the benefits of tourism developments. Furthermore, it is suggested that for sustainable tourism development to become a reality, local people and governmental authorities must show a willingness to participate, and be allowed to participate, in the shaping of the local tourism industry. The issue of local community access to the benefits of tourism development is a critical one. This is especially true of Developing Countries, since the general concept of sustainable development recognises the need for economic growth in these areas so that the quality of life can be enhanced and human aspirations satisfied. Concern over the protection of environmental resources (particularly natural resources) could be taken to the point where innovation and appropriate tourism development is stifled, thus removing the opportunity for the poor in the current generation to benefit from tourism development. Striking the right balance between the creation of benefits for the current generation (especially the poor) and the protection of wealth-generating resources for future generations, goes to the heart of the issue of sustainable tourism development. The need for an appropriate balance of concerns is summarised, succinctly, by Pigram (1990) who writes:

> Whereas sustainable tourism represents the cautious path to follow, prudence should be tempered by receptiveness to initiative and a willingness to judge developmental innovations from the standpoint of environmental acceptability.
>
> (Pigram 1990: 6)

This view appears to be broadly in line with the resource-conservationist, managed growth world-view outlined earlier. Whilst rejecting the extreme resource-exploitative world-view, Pigram also rejects the extreme resource-preservationist paradigm, and writes, '"Ecological determinism" alone is no more defensible than "economic determinism"' (Pigram 1990: 6). Such an interpretation also agrees implicitly with the working definition of sustainable tourism development provided at the beginning of this section.

Pigram's advocacy of sustainable tourism development as the cautious and prudent path, relates to inter-generational equity concerns. It is argued that sustainable tourism development should recognise non-utilitarian or 'hidden' values in environmental resources. According to Pigram (1990) these values include:

existence value – the satisfaction of knowing that a resource is being preserved even if there is no intention of putting it to use;
option value – the option of alternative future uses of the area if it is preserved; and,
bequest value – the satisfaction gained from the knowledge that a resource is not being used or developed to its theoretical maximum capacity, in the interests of future generations.

Pigram argues that the tourism industry should adopt a 'safe minimum standard' approach to development which minimises the risk that irreversible changes will foreclose these hidden values for future generations. The notion of avoiding irreversible changes to environmental resources through tourism activities is in keeping with the views expressed in the broader environmental management literature (see, for example, Pearce *et al.* 1989) and has been outlined previously with reference to the general concept of sustainable development.

Tourism development as it progressively transforms local economies and societies should be environmentally sustainable both in the context of existing tourist areas and in, as yet, undeveloped or under-developed destinations. Alternative tourism in new, or relatively new, destination areas is considered later in this chapter. At this stage, it is perhaps worth examining an example of a recent tourism strategy adopted at an existing mass tourism resort, within the context of the facets of sustainable tourism development described above.

In this respect, Morgan (1991) provides a critique of recent proposals aimed at re-vitalising mass tourism in Majorca. Majorca is the largest of Spain's Balearic islands and has long been a popular beach holiday destination. Recently, however, tourist flows have been declining (e.g. a 6 per cent fall in foreign visitors in 1989 compared to the previous year) and the island can be viewed as having reached the mature/decline stage of the tourism life-cycle model. Problems which are seen to have contributed to the downturn include an over-crowded, over-commercialised, 'tacky' and noisy image, combined with environmental deterioration, particularly through uncontrolled hotel construction, resulting in noise, dust, the blocking of views and the spread of tourism infrastructure to previously unspoiled areas with a consequent loss of scenery and wildlife resources. In an attempt to tackle these problems, public sector bodies have embarked upon environmental and infrastructure improvement programmes and adopted development control planning procedures.

In large, existing resort centres, measures have typically involved tree planting, the creation of parks, pedestrianisation, traffic calming, the creation of off-street car parks and controls over the siting and appearance of new hotels. Such measures appear necessary and laudable. However, as well as measures adopted in large existing resorts, there exists a parallel strategy to draw visitor attention away from large resort centres by publicising the island's other attractions. The island is being re-marketed with tourists and potential tourists re-orientated towards new attractions. Much of this re-marketing has been based on the high quality of the natural environment in other areas of the island. For example, the mountain scenery and unspoilt villages along the island's west coast, the wildlife to be found in mountain areas and the Albufera Marsh nature reserve, and more modern, architecturally and environmentally sensitive resorts on the east coast. Similarly, in order to attract more 'up-market' tourists, marina and golf-course developments have been encouraged (e.g. planning restrictions have been *eased* for accommodation developments linked to golf courses).

A generous interpretation of this dual strategy might emphasise the attempt to ease tourist pressure in large existing resorts, combined with environmental improvements in these centres. However, unless developments associated with the promotion of other attractions on the island are carefully managed and controlled (which does not appear to be the case in the Majorca strategy), then they will not fulfil the criteria for sustainable tourism development. Indeed, one could interpret the promotion of alternative attractions in this way as panic-induced, rather than being driven by environmental concerns. The ill-considered promotion of new areas and activities for tourists should be avoided. Sustainable tourism development is not about new marketing strategies, selling new features for exploitation. It is not about creating cycles of 'boom and bust' in ever new locations, initially offering something different to attract the tourist, but ultimately leaving behind a growing trail of environmentally degraded areas, no longer attractive to tourists or the tourism industry because the supporting environmental resources are no longer viable. In the case of Majorca, one must ask, for example, are fresh-water supplies adequate to sustain golf-course developments over the long term without disrupting the supplies for other activities? Or, how will oil pollution from marinas impact upon the local fishing industry; in other words, will economic diversification be sacrificed over the long term in order to promote continued growth in tourist flows over the short term?

The kind of attitude apparently embodied in the Majorcan strategy still appears to be all too prevalent amongst tourism developers and local public sector authorities alike, and corresponds to the resource-exploitative, growth-orientated world-view interpretation of sustainable development. This approach effectively ignores the constant natural assets rule, inter-generational equity of access to natural resources and the need to minimise irreversible losses for future generations. In the case of Majorca, sustainable tourism development appears to have been taken to mean tourism which merely strives to maintain or enhance short-term economic growth without a complementary and comprehensive assessment of environmental impacts. As Romeril

(1985) points out, travel brochures and magazines often advise tourists to visit 'X' now, before it becomes popular (and by inference spoilt). Thus begins the transition of an area from unspoilt to spoilt, and so the search for ever more remote and secluded sites begins again. Butler (1993) has recently described this approach as the remnants of a 'frontier' mentality, such that when a problem arises, one can always move on and leave the problem behind. Such an attitude is the antithesis of sustainable tourism development, and, potentially, threatens environmental quality around the world.

Sustainable tourism development must attempt to tackle existing environmental problems *in situ*, rather than encourage or facilitate the displacement of environmental problems elsewhere. With this in mind, Smith and Jenner (1989) use the example of Venice. As stated in Chapter 2, Venice, along with other Adriatic resorts, has been suffering lagoonal algal blooms in recent years, making it a less attractive destination. One proposed 'solution' to this problem is the construction of a new island city for tourists at sea, beyond the algal blooms. Smith and Jenner (1989) argue that the real solution to the problem is not the construction of a new city (which may suffer a similar fate if current waste disposal practices are retained) but rather lies in redressing the ecological imbalance which has led to the problem. The reader may be familiar with the much quoted environmental slogan 'prevention is better than cure'. It also follows that 'cure is better than displacement'.

As well as dispersing tourists and tourism developments geographically, attempts have also been made to spread tourist demand more evenly throughout the year, in an effort to reduce seasonal pressures on the environment, especially in resort centres (OECD 1981a; OECD 1981b). This approach may be combined with new marketing approaches designed to spread demand geographically as well. Butler (1991), however, argues that the dispersal of tourists in space and time is not amenable to sustainable development, because it could result (indeed, has resulted) in more profound and permanent changes to the environment over a wider area than when tourists are confined to small areas, in large numbers, for usually brief periods. Marketing strategies aimed at achieving the greater temporal and spatial dispersal of tourists need to be examined very closely with regard to the principles of sustainable tourism development.

Moreover, as reported in Chapter 2, the impacts of tourism on the environment are not restricted to destination areas. Relatedly, sustainable development is a global endeavour and recognises the links between nations and national economies. Tourism is a global phenomenon, yet much of the literature on sustainable tourism apparently fails to recognise that destination areas cannot exist in isolation. There is a danger that in focusing down to the level of a particular destination area, in terms of the implementation of policies for sustainable tourism development, the wider links that sustain the area will be forgotten. Even if a destination area becomes completely self-sufficient in its resource requirements, such an area will still 'generate' environmental impacts through tourist travel. Similarly, unless all waste products generated by tourists and tourism in the area are somehow eliminated, re-used or recycled, the area will affect the quality of resources in the wider environment, even potentially at a global scale. As with the working definition of sustainable tourism development offered at the beginning of this section, it is important to make explicit reference to the potential role of the tourism industry in the protection of resources on regional, national and international scales, as well as at destination areas. While much can be done, potentially, at destination areas to minimise wider environmental impacts, some aspects of tourism cannot help but contribute to wider environmental problems.

For example, the combustion of fossil fuels to generate energy is necessary for all aspects of tourism; from the production of tourist brochures, through the operation of computer terminals by travel agencies, through tourist transportation modes, and through to the heating and lighting of tourist facilities. Thus, tourism contributes to the depletion of global fossil fuel supplies, the global problem of atmospheric warming and to the trans-national problem of acid deposition. Yet, the conservation of natural resources, including non-renewables, is fundamental to sustainable development. Potentially, tourism could exert a significant influence on the conservation of fossil fuel supplies and on the reduction of atmospheric emissions. The tourism industry should be willing to contribute positively to regional, national and international policy initiatives on the environment and could exert considerable influence on policy-makers in lobby-ing for environmental initiatives. Indeed, with proposals for some form of 'energy tax' receiving ever greater attention from national and international governmental agencies, it would appear prudent for tourism and other authorities to encourage the adoption of energy conservation measures. These might include the construction of tourist buildings with good heat insulation properties, the use of fuel efficient vehicles and other technologies, and the limitation of tourist use of private cars in certain areas. Relatedly, Wheatcroft (1991), in considering the relationships between environmental quality, airlines and tourism, argues that it is essential for airlines and other sectors of the tourism industry to develop policies which will overcome the objections of environmentalists to their further growth. It is suggested that the future growth of the air industry could be seriously threatened by restrictions to protect the environment, which would impact upon the expansion of world tourism.

Recently, the English Tourist Board has been involved in the production of a guide for tourism businesses on practical measures for the achievement of sustainable tourism development (ETB *et al.* 1992). As a guide to sustainable tourism development, the publication lacks an in-depth exploration of the meaning of sustainable tourism. Other than equating sustainable tourism development with 'environmentally friendly' tourism and references to the importance of a stewardship ethic and the need for economic growth to take more account of the environment, the phrase receives little attention. However, the document provides an interesting example of recent thinking, particularly given its practical bias and because considerable attention is given to the wider impacts of tourism. Much emphasis is also given to the practical benefits for tourism businesses of 'going green'. These include:

- increased competitiveness, raised quality and a better position in the market;
- greater overall efficiency;
- improved image, credibility and a better basis for growth;
- lower raw material and waste disposal costs in the longer term;
- a better working environment for staff and a higher quality environment for local communities; and,
- opportunities for developing new services and products.

(ETB *et al.* 1992).

Table 3.2 gives a summary of some of the suggested actions to be taken by tourism operators to ensure that wider environmental impacts are minimised. Unusually, the document attempts to inter-relate tourism's future success to the tackling of global environmental problems. Examples cited include the threats to coastal and ski resorts from global warming, acid deposition damage to historic buildings and monuments, and the potential decline of 'sun and sea' holidays through ozone depletion and the increased risk of skin cancers.

The seven principles of sustained tourism, as outlined by ETB *et al.* are as follows:

- The environment has an intrinsic value which outweighs its value as a tourism asset. Short-term considerations should not prejudice its long-term survival and enjoyment by future generations.
- Tourism should be recognised as a positive activity with the potential to benefit the community and the place as well as the visitor.
- The relationship between tourism and the environment must be managed so that it is stable in the long-term. Tourism must not be allowed to damage the resource, prejudice its future enjoyment or bring unacceptable impacts.
- Tourism activities and developments should respect the scale, nature and character of the place in which they are sited.
- In any location harmony must be sought between the needs of the visitor, the place and the host community.
- Some change is inevitable and change can often be beneficial. Adaptation to change, however, should not be at the expense of any of these principles.
- The tourism industry, local authorities and environmental agencies all have a duty to respect the above principles and to work together to achieve their practical realisation.

(ETB *et al.* 1992)

Some claims are, however, being made that existing alternative forms of tourism may already both represent sustainable tourism development and conform to the kind of principles outlined in the list above and previously. The phenomenon of alternative tourism is examined in the following section.

ALTERNATIVE TOURISM

In recent years, there has been a rapid rise in interest in alternative forms of tourism. These are frequently presented as

Table 3.2 Examples of practical measures for businesses to minimise the environmental impacts of tourism beyond the destination area

Energy consumption	Transport	Purchases
• installation of insulation (especially roof spaces and hot water tanks) and draughtproofing of doors and windows • encourage use of showers rather than baths • use of low energy light bulbs • purchase electrical appliances with high energy efficiencies • heating which can be adjusted downwards by guests • exploration of new energy efficient technologies, e.g. heat recovery systems from kitchens, use of solar water heating, etc.	• encourage walking, cycling or use of public transport rather than private cars • choose fuel efficient vehicles with catalytic converters and which run on unleaded fuel • Use of diesel-powered vehicles • Reduce travelling speeds • Send waste oil, batteries and used tyres for recycling or safe disposal	• buy CFC-free aerosols, refrigerators and insulation and reduce purchases of plastics • replace disposable utensils with re-usable ones where possible • purchase recycled paper and paper products • purchase biodegradable materials where possible • purchase wood from sustainable plantations and avoid tropical timber unless it comes from properly managed plantations

Source: ETB *et al.* (1992)

alternatives to traditional mass (or hard) tourism, or urban tourism. Factors responsible for the enhanced awareness of alternative forms of tourism include a greater awareness of the environmental impacts of tourism, a growing demand from tourists for new tourism experiences, increased attention to the integration of environmental conservation and economic development policies, and a tourism industry concerned about future trends in the tourism market. Here, the term 'alternative tourism' is used as a collective expression of a range of terms which have recently appeared in the tourism literature. These terms include soft tourism, eco-tourism, green tourism, low-impact tourism, alternative tourism, nature tourism, gentle tourism, progressive tourism, responsible tourism, appropriate tourism and even sustainable tourism (Mader 1988; Himmetoglu 1992). In aggregating these terms under the single banner of 'alternative tourism', it is recognised that the detailed nuances of any differences in usage of the terms is lost. However, despite the different emphasis that each term may place on facets of tourism activities and tourist types, much common ground exists between these alternatives in terms of the underlying approach to tourism development. Frequently, alternative tourism has been presented as being synonymous with sustainable tourism. It may be that, within a given set of circumstances, alternative tourism may prove to be environmentally sustainable in some areas in the future, but to automatically equate alternative tourism with sustainable tourism, as previously defined, is premature and potentially dangerous. Alternative tourism may be the means to an end (sustainable tourism), but the terms should not be confused.

Alternative tourism has a number of characteristics. It is small scale, frequently developed by local people and typically involves travelling to relatively remote, undisturbed natural areas with the objective of admiring, studying and enjoying the scenery and its wild plants and animals, as well as any cultural features found there. It aims to conserve the environment and sustain the well-being of local people (Butler 1990). Thus, there are many of the features and principles which characterise sustainable tourism: conservation of natural resources, respect for limits to growth, respect for local culture, and local community involvement in tourism. The distinction between mass and alternative tourism is highlighted in Table 3.3, which considers some of the attributes of both types. Potentially, the management principles underlying alternative tourism do appear to represent an environmentally sustainable future for tourism development.

In essence, alternative tourism offers a specific role in terms of the scale of activity involved. For the tourism entrepreneur, it involves the specialist firm rather than the large operator. Clients tend to be individuals rather than large groups, accommodation is small scale and local rather than based on large hotel chains. Laarman and Durst (1987), suggest that the key facets of alternative tourism include its health-minded orientation, the direction of economic activity to remote communities and attention to threats to wildlife. The emphasis is on small-scale activity, in

Table 3.3 Attributes of mass and alternative tourism

	Mass tourism	Alternative tourism
General features	rapid development maximises uncontrolled short term sectoral	slow development optimises controlled long term holistic
Tourist behaviour	large groups fixed programme tourists directed comfortable and passive no foreign language nosy loud	singles, families spontaneous decisions tourists decide demanding and active language learning tactful quiet
Basic requirements	holiday peaks untrained labour publicity clichés hard selling	staggered holidays trained labour force tourist education heart selling
Development strategies	unplanned project-led new buildings outside developers	planned concept-led re-use of existing local developers

Source: modified from Himmetoglu (1992)

areas where (immediate) mass tourism is seen to be unacceptable. The following list shows Rauhe's (1992) idea of features required for an outline proposal for an alternative tourism planning model.

- A special sense of place must result that enhances local heritage and environment;
- the focus must be on the preservation, protection, and enhancement of the resource quality;
- local attributes must be complemented;
- local endorsement of growth and development is necessary;
- alternative tourism must be sustainable;
- proposals must be sensitive to living patterns of the local citizens;
- support must be mutual among all parties that are involved and/or affected;

- the standard of living must be improved (but how will this be defined?);
- cross-cultural understanding must be promoted;
- priorities must be established (but by who and for what?);
- carrying capacities must be determined, not only for natural systems but human systems as well;
- all parties involved or impacted must be convinced that the net outcome will be positive or at least neutral; and
- the community must be receptive to change and see alternative tourism as a constructive means of facilitating positive change.

Arguably, the key driving force behind the surge in interest in alternative tourism during the 1980s and beyond has been the perceived need for new tourism marketing strategies prompted by the changing needs and desires of many tourists themselves. Apparently, more and more people may be described as 'alternative tourists'. These can be characterised as people who:

- try to avoid the beaten track;
- go places nobody has set foot in before;
- bring a sense of adventure;
- seek to forget civilisation for a while;
- establish more contact with local people;
- try to do without tourist infrastructure;
- get more information before and during trips;
- travel alone or in small groups;
- are generally well educated;
- have an above average income; and,
- tend to remain in the country for more days than more traditional tourists.

(Laarman and Durst 1987)

Indeed, it has been suggested that the alternative tourist is guided by a need to feel as distant as possible from mass tourism (Krippendorf 1987). Whatever the characteristics and categorisations of alternative tourists, alternative tourism has created, and will continue to create, opportunities for tourism development in sensitive, unique and remote natural areas, particularly in Developing Countries. A number of positive benefits may ensue. Increased funds for parks and nature reserves through tourist receipts, for example. The generation of new jobs within local communities as tour guides, handicraft makers, hospitality workers, etc. Such jobs may co-exist more easily with the needs of conservation than pre-existing forms of employment (e.g. in the logging industry). Environmental education of visitors may result in greater concern for environmental issues. In short, alternative tourism may become a vital mechanism for environmental education, the protection of ecologically valuable habitats and job creation and economic development in many areas around the world.

On the surface, alternative tourism appears laudable, with commendable aims. Leaving aside the argument that any form of tourism will generate environmental impacts beyond a destination area (e.g. through long-haul air flights), great caution is required in the promotion of alternative tourism for a number of reasons. These can be summarised as fears over:

- the underlying rationale for the adoption of alternative tourism;
- the nature of alternative tourism itself;
- the lack of knowledge concerning the practical implementation of alternative tourism;
- the over-polarisation of debate between mass and alternative tourism; and,
- the possible inclination to turn small-scale into large-scale operations.

There is a sense, in reading the tourism literature, that following the now well-known vagaries of some mass tourism, alternative tourism is seen as the new panacea of modern tourism. A form of tourism capable of acting like a 'magic bullet' which homes in on areas seeking (or earmarked for) economic investment and development, without causing unwanted and life-threatening side-effects. Whilst not wishing to put a damper on the growing momentum behind the notion of alternative tourism as such, a degree of healthy scepticism, and perhaps suspicion, is surely warranted. The apparent ease with which sectors of the tourism industry and decision-makers in local and central governments have embraced developments which exhibit alternative tourism credentials of some kind may reflect a primary motive other than concern for the environment. Much of the discussion of alternative tourism has considered the development of the concept as a new marketing opportunity which aims to maintain or develop market share or returns to developers, rather than focus primarily on the issue of sustainability and the quality of the tourism environment. In short, there is at least the danger that alternative tourism will turn out to be little more than marketing hype to foster tourism in areas where mass tourism would be unacceptable, at least over the short term.

It seems almost inevitable that tourism, and especially forms of alternative tourism, will encourage larger numbers of people to visit more and more remote areas, less and less used to coping with modern industrial human activities and attitudes. As ecologically diverse and, therefore, valuable natural habitats become rarer, threats to their integrity or even continued existence become more important. It would indeed be a tragedy if tourism, of whatever kind, started, hastened or added to the degradation of such areas. Unfortunately, if alternative tourism proceeds under little more than a banner of 'green-ness', without accompanying controls and restrictions, and even with the best will in the world, environmental degradation is almost inevitable. Allowing or encouraging certain types of tourism development because they appear 'green', or conform to criteria identified as being of an alternative type is dangerous, if for no other reason than that environmental impacts are frequently very difficult to predict and their accurate assessment requires detailed local knowledge. Alternative forms of tourism could also be used merely as a means of fostering development in new locations to maintain tourist flows to a region which contains other centres of declining popularity.

Warnings of adverse consequences resulting from decisions based upon the shallow acceptance of alternative tourism as 'good' can be found in the literature. Ataby (1992), for example, with reference to alternative tourism developments in the Black Sea region of Turkey, argues that such developments can only be successful (sustainable) if planned carefully in line with a proper ecological evaluation of the region. Even if alternative tourism is implemented successfully in one region, this does not necessarily mean that the approaches and lessons adopted there can be transferred elsewhere. Not all destinations exhibit the same degree of fragility or resilience. Some may permit only very low levels of tourist activity, while other areas may permit none at all. It could be argued that nature reserves of global ecological importance, for example, should be just that, and not expected to generate income through any kind of tourism (Pigram 1990).

Munt (1992) argues that the desire of tour operators and tourists to penetrate new areas through alternative tourism is in itself a contradiction of the concept of sustainable development.

Research in the field of alternative tourism and environmental quality still appears to be at the stage of the formulation of appropriate principles and policies. There is little knowledge of the practical implementation of alternative tourism, and still less on the potential problems, implications and costs which will be associated with it (Butler 1989). Thus, it is impossible to equate alternative tourism with tourism which is environmentally sustainable. Until real evidence comes to light, perhaps not until the beginning of the next century, that alternative tourism as practised really can be sustainable at the destination area, it would be prudent to treat all tourism development as potentially destructive, regardless of its associated typology.

In contrasting alternative tourism with mass tourism there is a danger that debate will become too polarised, with mass tourism regarded as environmentally unsustainable and alternative tourism as sustainable. It may be that in the future all types of tourism activity will become, or need to become, sustainable, or at least much more environmentally-conscious. Some authors stress the continuous nature of the tourist experience, rather than focusing on perceived extremes. Fennell and Eagles (1990), for example, use a three-fold categorisation of tourism activity, with 'eco-tourism' forming a bridge between adventure travel and tour travel. Even if one regards mass and alternative tourism to be at the extremes of tourism activity, one cannot rule out the possibility that sustainable tourism or forms of sustainable tourism will be found to lie between the two extremes. Butler (1989), for example, implies that all tourism activities may be made to operate on a sustainable basis, using resources in a low-consumptive manner, below thresholds of resource renewability. It is suggested that although alternative tourism seeks to avoid many of the environmental problems of traditional mass tourism, alternative tourism may prove more environmentally harmful than no development, or even limited mass tourism for some destinations. Perhaps a new kind of limited and controlled mass tourism will slowly emerge which combines the potential advantages of relative efficiency of resource use associated with large-scale operations, with the sustainable use of resources. Indeed, Klemm (1992) argues that the real challenge for the future is to provide sustainable tourism for the mass market. If sustainable tourism is regarded as the final goal, alternative tourism only represents a collection of activities which may define one path towards that goal.

Finally, much is made of the small-scale nature of alternative tourism. Leaving aside the argument that what is small-scale in one area may be potentially more environmentally degrading than a large-scale operation elsewhere, there remains the risk that small operations in environmentally sensitive locations may eventually turn into much larger and more destructive operations. Alternative tourism might be the 'thin end of the wedge', if large tour operators see large profit margins and local control and influence is inadequate. Even if each tourism operation in a given region stays small scale, a growth in the number of tourist choices may over-reach the ability of the region to retain its ecological or cultural identity. In other words, 'death by a thousand cuts'.

In summary, the concept of alternative tourism is appealing because it appears to offer an alternative for those who have criticised the impacts of traditional mass tourism and those who wish to see the development of new tourism markets. The under-lying philosophy of alternative tourism appears to have much in common with the concept of sustainable development. However, the environmental implications of alternative tourism will depend on how it is planned, implemented, developed and controlled, and not simply on a list of 'appropriate' alternative tourist activities, types of alternative tourist or a declaration of policy intentions. Alternative tourism, in its current state of development, does not necessarily represent a sustainable future for the tourism industry, and is, potentially, a considerable threat to sensitive environments around the world.

ISSUES IN THE IMPLEMENTATION OF SUSTAINABLE TOURISM DEVELOPMENT

Irrespective of the type of tourism, there is a range of policy instruments that decision-makers could employ in an attempt to place tourism development on a sustainable path. These embrace different degrees of intervention in the market system ranging from the traditional 'command and control' approach through appropriate legislation, to the use of less direct economic incentives aimed at encouraging the market system to behave in a more environmentally-conscious manner. Such instruments can be applied by decision-makers in both local and central government, for example, depending on the relative distribution of power in any given country. There is growing interest in the use of different policy instruments in the environmental management of resources, under a variety of circumstances. See, for example, OECD (1990) with reference to the management of the urban environment. Recently, Nijkamp *et al.* (1992) have presented an overview of these instruments in relation to tourism developments. Table 3.4 and Figure 3.2 summarise these approaches, and aspects of their relative merits. The following short review of the policy instruments is largely taken from Nijkamp *et al.* (1992). Some of these instruments have already been mentioned in Chapter 2, with reference to environmental impact amelioration measures.

Information and education from (local or central) government and tourism agencies can make the local public, tourists and companies more aware of the environmental problems associated with tourism, and their role in generating and alleviating such problems. For example, information on the amount of waste tourists produce and the costs they impose on local inhabitants.
Subsidies belong to a group of economic instruments designed to re-orientate the market. The use of subsidies can make it relatively more expensive for companies to pollute the environment, for

Table 3.4 The potential advantages and disadvantages of different approaches to the environmental management of tourism

	For	Against
Government	• co-ordination	• less support for implementation
	• unification	• bureaucracy
Market Forces	• support for implementation	• economy-driven instead of ecology-driven
Direct	• result-oriented	• very strict
		• decreases flexibility
Indirect	• freedom/flexibility	• not result-oriented
	• space for creative ideas	

Source: Nijkamp *et al.* (1992)

Indirect	education/ information	infrastructure	free market
	subsidies/taxes/ pricing	agreements	niches
Direct	legal instruments	permissions/quota	investments
	Government		*Market forces*

Figure 3.2 Overview of the main policy instruments in tourism management
Source: Nijkamp *et al.* (1992)

example. Thus, government can stimulate and foster environment-friendly behaviour. Another example might be to decrease the price of tourist facilities in less ecologically vulnerable areas. Similarly, *taxation* tries to discourage poor environmental practices. For example, through the imposition of a tourist tax to discourage tourism in a specific area, or through taxes on the use of fossil fuels. Tourist taxes can be levied in order to help finance environmental initiatives.

Legal instruments can take many forms, from the development of an efficient development control local planning framework, to the compulsory use of Environmental Impact Assessment (EIA) for certain developments, to the imposition of liability on companies for the use or pollution of natural resources. Legal instruments can, therefore, be employed to ensure that the 'polluter pays', or that a hotel is metered so that the more water (for example) it uses, the more it pays (i.e. the 'user pays'). It is even possible to use legal instruments in such a way that companies have to demonstrate, e.g. through regular environmental audits, that their products are not harmful to the environment.

Infrastructure such as waste treatment facilities or public transport, can be supplied by public authorities to enable companies and tourists to behave in a more environment-friendly manner. Infrastructure provision can also be supplied through public/ private partnerships, perhaps increasing efficiency.

Agreements can be made between the public and private sectors concerning a range of activities, e.g. the release of pollutants to the environment. Agreements are more flexible than strict regulations or quota, but governments can always fall back on laws if operators break agreements. An agreement might stipulate the maximum number of hotel rooms or the maximum height of new tourist buildings, for example.

Permissions or quota can be used to limit the absolute amount of pollution, for example, from tourist operators. Alternatively, these can be used to set the maximum number of tourists permitted in an area at a given time. It is even possible to make permissions tradeable between tourist operators: permissions can be sold at 'auction' giving 'tourist quota'.

Free market means that there is no large intervention in the market system, either by government or large investors.

Niches are fractions of the total market. A group supplier of tourist facilities can, for example, decide to focus on a certain segment of the tourist market, e.g. nature tourism or health tourism. Such concentration of effort can more readily direct investment at the type of tourism most suited to the environment of an area.

Investments from large tourism organisations will very much determine the image of tourism in an area.

Much research is urgently needed on the potential use of the above instruments, to discover, for example, which are most appropriate in different situations; whether some are more suited to the long term or short term; whether they can be used in conjunction, giving a 'suite' of policy instruments; and, what undesirable side-effects their use might have. Potentially, these policy instruments can be adopted before tourism develops, or retrospectively, and can be applied to any type of tourist activity. While some commentators (e.g. Butler 1991) argue that the theory of sustainable tourism development will be extremely difficult or impossible to implement in existing mass tourism centres, these policy instruments at least offer some hope of retrospective success, as well as providing a policy framework for areas yet to be developed for tourism.

Although the need for tourism development to become environmentally sustainable has received much support across the globe, there remain great difficulties in the practical implementation of relevant principles and policies. This applies to both traditional mass tourism and alternative tourism. Among these difficulties are a number of inter-related factors, including ignorance of tourism's impacts, diversity of interests and attitudes, and the diversity of the tourism industry itself. Unfortunately, many tourists, operators, decision-makers, etc. remain comparatively ignorant of the potential impacts of tourism on the environment and the long-term reliance of tourism success on the maintenance of high environmental quality. Even if problems are much better appreciated, there still remains the task of convincing all those involved of the good sense in embracing sustainable tourism development policies in practice. Changing attitudes and creating the will to act are not easy. Pigram (1990), for example, argues that developers are unlikely to implement sustainable tourism policies unless coerced, because the basic profit motive is geared to ensuring short-term economic returns rather than long-term resource conservation. Thus, local entrepreneurs will not appreciate that 'enough is enough' while the opportunity still remains to increase their standard of living, and absentee development organisations are likely to have even less of a motive for any such 'altruistic' concerns (Butler 1991).

Much can be made of the potential power of the consumer (tourist), apparently increasingly concerned with environmental matters, in forcing the industry to act sustainably through the rejection of environmentally degraded destinations or poor environmental practices. However, despite the expectation that tourists should be strongly supportive of measures designed to protect the resources they enjoy, it has been argued that the reality falls far short of expectation (Butler 1991). This may be because tourists only stay in a destination for a few days or weeks (and may never return), and so are unlikely to feel really involved in the long-term fate of the area. Indeed, they may feel that it is their right to utilise the various resources on offer to the maximum having paid for the privilege. (Although, of course, part of the problem is that the full costs of environmental degradation caused by tourists are not internalised into the market, so that tourists and the tourism industry are not forced to include environmental costs in pricing mechanisms. In other words, tourism still relies to some extent on free environmental services.) Butler (1991) argues that the holiday is now almost regarded as a basic need by many people, and that it would be naive to believe that the use of persuasion to curtail, control or even re-orientate how tourists choose to fulfil this need will meet with swift success. Even assuming heightened environmental awareness and the will to act from all sides, implementing sustainable tourism development policies will still be fraught with difficulty due to the diversity of the tourism industry itself. The prospect that sustainable tourism development will emerge via some form of 'osmosis' involving a large number of individual firms, widely scattered markets, competing transportation agencies, different types of tourists, varying levels of government with different priorities and differing policies towards tourism, appears somewhat optimistic (Butler 1991).

Given some of the difficulties outlined above, it is all too easy to regard the concept of sustainable tourism development as merely a laudable goal. Perhaps many agencies and organisations involved in tourism will sign some charter of principles for sustainable tourism (in order to display green credentials), but secretly regard the idea as unworkable in practice and continue much as before. Pigram (1990), for example, suggests that some 'hard-headed' developers perceive sustainable tourism development as a Utopian ideal of no practical consequence, while for others it requires profound changes to economic investment patterns which are too far-reaching and redistributive to be implemented. One could envisage the sinking of a developer's heart on reading the view of Tananone (1991), for example, that sustainable tourism development means not allowing large-scale privatisation of land ownership, or stopping and reversing the process if it has begun. In other words, 'Without community land, there can never be community development' (Tananone 1991: 9). Others, however, might argue that such a view may result in (or has resulted in) the 'tragedy of the commons' with respect to tourism, due to a lack of assigned responsibility over common resources (Butler 1991). Such a diversity of opinion on the implications of sustainable tourism development perhaps reflects the infancy of the concept, and further highlights the urgent need for research on the implementation of appropriate policies.

Sustainable development and sustainable tourism development, as defined and discussed above, do represent profound challenges to traditional patterns of economic investment and growth and do require acceptance and co-operation between the various constituencies involved in tourism. This is not easy to achieve. It appears inescapable that tourism developments need to be planned and controlled at the local level, by those in the public sector with clearly defined responsibility and the power to implement co-ordinated planning and development control strategies. Reliance on local initiatives and self-regulation by the tourism industry without co-ordinated and pro-active planning will not result in sustainable tourism development. Local authorities, through the production of integrated plans and development control powers, are best placed to assess the characteristics of the local environment and the priorities, needs and attitudes of local people to tourism and other industries. Without such strong local control, it is very difficult indeed to envisage the emergence of tourism which successfully merges into the environment of destination areas.

With reference to wider environmental concerns, beyond a destination area, it must be hoped that through time local authorities will respond positively to national governmental initiatives aimed at sustainable development (or vice versa), as national governments in turn respond to policies proposed by international governmental and non-governmental organisations. Such positive change will not be easy and will not occur rapidly, but the complex nature of the practical implications of sustainable development should not be allowed to prevent appropriate actions being taken now. Sustainable tourism is a long-term goal, but action can be taken now to put the tourism industry on, at least, the path towards environmental sustainability. The following chapters examine the use of planning and Environmental Impact Assessment as pro-active management tools for tourism.

Chapter 4

Planning for sustainable tourism development

Howard Green

INTRODUCTION

Many of the objectives behind the promotion of tourism developments will, potentially, conflict with environmental sustainability goals, as countries, regions, groups and individuals develop tourist activity with particular interests in mind. The rationale behind this chapter is that the incorporation of tourism development considerations into an efficient land use planning system can aid in the resolution of many such conflicts. Land use planning should be seen as a central concern in the control and development of land, and tourism is one sector amongst the many which need to be integrated, controlled and managed within a comprehensive land use planning system. A formal, statutory land use planning system has the capacity to make a significant contribution to the realisation of sustainable tourism development. As noted by Healey and Shaw (1993), for example, the key tasks of conserving resources and landscapes, influencing the locational distribution of activities, finding appropriate locations for specific types of development and encouraging developers to adopt particular approaches to development, are all fundamental to land use planning systems. In the case of the UK, several authors have shown the planning system to be particularly effective in these contexts (e.g. Healey *et al.* 1988).

The mere presence of a land use planning system, however, does not automatically ensure that the environment will be better protected; commitment, education and the involvement of all interested parties are vital to successful development decisions. The way the system is operated and implemented are of equal importance. These, and other, important themes are developed throughout the chapter in preference to a detailed discussion of particular land use planning processes.

PLANNING AND TOURISM

The notion of planning is not new to tourism. Care must be taken, however, to differentiate a discussion of planning in the general tourism context from land use planning. Tourism planning includes a very diverse set of activities undertaken by many different groups representing different interests. Operators, for example, concerned to develop markets and market share, are involved in the planning of marketing strategies. Individual developers engage in the planning of tourist facilities, covering the layout of particular development proposals. Governments, perhaps anxious to expand the income from tourism, may plan strategies and policies at both national and regional levels to facilitate tourism development.

Each of these activities can be described as tourism planning, or perhaps more appropriately, the planning of a specific aspect of tourism. Each represents a narrow approach to tourism planning. If such narrow concerns dominate much tourism 'planning', it is not difficult to appreciate why this should be the case. Unlike other forms of economic activity, such as manufacturing, tourism is a relatively new sector of many national economies which has yet to be fully assimilated within statutory systems of development management and control. Many local and regional plans fail to deal specifically with tourism as an issue in a positive way, guiding the development of tourism facilities. Likewise, tourism involves a very diverse range of interests and organisations of different sizes, structures and constitutions, each with its own objectives and policy agendas. In some of their activities there is an interest in coming together and acting corporately. The development of joint marketing initiatives, for example, may encourage a joint planning approach. In other areas, however, tourism initiatives will be the responsibility of the individual developer or agency, frequently operating outside a formal planning framework.

More recently, there has been a move to view tourism planning as one element of a wider socio-economic setting, and as part of a land use planning process in which tourism is recognised as one of many elements for consideration (e.g. Cronin 1990). Such a change of emphasis can be attributed to a number of factors.

The rapid growth in tourist numbers at many destinations has put stress on the infrastructure of host communities and regions which has affected the performance of other sectors of the economy (e.g. through increased road traffic congestion). Such impacts are beginning to force operators and decision-makers to evaluate tourism developments within overall development objectives. Tourism competes along with other sectors for the resources on which it depends. It cannot, therefore, be seen as a self-contained set of activities with its own narrow policy agenda; but rather as part of the wider set of activities which need to be planned for and managed as an area develops. Heeley (1981) stresses this aspect of tourism planning in a discussion of the policy development process in the UK. It is noted that tourism is:

> an amalgam of economic, social and environmental considerations, involving a range of agencies in both the public and private sector. . . . It overlaps with policy fields such as transport, conservation, rural development and so forth, so that only a small proportion of the sum total of plans affecting tourism are exclusively devoted to it.
>
> (Heeley 1981: 61)

In a review of tourism planning approaches, Pearce (1989) also widens the scope of discussion by reference to the work of Getz (1987) and Murphy (1985), and cites the view of Hall, that planning is, 'an ordered sequence of operations, designed to lead to the achievement of either a single goal or to a balance between several goals' (Hall 1970: 4). Thus, planning is a process framework within which goals, for tourism and other sectors, are achieved. Braddon (1982) argues that, ideally, tourism planning should be integrated with all socio-economic activities and at all levels of involvement, so that tourism becomes one element in the planning (including land use planning) process. These views of tourism as part of the wider economy emphasise the importance of land use planning to environmentally sympathetic tourism development. Whilst it may be appropriate to consider tourism planning as a distinct activity, it should be an integral element of the land use planning process, adopting the same instruments and techniques of that process. Generally, land use planning, if implemented with a commitment to and understanding of environmental concerns, offers an adequate framework of environmental management instruments and techniques, although the planning of tourism may require specific additional approaches and techniques such as those of resort planning (Inskeep 1991).

LAND USE PLANNING

Land use planning is the task of developing a framework of land use for an area which balances the resource base and physical capacities against the different interests that are involved in development. A land use planning system can help by assisting decision-makers to think clearly about land use objectives and options, and to weigh these against other policy objectives, including those derived from principles of sustainable development (Haywood 1988). It is particularly in influencing the location of activities and associated infrastructure that land use planning can play an important role (Wood 1989). This anticipatory philosophy is a key component of a land use planning system (Healey *et al.* 1982) which allows potential problems to be recognised and appropriate management strategies to be introduced before development takes place. Once development has taken place, consequences are more difficult to control, although specific controls may be used in particularly sensitive locations.

The land use planning process can operate on several scales, from international to local, giving a hierarchical structure as illustrated in Table 4.1. Although a hierarchical framework has a certain elegance, it is rarely operated rigidly in practice. Rather, different planning approaches are seen to operate at different levels. In this idealised structure, national plans inform regional plans, which in their turn provide the framework for more local plans. Each level in the hierarchy will present a different level of detail against which to judge development decisions, normally the responsibility of a public authority. The actual authority involved will reflect the administrative structure of the country involved. At the national level, for example, some countries have a Ministry of Tourism (or equivalent) which will be the responsible body for tourism inputs into national plans. Examples of this structure are found in Turkey and Malaysia. In others, tourism is subsumed within other ministries, such as employment or industry, with an agency providing the specific tourism advice to the system. The nature of this relationship will be an important factor behind the importance which tourism has within the planning process.

Table 4.1 A model land use planning structure

Policy level	Function
Supra-national policies	provide guidance on policy directions
National plans and policies	establish national goals, develop policy and broad strategies for implementation
Regional plans and strategies	formulate general policies and plans for socio-economic and physical development
Development plans/local plans	district-wide land use plans which may include detailed development proposals or zoning of land
Development controls	the co-ordination and approval of individual development proposals

Tourism must be incorporated into land use planning policies, and hence the influence which the tourism lobby has over those responsible for their development is of particular concern. At the national level, inter-ministerial working is important. Organisations such as DATAR (Délégation d'Aménagement de Territoire et de l'Action Régional) in France, may be particularly appropriate models of organisational structure in which sectoral interests and land use policies can be brought together (Punter 1989). At the regional level, international comparison is difficult because of the variety of approaches taken in different countries. For some, such as the United Kingdom, the lack of a regional tier in administration results in only weak guidance at this level; in others such as Germany, the *Länder* create what amounts to a form of regional government. Between these two positions, countries such as France have a regional structure which permits plan-making, albeit with only limited spatial or land use content, by an elected assembly.

Rarely is a rigid hierarchical system of planning found and there are considerable variations between individual countries depending frequently on the administrative structure of the country and the competencies associated with each level of administration. A structure of national, regional and local planning has enormous appeal, but different and changing responsibilities can easily destroy the neat nesting of decision-making and implementation.

No matter what scale the planning process operates at, decisions about programmes and projects refer to place and hence provide the link to land and the environmental context.

NATIONAL PLANS AND POLICIES

National development goals provide a framework within which sectors, including tourism, can plan (Acerenza 1985). Approaches to national planning in this way range from the rigorous five-year national planning process, to the more liberal approach in which the broad parameters are established as policy guidance. The five-year plan may be mainly economic in nature, involving the sectoral allocation of resources, or may include consideration of spatial organisation and spatial distribution of resources without detail of precise locational impacts. The framework adopted in the five-year development plan process in Turkey, illustrates an essentially economic approach. In an analysis of the process since the first five-year development plan in 1963, Ors (1991) illustrates how a tourism strategy has evolved within this planning framework. The importance of tourism has increased throughout the period of the plans, reflected in the increasing emphasis given to tourism considerations. The five-year planning approach adopted by Malaysia is similarly economic in nature, but through the work of the Tourism Development Corporation a more spatially-oriented approach has evolved in association with a tourism development plan (TDC 1975). The latter explicitly seeks to provide a basis upon which Malaysia may develop its tourist potential in an orderly and balanced manner within the framework of the national five-year plan. The tourism development plan defines six geographical regions in the Peninsula as tourist areas which are both consistent with creating greater tourist diversity and with the national strategy of narrowing rural/urban and regional imbalances in economic development. Similar connections between national planning and spatial implementation are made by Choy (1992) in a discussion of development in Hawaii. Here, Visitor Destination Areas (VDAs) provide the link between the national level and physical development on the ground.

Many countries, however, still apparently lack the political resolve to put in place appropriate national plans for development, perhaps especially plans which limit or direct tourism investments. Although there may be numerous practical constraints in many Developing Countries which lack the (immediate) institutional basis to introduce such planning (Gunn 1988), an economic imperative is frequently apparent. For any country faced with the real or perceived fear of revenue loss resulting from refusal of permission to develop, issues of control may become of secondary importance (Stroud 1983). Governments may well be reluctant to implement a rigorous approach to tourism planning or to introduce regulations, land use laws and effective control over development. Unless politicians embrace environmental concerns in development planning, there can be no hope of sustainable development.

Even national planning, however, may be too restrictive for tourism developments in some parts of the world where policies need to be framed in an international context (WTO 1980). This is particularly appropriate for small island states such as those in the South Pacific, or where the tourist resources cluster around or across frontiers, as in the case of the Alps and the Mediterranean coast. The Blue Plan, an international attempt to investigate the future of the Mediterranean environment, is perhaps the most ambitious attempt to plan at an international scale, involving seventeen countries co-ordinated by the United Nations Environment Programme (Grenon and Batisse 1990). The plan, which deals with all aspects of Mediterranean activity, includes a chapter, although of only limited scope, on the future of tourism. The ultimate implementation of such strategies is, however, dependent on the planning structure and processes of individual countries, and a commitment to use tools and techniques of land use planning at a local level. Many other examples of international planning are little more than marketing and promotion exercises, having more to do with economies of scale than a concern for ordered development. This is particularly the case with tourism resources such as the Andes route in South America and the Maya route promoted jointly by Honduras, Guatemala and Mexico.

LAND USE PLANNING AT THE LOCAL LEVEL

It is at the district or local level that effective land use planning can provide the day-to-day framework within which decisions about land use allocations can be made, implemented and subsequently monitored. At this level, decisions about tourism development can take their place alongside other activities as policies for land use in a locality are developed. Most Developed Countries have such a system, although there is considerable variability in the scale (e.g. neighbourhood, town or county), legal status and flexibility of operation. To be effective, such a system needs the backing of law or statute, it needs appropriate mechanisms for controlling development and enforcing decisions, and yet it should be flexibile enough to respond to change. It must also recognise tourism activity as an activity worthy of inclusion.

The land use planning framework involves three key elements:

1 the preparation of plans;
2 the control of development; and,
3 the enforcement of decisions.

Such a system is charged with ensuring that developments are appropriate to the plan area, taking into account current capacities for transport, waste disposal, noise and aspects of facility design, for example (Williams 1992). The effectiveness of the system will depend on the level of rigour with which each is applied, within the overall structure of the planning system adopted by a particular country. The land use planning system in England and Wales, for example, was laid down in various Town Planning Acts (Cullingworth 1988), providing a structure at the level of the district (local plan) and the county (structure plan) for the preparation and implementation of plans, the control of development and the enforcement of controls. This structure reflects the administrative structure of England and Wales, based on a two-tier county/district model. Scotland, however, has a different system which accords with the regional and district structure of administration in Scotland. Other countries adopt different structures. In France, for example, the POS (Plan d'Occupation des Sols), the equivalent of the local plan, is developed at the level of the commune, of which there are over 36,000! (Davies et al. 1989).

A structure plan provides the strategic guidance for local land use initiatives, and many of them (or their equivalents) were introduced in the late 1960s in many European countries as a result of increasing affluence, car ownership and pressures for housing, all of which created great impetus for development (see, for example, MHLG 1965). In theory, structure plans provided the framework for land allocation policies which could influence the location and development of all sectors within the economy of the area. Their introduction was to provide the framework and statutory basis for local plans, which in turn provided the necessary further guidance on development control. Where tourism is a key sector, then allocation policies in the structure plan would pay due regard to the needs of tourism. The economic problems associated with the oil crisis in the 1970s removed much of the pressure for this type of plan, and although structure plans were still produced, their relevance in the 1970s and early 1980s across Europe was diminished. More recently, however, interest has increased again in the preparation of structure plans as development pressures have once more created a need for the strategic planning of land use. In England and Wales, a new form of strategic plan, the UDP (Unitary Development Plan) has been prepared in certain metropolitan areas. It is notable that these new plans, many of which address the strategic issues raised by tourism developments, are taking a considerable length of time to prepare (Whitney 1993). One of the major criticisms of strategic planning, that of delay in plan-making, still appears to be present. However, the approach adopted in the English city of Leeds (LCC 1990) recognises the inter-relations between tourism and the rest of the economy, concluding that leisure and tourism are complex and dynamic activities which affect the perception of Leeds as a place to live, work and visit, and hence are integral elements of the UDP process.

Strategic plans need national and regional guidance. Such guidance may arise out of a hierarchical approach to plan-making, in which nationally defined allocations are translated first at a regional level, and then at a more local level. In the case of the UK, policy guidance is provided by the Department of the Environment (DoE) in the form of Circulars and Planning Policy Guidance (PPG) notes. These documents outline the way in which government would wish planning authorities to develop and implement their strategies. It is the responsibility of planning authorities to interpret the guidance in the context of local conditions.

In 1992, the UK Department of the Environment issued a Planning Policy Guidance note (PPG21) specifically relating to tourism (DoE 1992). This document sets out the UK government's views on how the planning system should respond to tourism development pressures. The government recognises the interplay between the demands of the industry and the environment when it states:

> The Government's policy is that the tourism industry should flourish in response to the market, whilst respecting the environment which attracts visitors but also has a far wider and enduring value. Policies for this purpose must be fully consistent with the Government's environmental strategy as set out in the White Paper, 'This Common Inheritance' and must take full account of the particular needs and character of individual areas.
>
> (DoE 1992: 50366)

Other guidance may come from the regions themselves, either as formal regional plans or as indicative statements on the types of development to be encouraged. Recent research in the UK has shown the importance of guidance of this nature (Whitney 1993). Comment from Malaysia, however, has highlighted the problems which may occur when regional priorities differ from those at the centre, and where local implementation differs from national or regional priorities. Wahab *et al.* (1992) describe how the tourist development plan produced by the Malaysian Tourist Development Corporation (established in 1972) has hit serious difficulties of implementation because many of the districts responsible for plan preparation in the hierarchy do not regard tourism as particularly important (see Table 4.2). These contradictions illustrate the need to clarify the relationship between tourism and other elements of the area being developed, and the priorities of the different decision-makers.

Local plans appear in different guises in many countries and with various approaches, from the tightly prescriptive and controlling to the broader brush framework. Differences in approach frequently reflect the national context and administrative structure of the country involved and the place accorded to planning within the administrative structure. Healey (1983) argues that a local plan is a tool, a means of achieving some purpose or policy, and should have four key purposes:

1 to apply the strategy of the structure plan;
2 to provide a framework for development control;
3 to provide a basis for co-ordinating development; and,
4 to bring local and detailed issues before the public.

Table 4.2 The importance of tourism in Malaysian Structure Plans

Local authority area	Key issue	Non-key issue
Alor Setar		x
Kangar		x
Seberang Perai	xx	
Penang Island	xxx	
Ipoh		x
Kuala Lumpur	xxx	
Shah Alam		x
Keland	xx	
Bangi		x
Seremban		x
Central Malacca	xx	
Johore Bahru	xxx	
Kuantan	xx	
Kuala Trengganu	xx	
Kemaman		x
Kota Bharu	xx	

Key: x – not an important sector
   xx – important sector
   xxx – very important sector

Source: Wahab *et al.* (1991)

These issues, especially development control and public involvement, are discussed in more detail below.

Development control

The control of development is fundamental to land use planning. Development control has been defined by Harrison as:

> the activities whereby applications for development or change in the use of land and buildings are considered by planning staff, and other persons, and decisions issued.
>
> (Harrison 1987: 5)

As tourism activities affect the way land and buildings are used and developed, development control is potentially a powerful tool in the planning of tourism facilities and activities. For the purposes of land use planning, 'development' is defined and interpreted in various ways partly reflecting the different approaches taken to planning in different countries (Davies *et al.* 1989). Whilst differing in precise detail, most countries with a statutory land use planning system incorporate material changes in land or building use, and various building, engineering and other operational activities (e.g. mining) into definitions of development. Many countries exempt particular types of activity from planning and development controls. Again, these vary from country to country. The following list gives an idea of the type of activity typically exempt.

• Agricultural use of land and associated activities. The inclusion of agricultural buildings varies between countries.
• Existing uses and the renewal of those uses after substantial damage involving demolition or substantial rebuilding.
• Temporary buildings, fences, sheds and other minor structures.

Changes in the use of land by modification to buildings and works is controlled in most countries by the planning system. However, the degree of control, as exemplified by the degree of change which can take place without permission, varies. The relaxation of change of use regulation has been an important element of modification to the planning system in England and Wales in the 1980s (DoE 1985). The importance of change of use in tourism development is frequently observed in rural environments where agricultural buildings are to be modified to be used in tourism contexts, e.g. barns or other outbuildings converted to holiday cottages, *gîtes* or craft workshops. In these examples, planning permission from the local planning authority would (rightly) frequently be required, and the local planners would need to be convinced that there would be no significant associated changes which would affect the local area. Such changes, or 'material considerations' as they are referred to in the UK, might include increased noise, traffic generation, loss of amenity and modification to the rural economy. Environmental concerns have become increasingly important in the control of development in both Europe and the USA in recent years, and have been embraced within the planning systems of many Developed Countries. The use of Environmental Impact Assessment (EIA) as a development control planning tool, for example, has received much attention, and is described in detail in the following chapter.

Protection and designation

Development control measures are frequently enhanced in certain circumstances where it is appropriate to offer special protection to particular environments, or environmental assets. This is increasingly being achieved by the designation or zoning of specific areas in association with additional development control measures. Many types of environment or environmental features can be, and are, protected by generic land use planning controls and regulations. In the UK these typically include the following.

Ancient monuments – monuments of special importance are identified and given special consideration in development decisions.

Listed buildings – particularly important in urban tourism, buildings are identified as having special architectural or historic interest.

Conservation areas – this approach is adopted for areas which contain groups of buildings and associated urban spaces which have architectural and historic significance. Designation is intended to maintain and enhance an area's character.

Trees and woodland – some planning systems allow for the protection of individual elements such as trees and woodland through the use of preservation orders.

Areas of outstanding natural beauty – areas of this type are seen as contributing to the wider enjoyment of the countryside, but are probably not of national significance. Nevertheless their designation gives them special protection.

Coastal zones – specific protection for coastal areas is afforded by the use of special powers. Coastal zoning such as the heritage coasts in England and Wales (covering some 1,300 km of coastline), can provide a significant level of protection from inappropriate tourism developments.

(Countryside Commission 1992a)

It is notable that, generally, the majority of specific protection to environmental elements provided for within planning systems deals with the rural environment. This is emphasised by the use which many countries make of national park designations which permit large areas of rural landscape to be designated as a whole (MacEwen and MacEwen 1982; Aitchison 1984). In England and Wales, the control of national parks is established within the various Town and Country Planning Acts; control is achieved by designation and legislation rather than by state purchase and control of the land itself. The legislation requires the planning authority for the national park to produce two documents: a structure plan, which includes policies and proposals relating to activities which are controlled by the various Planning Acts, and a national park plan, which emphasises the development of policies for the management of the park. The distinction between the two concepts, planning and management, is not always that clearly specified. In this context, 'planning' provides the basis for policies and decisions affecting the physical, social and economic environments. Management, on the other hand, means the organisation and provision of services and facilities including the management of land and resources.

Frequently, the zoning of tourist activities (or their exclusion from specific zones) is used as a means of preventing unacceptable intrusion and pressure. Healey (1983) suggests that zoning in land use planning systems will increase in the future as environmental conservation concerns grow, while Marsh (1983) provides a discussion of the use of zoning in the development of a national park plan in Canada. Frequently the concept of zoning with specific relevance to tourism is associated with coastal areas where significant resort development has taken place in the last 20 years (e.g. Baarse and Rijsberman 1986; Salm 1985; Waite 1982). The application of protection measures, both statutory and management, has also been discussed in other areas (e.g. Pivert 1987, with reference to the Ardeche region of France; Ostrowski 1984, with reference to the extensive legislation which is found in Poland aimed at the protection of natural resource attractions).

Decision-making

The mechanisms and agencies involved in the control of development are fundamental to the level of control achieved and will vary from country to country, reflecting the approach to planning adopted. Approaches can be broadly divided into two categories: an administrative approach and a political approach. In the administrative approach, an application for development is considered strictly in the context of existing regulations, which may be in a variety of forms including local plans or zoning ordinances. Whether the proposal complies with the plan or not will determine whether it is approved. Little discretion is available in this approach; approval of non-conforming proposals will require modification to the plans rather than the application of discretion (Booth 1991). The political approach, on the other hand, considers applications for development on their merit and is one in which discretion may be exercised. Typically, decisions are taken by a committee of the local council, although in some cases this power may be delegated to planning officers working for the local planning authority.

Thus, although all planning controls will be open to interpretation, some systems are also open to discretion in implementation. In certain countries, particularly where zoning forms the basis of local planning and development control, discretion is more limited, although even in these cases there is usually some flexibility (Booth 1991). Where a particular system allows for considerable discretion, people's experience and view of the system may be markedly different, perhaps reflecting the differing degrees of discretion employed by different local planning authorities. Possible contrasts in the use of discretion are highlighted in Davies and Healey's (1983) caricature of contrasting stereotypes of planning authorities in the UK. In one, planning is:

> flexible, responsive and innovative . . . it recognises the importance of statutory planning procedures but is not confined by them.

In another, by contrast, planning is:

> an isolated activity, dependent at best on an uncertain relationship with political and corporate leadership.
>
> (Davies and Healey 1983: 10–11)

Discretion is important if total uniformity is to be avoided. It is important in tourism development because no two tourism destinations are the same. However, it introduces uncertainty to the development process which can undermine developer confidence. Green and Foley (1987) note that even a change of case officer involved in a project can lead to a different interpretation of regulations.

Once planning regulations have been decided, then attitudes towards planning and a particular planning system are ultimately underpinned by the degree to which the planning system is committed to ensuring that regulations and development decisions are carried out. Without mechanisms for enforcement, the control of development cannot be assured. Enforcement decisions may involve the demolition of offending developments or taking legal action against offending individuals or companies, for example. All too often, a planning system falters through lack of effective enforcement action. Henry (1988), for example, discusses the ways in which land use planning regulations can be bypassed by tourism developers in Jamaica. Although planning controls have helped in positioning new hotel complexes in appropriate settings, there are several examples of developments which have not been controlled. Many developers are unhappy with the regulations, particularly as they relate to development density and building height which restrict their rates of return. Consequently, many hotels have been built which defy the planning regulations, some having never been submitted for planning approval. As noted earlier, the pressures on governments and local authorities can mean that the commitment to a system of control may falter in the face of economically attractive development opportunities.

Design, design guidance and the planning process

Issues of design are fundamental to discussions of the maintenance or enhancement of environmental quality. What constitutes 'good design' and the control of design will always be matters of debate, and have been much discussed in the literature (Booth and Beer 1983). Frequently, conflicts arise between the vernacular and the modern. Holloway (1991) argues that modern buildings and settings, if exciting and well designed, can play a significant role in generating tourism, as can vernacular architecture. The need for great care in design is taken up by Jamieson (1990) in a discussion of the role of design in the development of historic districts in Canada. Sympathetic development, it is argued, must take into account aspects of the wider social, economic and cultural environment. Ayala (1991) reinforces the importance of design to tourist resorts for the maintenance of a competitive position, arguing that visitors are attracted by good design. Similar comments are equally applicable to design in rural areas. The Countryside Commission demonstrates the importance of good design in a range of environments within the national parks of England and Wales (Countryside Commission 1992b).

The extent to which design becomes an element of the planning process and the manner in which it is influenced and controlled show major variations, both within countries as well as between them. The degree to which design considerations are taken into account will be influenced by a range of factors, including the nature of the individual planning system, the level of political commitment, development and commercial pressures and the individual discretion exercised by planning authorities themselves. For some practitioners and decision-makers the control of design is contrary to free market principles and can produce tensions between development and the environment. Booth and Beer (1983) note that over 86 per cent of all planning approvals carried conditions that were intended to modify the landscape design, layout and architectural detailing of developments. It is also significant that the UK Secretary of State for the Environment (a pioneer of de-regulation within the planning system) noted in Circular 22/80 that:

> Planning authorities should recognise that aesthetics is an extremely subjective matter. They should not therefore impose their tastes on development simply because they believe them to be superior. . . . Nevertheless control of appearance can be important especially for instance in environmentally sensitive areas such as national parks, areas of outstanding beauty, conservation areas and areas where the quality of the environment is of a particularly high standard.
>
> (DoE 1980: 3)

Increasingly, design guides are being developed to help communicate broad principles of what is appropriate to those wishing to develop. Although perhaps the most important of the design guides in use, such as the Essex Design Guide for residential areas in the UK, are not targeted at tourism development specifically, increasingly guides are being produced for the use of redundant buildings and the restoration of buildings in conservation areas (Essex County Council 1973). The Essex Guide is important because it identifies three important principles which have more general applicability. The first is that residential development has failed on both aesthetic and functional grounds. The second is the claim that a satisfactory environment is one which creates a sense of place which is related to the local area. The third emphasises that good design is not a subjective matter of opinion or taste but is based on well proven principles.

Frequently, tourism is not specifically identified as an element in design guidance, but can be associated with several aspects of design which do receive coverage. In their study of the use of design guidance in the UK, Chapman and Larkham (1992) note local authority use of guidance in the specification of materials, conservation areas, open space/landscape and the re-use of redundant buildings. However, they observe that the number of authorities using guidance is limited. Design guidance relating to tourism is normally related to specific aspects of the environment. It is, therefore, unlikely and also undesirable to find design guidance specifically targeted at tourism as an activity. Two guidance documents are worthy of note, however, because they relate to settlements whose primary role is tourism. The *Townscape Studies* produced for Jersey (States Planning Department 1984) provides comprehensive guidance for the settlements of St. Helier, St. Aubin and Gorey. *Thaxted, An Historical and Architectural Survey* (Essex County Council 1966), makes similar comment for the historic village of Thaxted.

Tourism in National Parks: A Guide to Good Practice (Countryside Commission 1992b) provides an example of guidance in which management practice and design guidance are linked. The document covers a range of issues including sensitive approaches to development, integration with the community, recreation and interpretation, conservation, information provision, and marketing. The document is specifically produced for those involved in the national parks in which tourism development is particularly sensitive and at the same time well controlled in existing legislation. The guide outlines three key principles for design in the parks which include observing the character of existing buildings, reflecting local vernacular styles and taking account of setting. It is doubtful if the level of detail provided by this document is adequate to influence developments and it will be necessary to supplement it with more detailed guidance at a more local level.

Although such guides are attempting to impose a level of aesthetic control, it is by no means agreed that such control is necessary. Indeed, some commentators argue that design control stifles innovation and encourages mediocrity (Beddington 1973; Manser 1979). However, there does appear to be a strong case for the use of guidance and aesthetic control in many countries where precipitous development, particularly by international hotel chains, has done little to improve the visual environment of many towns and cities.

There are opportunities for design guidance of more general applicability to assist in major tourist developments (Green and Hunter 1992b) and in other more specific aspects of environmental planning. Design guidance is not necessarily regulatory. A recent publication by the Forestry Authority in the UK provides practical design guidance for those involved in lowland management. It acknowledges that 'a good design is one that marries aesthetic principles with an understanding of ecological processes and economic realities' (Forestry Authority 1992: 2).

People and planning

Increasingly, a tourism backlash amongst host communities is drawing attention to the hostility of many local people to tourism (Witt *et al.* 1991). Travis (1988), for example, addresses this issue in the context of 'friendly tourism' in which tourists and locals are successfully integrated. As indicated in previous chapters, many authors have concluded that the sustainable development of tourism must involve local people in the decision-making process. Thus, researchers are examining the relationship between tourist and host community, in the hope of fostering mutually supportive interactions between tourists and locals (e.g. Zube and Busch (1990)).

Public involvement in land use planning decisions of relevance to the tourism sector can be achieved in a variety of ways. Bridge and Hutchinson (1988) describe how leisure activity can be better integrated into the community and outline the challenges facing individuals, agencies, associations and the communities themselves if they are to achieve a better harmony. Diatta *et al.* (1986) show how local people have been involved in the management of tourist activities in Senegal creating a more harmonious relationship between local people and visitors. The literature generally, however, devotes little attention to the direct involvement of people in the decision-making processes concerning tourism planning. This may be because the formal involvement of local people in the planning process is relatively recent in some countries. In other countries it is virtually non-existent. Public involvement is not simply a way of responding to pressure groups, but (more positively) of recognising that local people are expert in their own areas and have much to offer in the understanding of local situations and activities (Green and Hunter 1992a). The Skeffington Report (MHLG 1969) suggested practical ways in which planning authorities could implement public participation in the planning system in England and Wales. Approaches included the use of public meetings, formal exhibitions and public inquiries. As Mordey notes:

> with increased scope for participation, of course, planning aid became a more urgent item on the agenda, in recognition of the difficulties members of the public can have when dealing with the planning system.
>
> (Mordey 1987: 196)

The complexity of a planning system, even where adequate public consultation mechanisms are in place, will greatly limit its accessibility to many groups. Consequently, there is no guarantee that a formal structure will provide the level of public involvement appropriate to many tourism developments. Equally, as Mordey notes, even in 'well developed' planning systems there is variation in both the legislation relating to public involvement and the procedures through which it is implemented. The Royal Town Planning Institute sums the situation in England and Wales up very neatly stating:

> The provisions in public legislation for the role of the public are based on the twin assumptions that local democracy works effectively and that all sections of the population have equal access to knowledge and resources. Both assumptions are now generally recognised to be unfounded in fact. Elected members cannot hope to adequately represent local views on specific issues. Experience has shown that the most articulate and resourceful sections of the population are most successful in having their views accepted.
>
> (Mordey 1987: 211)

Managing the tourist environment

The planning process is not simply a mechanism for prior control within the environment. Management is a key element of the implementation process which ensures that development objectives are met. In a discussion of the tourism impacts in the Pacific, Milne (1990) emphasises the central role which management plays. Many planning documents will be followed by management plans, as is the case with the national parks of England and Wales. All too frequently, matters of management are omitted in decision-making with minimal subsequent control.

In many specially designated areas it is important to stress the importance of management if we are to avoid a static view of the environment. Cullen emphasises this point in a consideration of heritage coasts in England and Wales when he states that, 'many local authorities see heritage coasts as another development control tool rather than an opportunity to provide local leadership and land management' (Cullen 1981: viii). In a dynamic environment, the impacts of decisions and activities may change so that it is necessary to develop management and monitoring tools and approaches so as to ensure the long-term implementation of decisions and the maintenance of the tourism environment.

Tourism management approaches and schemes are found in the contexts of both urban and rural environments. However, more attention has been devoted to management in rural rather than urban areas. The literature has many examples of rural management and coastal management (Milne 1990; Fagence 1990), but very little discussion of the urban context (Russell 1989). Although common approaches can be established, it is important to recognise that there are no common solutions. In establishing management plans and strategies, it is always important to recognise regional dimensions and the particular characteristics and circumstances of each area.

The management tools adopted are very varied, in part dependent on the required goal. Much of the discussion in the literature relates to management issues in rural areas such as national parks or coastal areas where the impact of tourist numbers on a fragile environment is regarded as being particularly important (see, for example, Thiele 1987; Woodley 1989). Here, problems of erosion and congestion are leading to drastic management solutions (Theile 1987). In many of the national parks, authorities are turning to measures to restrict visitors rather than manage their activities. Park and ride schemes, for example, which attempt to reduce car access, create their own problems of visual intrusion and erosion from car parks (Hick 1991). French (1991) argues that restrictions must be applied to manage visitor access. The impact of management measures on visitor behaviour and ultimately on the environment being managed is a subject of particular relevance to policy-makers and managers anxious to develop procedures to protect the tourist environment (Peltzer 1989).

The management agreement is a tool which is often used in situations where public authorities wish to influence the management approach taken by another agency. A management agreement can be defined as a formal written agreement between a public authority and a landowner, who thereby undertakes to manage the land in a specified manner in order to satisfy a particular public need, usually in return for some form of consideration.

Management in the urban environment has received less attention in the literature. Traditional aspects of urban management such as car parking provision, traffic management, refuse collection and street cleaning are taken for granted as management of the urban environment. Recently, the concept of town centre management has been introduced in an attempt to manage the urban environment to maximise its appeal for visitors. Town centre management is not uniquely about tourism environments, but rather deals with town centres and their associated buildings in order to make them better places to visit. It involves a planned and co-ordinated programme of policies and activities to establish, maintain and enhance the central areas of our cities (Balbock 1989). A number of functions and activities include:

- routine environmental maintenance such as litter collection and street cleaning;
- co-ordination of public authority services and public and private sector initiatives;
- the creation and maintenance of safe shopping environments;
- the integration of retail interests with leisure and service facilities; and,
- promotion of events and publicity.

The maintenance of the urban environment is normally the responsibility of those agencies in both the public and private sectors which are located in the town centre or which have a responsibility to its development but which frequently do not operate within an established framework unless the area is subject to some other type of control.

The approach of town centre management is particularly important in historic cities where the potential conflicts between visitors and technical capacity of the infrastructure or the environment is great. In such cases, management has to deal with the requirements of specific planning policy such as conservation areas. Here the management of the partnership between the public and private agencies can ensure that urban character can be reconciled with retailer identity and economic viability. The involvement of all parties in the development of the management strategy and the use of clear policies and guidelines is a key component of strategy (Purton 1992).

Monitoring and evaluation

For Turok and Wannup (1990), evaluation involves the monitoring and assessment of the impact and effectiveness of policies and programmes. Foley (1992) notes that it differs from policy appraisal which takes place before a policy is implemented. The tourism literature presents few examples of evaluation, nor is there discussion of the importance of evaluation and monitoring in a policy context. However, the monitoring and evaluation of actions is becoming increasingly important across a range of planning and development activities for three principal reasons: accountability, understanding and cost efficiency/effectiveness.

Accountability is increasingly important in most public sector decision-making situations (see, for example, DoE 1988). Transparency in decision-making is similarly important if local people are to be encouraged to take part in the process. Evaluation ensures that such accountability is the case. Better understanding of the impacts of policy is needed if the process of policy planning is to evolve in a well-informed manner. The process of evaluation will lead to both learning and better understanding. Robinson, Wren and Goddard (1987), for example, observe that there are too few rigorous evaluation studies which can provide the answers to questions about policy impact. Finally, efficiency and effectiveness became increasingly key reasons for evaluation as central and local governments strove to create greater value for money in the 1980s (Lewis 1986).

Monitoring and evaluation depends on the availability of appropriate and comparable data. In many areas of public policy, evaluation problems of data are frequently encountered and surrogates are used. Whilst Cronin (1990), for example, notes the development of consistent and comparable data in Canada, such developments are not universal and create problems for evaluations at intra-national as well as international levels. The quest for the standardisation of definitions and data collection methodologies is a long-term objective of many analysts.

However, in many cases data requirements are not found in nationally collected data sets and require independent survey.

Moore and Townroe (1990) note a range of practical, methodological and conceptual problems in evaluation. These include:

1 poorly specified objectives;
2 difficulties in measuring secondary effects; and,
3 problems of geographical definition and scale.

These problems should not discourage the use of evaluation in the planning process but rather inform the process and encourage the development of clear, explicit approaches which avoid unnecessary over-sophistication. As Robinson, Wren and Goddard (1987) observe there is a need to narrow down the complex overlay of policy measures to manageable proportions, using data which can be reliably and readily collected.

There is very little work which deals with the evaluation of planning structures and processes as they relate to tourism. The literature does, however, provide critical evaluation of relevant policies, as for example that of national parks policy in England and Wales (McEwen and MacEwen 1982), and the Department of Environment evaluation of tourism projects in the inner city (DoE 1990).

The UK Countryside Commission's evaluation of the heritage coast programme illustrates many of the difficulties of such an exercise, most notably the lack of policy objectives against which to evaluate success (Cullen 1981). It is noted that, although the stated objective of the policy is to conserve the natural coastal scenery and to facilitate and enhance its enjoyment by the public (Countryside Commission 1992a), there are a series of unstated objectives which may well be relevant to the programme of evaluation. Similarly, the Commission does not have explicit measures that can be used to assess the extent to which objectives have been achieved. The lack of post-development appraisal of individual projects is a matter of great concern, and is discussed within the context of Environmental Impact Assessment in the following chapter.

Education

The successful implementation of an environmentally-conscious planning system will depend on the awareness of all the actors, be they tour operators, developers, local residents, politicians, policy-makers or decision-makers involved with environmental concerns and imperatives. Consequently, the raising of ecological awareness will help protect the environment. Cronin (1990) discusses the development of an educational programme for tourism which would involve both the educational system and the professions in the development of courses for corporate and governmental agencies. Such an approach ignores the fact that tourism is only one element of the environmental debate, and that education must come through a variety of sources, some as part of national programmes, others associated with interpretation activities at individual sites.

Interpretation can play a major role in the education process both at individual site level and in terms of raising general awareness of management problems. Tilden defines interpretation as an educative activity whose objective is to reveal meanings and relationships through the use of original objects, by first-hand experience and by illustrative material, rather than simply to communicate factual information (Tilden 1977). At the level of the site, interpretation can help explain the significance of the site, how it developed, what there is of significance to see and how it is managed. At a more general level, it will assist in influencing the distribution of visitors as well as gaining support and enthusiasm for conservation. In the UK, interpretation plays a pivotal role at the interface between tourists and the environment. Interpretation centres and interpreters are part of the strategy of many of the key organisations concerned with visitors at important sites such as National Trust properties, English Heritage sites and in the national parks. Several private organisations are now developing similar interpretation strategies (Barrow 1992; PPJPB 1988).

Discussion of the role of interpretation in specific contexts is provided by Tiard (1987) for the Brotonne nature park, in which interpretation plays a significant role in protecting the area's cultural and historical environment. Similarly, Beauchamps (1983) outlines the approach in the Mercantour National Park in the southern French Alps. Alcock (1991) discusses the way in which educational and information services provided by the Great Barrier Reef Marine Park Authority helps in the management of the area. This theme is further developed, and the importance of environmental education and training is particularly stressed, by Gloor (1982) in a discussion of access to nature in mountain regions. The experience of the sense of place and the identification with the uniqueness of place which Hall *et al.* (1993) describe in a discussion of environmental education products in New Zealand, for example, are particularly important if we are to ensure that planning decisions respect and reflect local conditions.

Interpretation is generally intended for visitors; however, it is also available for local people. Gurung (1992) describes the development of environmental education in Nepal where it is given a high priority in the country's conservation policies. Programmes are run for villagers in and around Nepal's protected areas. In the newly designated Annapurna Conservation Area conservation education is the top priority. Although it has been stressed that approaches such as these are important to a better understanding of environmental issues, there has been very little research to evaluate the actual impact of interpretation on visitors' attitudes towards the environment, and subsequently on land use planning policies, programmes and decisions.

Partnership

Traditionally, the successful implementation and management of projects has involved a partnership between public, private and community sectors. There is a long history of both formal structures, such as joint venture agreements with companies where land assembly and infrastructure is an integral element of commercial development, and less formal agreements such as management agreements where co-operation is a vital element in the achievement of jointly held objectives. Although increasingly favoured in the 1980s in Europe and North America, the partnership approach has been present in many environmentally oriented policies and projects for some time. The interest in partnership in the UK, however, conceals a very fragmented pattern compared with North America and several Western European countries (Whitney and Haughton 1990). France, for example, has a long tradition of public/private sector collaboration in the form of joint development companies, the Sociétés de Développement Mixte (SEMs), which are active in a range of tourism and associated infrastructure projects (Ministère de l'Intérieur et de l'Aménagement du Territoire 1993).

Partnership is particularly important in areas of activity which involve a number of agencies and interests, where individual agencies do not have the necessary powers of control or where a controlling approach would be an inappropriate strategy to adopt. This is typically the case in the English national parks or heritage coasts. National park authorities own only small areas of the park and have limited budgets. To implement policy consequently involves partnership between landowners and those living in the parks at all stages of decision-making. The Peak National Park Plan emphasises the importance of partnership, saying, 'The very success of the implementation of the Plan depends upon large numbers of partners. Only with their active agreement and participation will this plan be implemented' (PPJPB 1978: 14). The parks authority consulted 136 agencies in the development of their proposals.

The Countryside Commission's policy statement on heritage coasts gives equal emphasis to the views and commitment of organisations and agencies with an active interest. In its statement of policies and priorities – 1992 (Countryside Commission 1992a) – it reproduces statements of commitment from 15 organisations representing the public, private and voluntary sectors. Murphy (1988) adds weight to the importance of a partnership approach to tourism development and planning in his discussion of development in British Columbia. In this context workshops are the mechanism to bring together the industry and community to develop appropriate forms of tourism strategies.

LAND USE PLANNING: INTERNATIONAL COMPARISON

This chapter has drawn together research work and legislative principles which deal with land use planning on an international level. It is particularly the case that the world-wide nature of much tourism activity invites cross-national comparison; the industry operates on many levels from the international to the local, and needs to have a common understanding of development and planning processes world-wide in order to make informed decisions. Cross-national study is consequently attractive because it offers the researcher four key opportunities which Wolman (1993) refers to as policy transfer, policy content, policy learning and systems understanding.

We must, however, proceed with care in the making of policy or process assumptions about other countries. Most important is the policy setting which will be shaped by a host of national attributes (political, cultural, social, economic, racial, legal, historical and geographical) which either individually or in combination will create unique situations. Even the nature and use of language can be an important obstacle to the translation of ideas, both within the same language and between different ones. As Booth and Green note, 'the apparently beguiling similarities (of approaches and systems) dissolve on closer inspection into a host of differences' (Booth and Green 1993: 1).

In developing a conceptual framework within which to consider policy, Wolman (1993) suggests that there are three critical questions which must be posed.

1 Are the problems in a particular country similar to those in the country of comparison?
2 To what extent is policy successful in the origin country?
3 Are there any aspects of policy which are critical to its success?

Wolman's questions highlight many of the observed differences in response to planning processes and policy development between countries. In many countries the commitment to structures is reflected in a polarisation between environmentalists and the tourist industry. Even in some Developed Countries there is a lack of political resolve to put in place appropriate national policies. In many Developing Countries, the imperative for economic development, wealth creation and employment growth jeopardises the establishment of appropriate frameworks for planning and development. As Gunn (1988) notes, many of these countries lack the essential mechanisms to ensure successful planning of tourism. This is reinforced by Wieberdink and Ketel (1988), who observe that it is generally accepted that in order to guarantee a sustainable development process, environmental politics must form an integral part of development policies.

In countries in which legislation provides the framework for control, its implementation is still vulnerable to political expediency or more general ideological influence. In the UK, for example, the Conservative Government, as a key element of its policy of deregulation in the 1980s, strove to weaken planning controls and constrain the power of the local authority in making planning decisions (Green and Foley 1987).

Earlier chapters have identified and emphasised the importance of both the positive and the negative impacts of tourism. The importance of these impacts will depend on the importance of tourism to the economy of the area concerned. In countries such as Turkey, where tourism is a significant instrument in development, the importance of environmental understanding has frequently been under-emphasised in tourism development decisions (Korca 1991). Political and economic necessity may colour the views taken by both policy-makers and developers in their understanding of potential impacts. Of the early attempts at tourism planning in Turkey, Alipour (1991) observes that significant problems in this field have been encountered because of a lack of policy decisions and tools to indicate the spatial distribution of resources and priorities. Similar comments can be made about legislative structures and technical capacity to assess impacts. Although in Western Europe and North America, legislation is in place, this is not the case world-wide. Nor can the presence of technical capacity be assumed.

Chapter 5

Environmental impact assessment and tourism development

Colin Hunter

INTRODUCTION

The focus of this chapter is the use of Environmental Impact Assessment (EIA) as a pro-active development control tool in the appraisal of tourism developments. Increasingly, the potential value of using EIA as part of the overall appraisal of proposed tourism developments is being recognised. Martin and Uysal (1990), for example, state that as a precursor to any tourism development, an EIA should be conducted together with an in-depth market analysis. Butler (1991) observes that traditionally in many areas and for many years tourism projects have rarely been reviewed for environmental impacts before development approval was given, and that where tourism planning exists it has largely been reactive rather than pro-active. Similar suggestions that EIA should precede approval of tourism developments have also been made (e.g. Holder 1988; Cronin 1990; Milne 1990). Indeed, Wheatcroft (1991) reports that a monitoring mechanism is under development by the World Travel and Tourism Council which involves a self-imposed EIA for all new tourism projects. These suggestions are in keeping with the view of the World Commission on Environment and Development that nation-states should make or require prior environmental assessments of proposed activities which may significantly affect the environment or use of natural resources (WCED 1987) (see Table 3.1). Potentially, EIA has an important contribution to make to the realisation of sustainable tourism development, because it may provide a means of translating the concept of sustainable development into action on the ground. It has been argued that EIA is not merely a procedure for identifying potential impacts, but is a means of integrating the concerns of economic development and environmental protection (Htun 1992).

Following some general background to EIA, this chapter examines the basic features of a generalised EIA system. Descriptions of commonly utilised EIA methods and techniques for the description and prediction of environmental change are then provided. The potential of EIA in allowing the greater involvement of local communities in development decision-making is then discussed in some detail. Finally, an overview of issues surrounding the potential use of EIA in the appraisal of tourism developments is provided at the end of the chapter.

BACKGROUND TO EIA

Environmental Impact Assessment, sometimes referred to as Environmental Assessment (EA), provides a framework for the prior assessment of the potential impacts of tourism development to allow the avoidance of unacceptable environmental degradation and the maximisation of potential benefits. EIA has been described as the embodiment of the preventative or precautionary approach to environmental management (e.g. Haigh 1984), and is one manifestation of the much quoted and lauded, 'prevention is better than cure' principle of environmental protection. Pearce (1989), for example, cites water pollution problems resulting from rapid increases in the number of tourists and inadequate treatment facilities, and suggests that:

> Economically, as well as environmentally, provision of adequate infrastructure from the outset will in the long run prove less expensive than the correction of environmental damage plus the eventual construction of the necessary plant.
>
> (Pearce 1989: 236)

EIA should, if operated properly, prevent lack of foresight from storing up environmental problems for the future, and can save the developer money over the long term. In any case, experience suggests that the financial cost of conducting a satisfactory EIA normally accounts for a very small proportion of the total capital cost of a new project (UNEP 1988).

The great majority of work on the assessment of the environmental impacts of development has been concentrated at the level of the individual project, whether for tourism or other types of development. It should be noted that EIA can also be utilised in the assessment of area-based policies, plans or strategies (Wood, 1992). However, the focus of this chapter is the use of EIA at the project level.

EIA is now an accepted part of the development control procedures of many of the Developed Countries around the world, whereby an Environmental Impact Statement (EIS), or Environmental Statement (ES), must be produced for certain types of development project according to the potential for environmental disruption. Potential disruption is usually related to such factors as the size of the project, the nature of the processes associated with a particular development and the planned location of the project. It may not be too long before EIA is formally adopted in a number of countries in the former Eastern bloc (Starzewska 1992) and in Developing Countries (Htun 1992; Moreira 1992).

Before embarking on a general description of EIA, it is worth making the point that any formal EIA system can only operate at an optimal level within the context of well-developed and properly implemented environmental and planning legal frameworks, both at national and local levels of government. Much of the description of EIA in operation given in this chapter assumes such a broad legislative framework and can, therefore, be viewed to some extent as an idealised description. In many Developing Countries, for example, there remain significant obstacles and constraints to the successful operation of a formal EIA system. These include a general lack of political will or awareness of the need for EIA, insufficient public participation in decision-making, lacking or inadequate legislative frameworks, lack of an institutional base, insufficient skilled manpower, lack of scientific information and data, and insufficient financial resources (Kennedy 1992). With specific reference to Latin American countries, Moreira (1992) argues that one of the main obstacles to the instigation of formal and comprehensive EIA systems is the authoritarian character of many of their governments, which deny a broad participation of social groups in decision-making and the free availability of information concerning development proposals. Since most Latin American countries have yet to formulate national environmental policies or legislation, Moreira (1992) further suggests that it would be more advisable, at the moment, for these countries to undertake a broad re-orientation of development policies at all levels of government towards environmental protection, rather than focus immediately on the adoption of some type of formal EIA system.

Although EIA comes in a variety of systems and procedures, utilising a wide range of methods, techniques and thresholds of implementation, most forms of EIA conform to four fundamental principles (Roberts and Hunter 1992).

1 They identify the nature of the proposed and induced activities which are likely to be generated by a project or the introduction of a process.
2 They identify the elements of the environment which will be significantly affected.
3 They evaluate the initial and subsequent impacts.
4 They are concerned with the management of the beneficial and adverse impacts which are generated.

Thus, at least in theory, EIA is not merely a method of analysis, but a comprehensive framework which identifies, analyses, evaluates and manages the impacts associated with the introduction and operation of a development project. The output from the EIA process, namely a detailed EIS, should provide the decision-maker with a rational basis upon which to make a better decision. The EIS is not, in itself, a decision. If an EIA has been used to appraise a particular project within the context of a broader area-based plan or policy framework, then the EIA may suggest to the decision-maker one of the following alternatives:

- that the proposed development is acceptable at the suggested site;
- that the proposed development is not acceptable at the site suggested but may be acceptable at an alternative site;
- that the proposed development is unacceptable at any site; or,
- that a modified proposal may be acceptable either at the site suggested, or at an alternative site.

In reaching one of these decisions, it is important to recognise that the standards and criteria adopted by the decision-maker will vary from country to country (e.g. according to national environmental legislation and policies) and even between different areas within one country according to local conditions, needs and priorities (Murphy 1981).

In more detail, EIA has recently been defined as:

> A process for identifying the likely consequences for the
> biogeophysical environment and for man's health and welfare
> of implementing particular activities and for conveying this
> information, at a stage when it can materially affect their
> decision, to those responsible for sanctioning the proposals.
>
> (Wathern 1992: 6)

It is apparent from this widely accepted definition that apart from
concern for human health and welfare, EIA has a bias towards
impacts on the biological and physical components of the natural
environment. It is important to recognise this bias because tourism development is often associated with a multi-faceted range of
potential impacts (see Chapter 2). Thus, EIA as currently
practised does not provide a comprehensive framework for the
integrated appraisal of tourism projects and, therefore, provides
only a partial mechanism for the pro-active management of
tourism. Although some researchers argue for the extension of
EIA to encompass a wide range of potential socio-economic
impacts (e.g. Davies and Muller 1983), it is normally apparent
in studying the majority of EISs that EIA still remains tied to its
roots. In fact, EIA has its origins in the USA where it formed
(initially a very small) part of the Cost–Benefit Analysis (CBA)
procedures of the early 1960s. Its primary function then, as now,
was to enable those impacts on the natural environment which
could not be measured in monetary terms to be included in the
project appraisal process. With the enactment of the National
Environmental Policy Act of 1969 in the USA (United States
Government 1969) which required the preparation of an EIS
by federal agencies for all major projects, EIA received formal
recognition as an environmental management tool. Some socio-
economic data are usually included in an EIS, since developers
are often keen to stress aspects such as job creation and economic
multiplier effects. Similarly, impacts on the built environment,
such as road infrastructure, frequently receive attention. Even
the more comprehensive CBAs often include some information
on environmental impacts (Wathern 1992). However, the routine
application of a fully integrated and comprehensive appraisal
system to the assessment of development proposals still appears
a distant prospect. The work of Nijkamp (1980) may provide the
basis of such an integrated system.

In July 1988, member states of the European Community (EC) formally complied with the EC Directive on EIA (CEC 1985). This important piece of legislation provides a relatively recent example of the types of impact considered appropriate in EIA. The Directive requires that effects on the following should be described and assessed:

- human beings, fauna and flora;
- soil, water, air, climate and the landscape;
- the interaction between the two groups above; and,
- material assets and the built cultural heritage.

Expressed in a different way, the types of impacts typically covered in EIA include impacts on receiving environmental media (air, water, land), living receptors occupying those media (human beings, flora and fauna) and the built environment (structures, buildings, monuments, etc.) (Lee 1989). Changes to these aspects of the environment brought about through a particular development project may be favourable or adverse. It is also important to note that the impacts to be assessed are not merely restricted to those which are of a direct and immediate nature; knock-on, secondary effects should also be considered, if significant. These may arise through environmental inter-relationships and inter-dependencies. Further complications may arise where the dividing line between environmental (using the term 'environmental' as currently understood in EIA practice) and non-environmental impacts is difficult to define. For example, if a project reduces an area of woodland, the resulting amenity loss has both ecological and social implications. In this case, the social impacts may also be considered. However, the employment effects of a new project, although of potential social and economic significance, do not, of themselves, constitute environmental impacts for the purposes of EIA. This said, given the commonly agreed need for the consideration of the environment, or the environmental impact of actions, to be holistic in nature, there are compelling reasons for redefining the coverage and competence of EIA to include detailed socio-economic changes. This has been recognised in the tourism literature (e.g. Duffield and Walker 1984; Cronin 1990).

As well as attempting to define the types of impact to be included in EIA, it is also necessary to adopt selection criteria which allow an initial screening of projects to determine those to be submitted for EIA. As indicated previously, calls for EIAs to be carried out for proposed tourism developments are found in the more recent tourism literature, but rarely are these followed by any explanation of which types of project should be selected. Selection criteria are necessary, although difficult to impose in a manner which will protect the environment under most circumstances. Very many tourism developments may not be of a nature to pose any significant threat to environmental quality. Small extensions to existing tourist facilities which do not constitute a change in use, for example, may require some form of regulation and planning permission from the local planning authority, but hardly merit a full EIA. However, it is difficult to formulate suitable screening criteria. Possibilities include the physical size of the project or its monetary cost. Clearly, these will not by themselves be adequate in all circumstances, as small and inexpensive proposals, in sensitive locations, may carry major impacts. Studies conducted to provide guidance in selecting projects to be subject to EIA highlight three criteria (Lee 1989). These are:

1 the size of the project, i.e. principally whether the physical scale of the project makes it of more than immediate local importance;
2 the environmental characteristics of the area in which it will be located, e.g. a sensitive environment such as a nature reserve; and,
3 the physical and process characteristics of the project, e.g. a project thought likely to give rise to particularly complex, dangerous or adverse effects.

To these considerations might be added the novelty of the project. Some tourism developments, perhaps particularly alternative developments in remote areas, may be such that there is little or no prior experience to draw on when trying to gauge their potential for environmental change. It would appear prudent to err on the side of caution in such circumstances and subject such projects to EIA, if possible.

Many countries have now developed lists of projects, based on criteria such as those given above, for which EIA is a development requirement. In Thailand, for example, the need for EIA is related to location based upon the identification of environmentally sensitive areas (Wathern 1992). The use of rigid criteria has, however, been rejected in some countries because of perceived inflexibility of operation. Canada, for example, has adopted a phased screening process (FEARO 1978). Under the EC Directive mentioned earlier, projects are divided into two broad categories or lists. Those in Annex 1 of the Directive (generally large industrial or infrastructure developments) are normally subject to a mandatory EIA in all member states. For those in Annex 2, requirement for an EIA is at the discretion of each member state. The projects in each category are given in the lists below.

According to Wathern (1992) the Annex 1 projects from the EC Directive requiring an EIA are as follows:

- Crude oil refineries (excluding undertakings manufacturing only lubricants from crude oil) and installations for the gasification and liquefaction of 500 tonnes or more of coal or bituminous shale per day;
- thermal power stations and other combustion installations with a heat output of 300 megawatts or more and nuclear power stations and other nuclear reactors;
- installations solely designed for the permanent storage or final disposal of radioactive waste;
- integrated works for the initial melting of cast iron and steel;
- installations for the extraction of asbestos and for the processing and transformation of asbestos and products containing asbestos;
- integrated chemical installations;
- construction of motorways, express roads and lines for long distance railway traffic and of airports with a basic runway length of 2100m or more;
- trading ports and also inland waterways and ports for inland waterway traffic which permit the passage of vessels over 1350 tonnes; and
- waste disposal installations for the incineration, chemical treatment or landfill of toxic and dangerous wastes.

Wathern (1992) cites the following categories of projects included in Annex 2 of the EC Directive

- agriculture;
- extractive industry;
- energy industry;
- processing of metals;

- manufacture of glass;
- chemical industry;
- food industry;
- textile, leather, wood and paper industries;
- rubber industry;
- infrastructure projects;
- miscellaneous; and
- modifications to Annex 1 developments.

The tourism industry is not referred to explicitly in either Annex as such. The huge variation in the size and type of tourism projects would make the inclusion of tourism in such a schedule extremely difficult and, perhaps, inappropriate. Aspects of development of varying relevance to the tourism industry do, however, appear. For example, explicit reference is made to holiday villages and hotel complexes under the 'miscellaneous' grouping in Annex 2. Yacht marinas are mentioned under 'infrastructure projects' in Annex 2, and other features, such as the construction of minor roads, which may accompany tourism development are also covered in Annex 2.

In other EIA systems, however, there are explicit references to tourism developments. Environmental conservation law in the Republic of Korea, for example, has required the preparation of an EIS for tourism complexes proposed by government agencies or government-funded institutions since 1981 (Htun 1992). This legislation does not apply to developments in the private sector. The legislative framework for EIA was established in Thailand in 1975. In 1981 a list of ten categories of projects to be subject to EIA was enacted, and this list includes hotel or resort facilities with more than 80 rooms, in environmentally-sensitive areas such as those adjacent to rivers, coastal areas, lakes and beaches, or in the vicinity of national parks (Htun 1992). Although not required by law, Uruguay provides another example of a Developing Country where several EIAs have been carried out for tourism projects (Moreira 1992).

BASIC FEATURES OF AN EIA SYSTEM

The fundamental features of a generalised and, to some extent, idealised EIA system are summarised in Table 5.1. Before proceeding to examine aspects of the system in more detail, it is

Table 5.1 Basic features of an EIA system

Types of items	*Main procedural elements*
• description of the main characteristics of the project • estimation of the residues and wastes that it is likely to create • analysis of the aspects of the environment likely to be significantly affected by the project, including a description of the baseline condition of these aspects of the environment • analysis of the likely significant effects of the proposed project on the environment including a description of the forecasting techniques and data used to assess these effects • description of the measures envisaged to reduce harmful effects (this may be extended to include a consideration of alternatives to the proposed project and the reasons why they were rejected) • assessment of the compatibility of the project with environmental regulations and land-use plans • non-technical summary of the total assessment	• the developer (often with assistance from consultants, regulatory bodies and other organisations) prepares an EIS which is submitted, along with the application for project authorisation, to the competent authority • the study is published (possibly after checking its adequacy) and is used as a basis for consultation involving both statutory authorities, possessing relevant environmental responsibilities, and the general public • the findings of the consultation process are presented to the competent authority • the assessment study and consultation findings accompany the proposed project through the remainder of the competent authority's authorisation procedure

Note: these basic features can be further elaborated by, for example, making arrangements for the preliminary screening and scoping of projects, for independent panels to vet the studies made for major projects and for monitoring the environmental consequences arising from the implementation of the project.

Source: adapted from Lee (1992)

worth making two points. Firstly, it is easy to view the process of conducting an EIA as a linear, one-dimensional progression through defined stages, such as those given in Table 5.1. While this simplifies a description of the EIA process, it does not necessarily represent the real-life situation. Commonly, there are cyclical as well as linear sequences of activities. These may arise through consultations between the developer and the competent authority (e.g. the local planning authority) responsible for sanctioning the project. Thus, feed-back is possible at any stage in the EIA process resulting in modifications to the project's design or operation. The second point relates to the timing of the commencement of the EIA. In Table 5.1, the EIA process is shown to begin with the preparation of the EIS. In reality, it is highly desirable for EIA to be considered early on in the project planning and design stage, so that the project planning and EIA processes overlap. Indeed, ideally, the EIA process should be closely integrated with the ongoing planning and design work on the project, so that the developer can take account of environmental issues when considering alternative forms of the project. In the long run, such integration can bring considerable benefits to the developer, including more effective compliance with environmental standards, improvements in the design and siting of plant, savings in capital and operating costs, speedier approval of development applications and the avoidance of costly adaptations to projects once in operation (Cook 1979; Dean 1979; Canter 1983). According to Lee (1989), EIA should be contributing to matters such as a review of alternative ways of meeting the developer's objectives (i.e. alternatives to the proposed project), a review of alternative locations for the project, and a review of alternative process designs, site layouts and ancillary facilities for the proposed project. In combination with technical, financial and other specialist studies, such information can aid the developer in finding the most appropriate form of the project to submit to the remainder of the EIA process and later to the competent authority for formal authorisation. Indeed, informal consultations with the competent authority may begin at the project formulation stage. Local community involvement is also a possibility at this stage.

Any formal EIA system hinges on the preparation of a detailed, written report of the environmental consequences of a development project: the EIS. This normally supports the developer's application for project authorisation, with both documents commonly being submitted to the competent authority for simultaneous consideration. The preparation of the EIA study report is normally the responsibility of the developer, and this is desirable and necessary for a number of reasons. Firstly, it avoids the unfairness of the public sector having to bear the cost of assessing what should be a profitable investment for the private developer. (Although under some circumstances, a local public authority may be both the proponent and judge of a development project. In these situations great uncertainty must surround the objectivity of the authority both in deciding if an EIA is necessary and in the conduct of the EIA.) Secondly, it ensures that the EIA is conducted by those with the greatest information on the proposed development. Thirdly, if the EIA and project formulation processes are to be integrated, as is advocated above, then responsibility for the preparation of the EIS must lie with the developer. For these reasons, the view of Milne (1990), for example, who suggests that governments carry out detailed EIAs of tourism projects before approving them, may be inappropriate. However, on the negative side, a developer cannot be expected to show objectivity in the conduct of an EIA and in the presentation of findings in the EIS. In other words:

> Without adequate safeguards, proponents may be tempted to regard EIA simply as a means of obtaining project authorization and present only those results which show proposals in a favourable light.

(Wathern 1992: 17)

For this reason, a formal EIA system should require developers to consider at least a minimum and proscribed set of environmental features which may be affected by development, as is the case with the EC Directive, for example. Also, it should be a requirement of the EIS that the data used to make predictions of potential impacts is provided, along with a clear explanation of the prediction techniques employed (see Table 5.1). Ideally, the preparation of the EIS will involve consultations between the developer (or the consultants employed by the developer to produce the EIS) and representatives of the competent local authority, as well as other environmental control authorities.

More generally, it is important that developers are made aware of the potential benefits of EIA. If fully integrated with project planning and design, EIA can bring savings in time and money as well as improving the image of the developer with an increasingly environmentally-aware public. Thus, it could be argued that developers who view EIA merely as a necessary 'add-on' to the process of gaining planning permission do themselves a disfavour. Even when, for the sake of national interest for example, a development is almost certainly going to be approved, applying EIA may still yield benefits. Mitigating measures, for example, identified during EIA may be incorporated more economically at the design stage than subsequently (Wathern 1992). Romeril (1985) cites an example of a tourism development at Saas Fee in the Swiss Alps, where the developer gained as a consequence of EIA. In this case, the EIA aided the developer in deciding to opt for a tourist railway rather than a standard lift installation. This alternative operation benefited the developer because the railway proved easier to maintain and was less affected by severe weather conditions, thereby allowing the tourist season to be extended.

The structure and content of the EIS should reflect the types of items given in Table 5.1. It is important to note that the EIS should only consider those potential environmental impacts thought to be *significant*. This implies some kind of prior 'scoping' of potential impacts so that only significant ones are covered in detail. Scoping is an important part of the EIA process and is discussed later in this chapter. Although the majority of EIA legislation and guidance restricts the EIS to the consideration of significant impacts, frequently little help is given in the interpretation of the word 'significant'. Lee (1989), poses the following questions as a guide to deciding on significance.

• Is the impact in question likely to threaten the attainment of existing or proposed environmental quality standards?
• Is it likely to conflict with the objectives, policies or plans of the authority competent to authorise the project?
• Is it likely to be an issue of concern to an environmental control authority because it may conflict with its environmental objectives, policies or plans?
• Is it likely to be an issue of concern either to national environmental interest groups or to the local community in which the project would be located?

In assessing and predicting the significance of impacts a number of other factors should be borne in mind. Potentially, impacts can arise at any stage in the life of a project. The nature and magnitude of these impacts may vary considerably and it is common to find that project impacts are considered during both construction and operational phases, for example. New impacts may also occur if a project is subsequently modified in terms of its scale or operational characteristics. Also, the implementation of one project may stimulate other developments, such as service facilities. The impacts associated with ancillary developments may be significant and, although frequently difficult to predict, should be kept in mind. Relatedly, the cumulative impact of a series of projects may be greater than the sum of the impacts from individual developments. Thus, impacts may become significant when a grouping of projects is considered together, but not on the basis of the effects of individual projects. Similarly, a point may be reached where one more tourism development in an area poses a significant threat to environmental quality.

Additionally, although it is useful in gauging the likely impacts of a proposed development to refer to prior impact studies conducted for a similar project and in a similar location, caution must be employed if this is done. As pointed out by Pearce (1989), it is imperative that any tourism impact study takes account of the specific environmental conditions which prevail at the location under consideration, and considers specific aspects of the development (i.e. stressor activities) within this context. Pearce (1989) cites the study of Kirkpatrick and Reeser (1976) who considered air pollution potential in the resort communities of Aspen and Vail in Colorado, USA. They found that due to topographic characteristics the pollution dispersal at the mountain resort sites was lower than in the Colorado Plains. This finding highlights the importance of considering the unique and specific characteristics of a development site during the EIA process.

Once a project is operational, regular temporal changes in the levels of environmental stress may be expected. This is especially true of tourism operations which frequently show a strong seasonal pattern. Seasonal influxes of tourists will increase the demands for and on resources, and the EIA should take account of these patterns. Again, it is important to be aware of local conditions, since in some locations the tourist season may coincide with the period when residents leave the area for holiday destinations elsewhere, thereby lessening the demands on resources (Pearce 1989). As was pointed out in Chapters 2 and 3, tourism impacts are not restricted to destination areas, and determining the geographical size of the area around a proposed development to be considered in the EIA may be problematical. The necessary size will depend on the characteristics of the development and of the local environment; for example, the dispersion patterns of various pollutants, the relative importance of primary, secondary and tertiary impacts and the specific locations of important ecological, archaeological and cultural sites in the vicinity (Htun 1992). In this way, a broader perspective in the appraisal of an individual tourism project may, for example, lead to more ameliorating measures being suggested and implemented.

On completion, the EIS usually accompanies the developer's application for project authorisation to the competent local authority. At this stage in the EIA process it is common for the EIS to be made public, although some prior consultation between the developer and the competent authority regarding the quality of the EIS may occur. Some independent review organisation or panel may also evaluate the EIS once it has been submitted to check that it is of a standard which can be used as a basis for public participation and decision-making. As a consequence of consultations between the developer and the competent local authority, the general public and other environmental control agencies, the detailed specification of the project may be altered by including additional impact amelioration measures, for example. Following consultation, the competent authority will reach a decision on the proposal, with details of the decision often being made public. The competent authority may impose planning conditions on consenting to the development, such as the regular monitoring of actual environmental impacts. In the Rastus Burn ski-field development in the Remarkables near Queenstown in New Zealand, for example, stringent conditions were imposed on the construction of the associated access road as a result of EIA (Pearce 1989).

EIA METHODS AND TECHNIQUES

There are a large number of diverse assessment methods which can be employed throughout the EIA process. A detailed review of these would run to a large volume and is not the aim of this section. This section considers only a small number of assessment methods and gives illustrations from the tourism impact literature, where possible. EIA assessment methods can be categorised according to the specific task under consideration at a given stage in the EIA process. The following list shows a classification of EIA assessment methods by task (Lee (1989).

- Identification methods – to assist in identifying the project alternatives, project characteristics and environmental parameters to be investigated in the assessment.
- Data assembly methods – to assist in describing the characteristics of the development and of the environment that may be affected.
- Predictive methods – to predict the magnitude of the impacts which the development is likely to have on the environment.
- Communication methods – to assist in consultation and public participation, and in expressing findings of the study for decision-making purposes.
- Management methods – to assist in managing the scoping of the study, the preparation of the impact study, the efficient conduct of the consultation process, etc.
- Decision-making methods – to assist decision-makers in assessing and understanding the significance of environmental impacts relative to other factors relevant to a decision on the proposed development.

Such assessment methods are not unique to EIA and have been developed in a wide range of traditional disciplines (e.g. natural sciences, engineering, social sciences, management sciences and land use planning). EIA is a strategic route which brings together these different methods as required. However, in the EIA literature much is often made of overall or comprehensive 'EIA methodologies'. These are primarily designed to assist in the identification and presentation of significant impacts and as such provide a partial framework to assist in the conduct of an EIA. Frequently, a distinction is made between the overall methodology adopted for a particular EIA and the constituent techniques used to evaluate specific impacts, such as visual intrusion, water pollution and ecological disturbance (e.g. Lee and Wood 1980). While there is some merit in distinguishing between methods and techniques in EIA, the concept of an overall EIA methodology has come in for recent criticism. Lee (1989), for example, argues that such methodologies are not comprehensive and do not address all of the assessment tasks in EIA, and are not original nor restricted in their use to the EIA process. Thus, Lee (1989) makes no distinction between methods and techniques, but prefers to use the term 'method' according to the nature of the task being undertaken. However, in deference to the majority view, the following pages provide separate overviews of some of the methods and predictive techniques frequently employed in EIA.

EIA methods

As EIA has become a formal requirement for certain develop-ment projects in more and more countries around the world, there has been a growth in interest in methods designed to aid in the preparation of EISs. Much of this work originates in the USA. Such methodologies have been described using alternative names, including: technologies, approaches, manuals, guidelines and procedures (Bisset 1992). According to Bisset (1987), these methods can be defined as:

> Structured mechanisms for the identification, collection and organization of environmental impact data. In addition, methods are means whereby information is presented in a variety of visual formats for interpretation by decision-makers and members of the public.
>
> (Bisset 1987: 8)

Some of the more common methods are outlined below.

Checklists

One of the oldest of the EIA methods, the checklist is still widely used, although in a variety of forms. A checklist provides a specific list of environmental parameters which may be affected by a project. Its use should ensure that no aspect of the environment that may be affected is omitted from investigation, whilst also focusing attention on those parameters which may be signifi-cantly affected. A simple checklist is merely a listing of relevant environmental parameters with no additional information on how the impacts on the chosen parameters are to be measured and interpreted. A descriptive checklist is more refined, and provides some guidance on the assessment of impacts. Typically, this involves guidance on the appropriate environmental measure-ments which need to be made and the techniques to be employed in the prediction of project-induced environmental change. Checklists can be made more elaborate still if they incorporate a scale for the presentation of impact magnitudes (a scaling checklist) and/or other impact characteristics, such as reversibility and whether the impact is short term or long term. If each environmental parameter is evaluated subjectively in terms of its relative importance with respect to every other parameter, then the result is a scaling–weighting checklist.

The almost inevitable end-point of the adoption of scaling and weighting is the construction of a complex, quasi-mathematical index of impact, whereby individual impacts are transformed into units on a common, notional scale, weighted in terms of relative importance, and then manipulated mathematically to form some index of total impact (Bisset 1992). Thus, a 'quantitative' evaluation by decision-makers of alternative projects or project specifications is possible. In some cases, a sub-total score for each major component of the environment (e.g. built environment impact or natural environment impact) can be derived, allowing the explicit trade-off of 'sectoral' impacts by decision-makers. Examples of such approaches include the Environmental Evaluation System (Dee *et al.* 1973) and the Water Resources Assessment Methodology (Solomon *et al.* 1977). Some attempts have been made to broaden the basis of the way in which potential impacts are weighted relative to each other, by extending the composition of a 'weighting panel' to include representatives of government, industry, pressure groups and the local community, as well as those experts working on the particular EIA and/or those responsible for developing the method (e.g. Sondheim 1978).

Simple, descriptive and scaling checklists are easy to understand and use, and are all useful for structuring the initial stages of assessment by acting as a guide and ensuring that no vital aspect of the environment is omitted from the EIA study. However, it has been argued that these basic forms of checklist tend to be rigid and derived from some generic list of environmental parameters. Thus, there is a danger that they may lack the flexibility required to assist in the assessment of widely different projects with diverse characteristics (e.g. Bisset 1987). The more complex scaling–weighting checklists allow the results of EIA to be amalgamated and manipulated to produce some final score (or set of scores) to ease the decision-making process. A numerical 'answer' can be very attractive. However, scaling–weighting checklist methods which produce a final index of impact have been strongly criticised for a number of reasons. There is a danger that quantification is equated with objectivity (and therefore 'correctness') in the minds of decision-makers and others. The relative weighting of impacts is a subjective exercise, and, moreover, is often restricted to a small number of specialists. But this inherent subjectivity and bias can all too easily be hidden by the computations associated with the quantification of environmental changes. The complexity of such methods may also inhibit public participation in the EIA process, and limit the degree to which the results of an EIA can be questioned by the public (Bisset 1978). Additionally, there may be a tendency to consider only those impacts which are relatively easily quantified. Alternatively, there may be a great temptation to attempt to quantify aspects which, in the view of many, are essentially unquantifiable, as is the case with aesthetic change (Bisset 1992).

Table 5.2 provides a tourism-based example of a simple checklist, while an example of a scaling checklist is given in Table 5.3.

All checklists, however simple or complex, only deal with

Table 5.2 Extracts from a checklist of the potential environmental impacts of a marina/resort complex

Category of impact	Planning and design phase	Construction phase	Operational phase
I Noise impacts			
A Public health			
B Land use			
II Air quality impacts			
A Public health			
B Land use			
III Water quality impacts			
A Groundwater			
1 Flow and water table alteration			
2 Interaction with surface drainage			
B Surface water			
1 Shoreline alteration			
2 Flood characteristics			

Source: modified from Williams (1987)

Table 5.3 Extracts from a scaling checklist of the general impacts of tourism in the Patara Valley, Turkey

Potential impact of development	*Classification of impact*	*Description of potential impact*
PHYSICAL IMPACTS		
Greater numbers of buildings	I D Elt	Inappropriate design; poor building standards etc.
Increased amounts of sewage	I ID C EI EE	Lack of organised sewage treatment system; effluent seepage from septic tanks; poor enforcement of building standards, etc.
Increased demand on water supply	R D C	Water demand exceeds supply during tourist season; sinking of boreholes in uncontrolled manner, etc.
SOCIAL IMPACTS		
Use of DDT for the control of mosquitoes	I ID C EE Elt	DDT is a known carcinogen and teratogen; continual exposure puts health of indigenous population at risk.
Topless sunbathing	R D EI EE	Practice gives great offence to older people and local women; attracts groups of local men who create a nuisance, etc.

Key:
I=Irreversible   D=Direct   ES/EI=Exposure superficial/intensive
R=Reversible   ID=Indirect   EL/EE=Exposure limited/extensive
C=Cumulative   Est/Elt=Exposure short-term/long-term

Source: modified from Morrison and Selman (1991)

aspects of the environment. However, environmental changes are brought about by aspects of the development. Checklists do not incorporate any sense of cause and effect which demonstrates how an environmental feature is affected by one or more features of the development project. This limitation has led to the development of interaction matrices, described below, which together constitute probably the most widely used EIA methodology (Bisset 1987).

Matrices

A matrix method basically consists of a list of project activities ranged against a checklist of environmental features that might be affected. Project activities can be given a temporal aspect by dividing activities according to the stage of the project, for example the construction and operational phases, and/or by indicating the short- or long-term nature of the impact. Entries in the cells of the matrix can be qualitative or quantitative estimates of the strength of the significant cause and effect relationships portrayed. At its simplest, a matrix will merely indicate (e.g. with the use of a cross) those relationships thought to be significant. This is termed a simple interaction matrix (see Tables 5.4a and 5.4b). Table 5.5 provides an example of a matrix where qualitative estimates of impact significance have been used. Where estimates of impact strength are quantitative, a weighting scheme may again be employed to formulate some total impact score in a quantified and graded matrix. Frequently, the interactions between project activities and environmental aspects are assessed in terms of their magnitude and importance. This is the case in the most famous matrix, the Leopold matrix, developed for the Geological Survey of the USA (Leopold *et al.* 1971). In such a matrix, an interaction cell is divided by a diagonal line with impact magnitude occupying the upper triangle and impact importance in the lower triangle (see Figure 5.1). Magnitude refers to the scale or extensiveness of the interaction, while importance indicates the degree of significance of the interaction. Both can be gauged on a scale of 1–10 by those responsible for producing the EIS. Many further refinements are possible. Relative weights can be assigned to each development activity, for example.

Unless matrices become very complicated, they offer a means of

Table 5.4a Impact matrix for the construction phase of a tourist railway development in Norfolk, England

Aspects of the environment	Nature of development work		
	Tunnel	Stations	Clearance and track laying
Noise	x	x	x
Dust/mud	x	x	x
Vibration	x		
Traffic	x	x	x
Visual	x	x	x
Ecology			x
Economic	x	x	x
Recreation	x		x

Source: modified from Farrington and Ord (1988)

identifying major cause–effect relationships, whilst being relatively quick and easy to formulate and easy to interpret (Lohani and Halim 1987). Complex weighting matrices involve the attractions and criticisms outlined previously for scaling–weighting checklists.

Table 5.4b Impact matrix for the operational phase of a tourist railway development in Norfolk, England

Aspects of the environment	Nature of source		
	Operation of trains	Stations	Track/bridge maintenance
Noise and vibration	x		
Smoke	x		
Sparks	x		
Dust	x		
Waste	x	x	
Visual	x	x	
Recreation	x	x	
Economic	x	x	x
Ecology	x		x
Safety	x	x	
Traffic and access	x	x	

Source: modified from Farrington and Ord (1988)

Table 5.5 Extracts from a matrix showing the general impacts of tourism in the Patara Valley, Turkey

Aspects of the environment	Aspects of tourism development							
	Noise	Lights	Roads	Buildings	Sewage	Water supply	Traffic	More incomers
Landscape		*	**	**				
Archaeological site			**	**				
Wetland ecosystem			*	**	**	**		
Valley fauna			*	**		*	*	
Flora			*	**				
Beach	*			**				**
Beach fauna	**	**		**			**	**
Local economy	**			**	**	**	*	**
Culture	**			**	**			**
Water quality					**			
Air pollution							**	
Health	**		**	**	**	**	**	
Land use						*		++

Key:
*low adverse impact
**high adverse impact
++ beneficial impact

Source: modified from Morrison and Selman (1991)

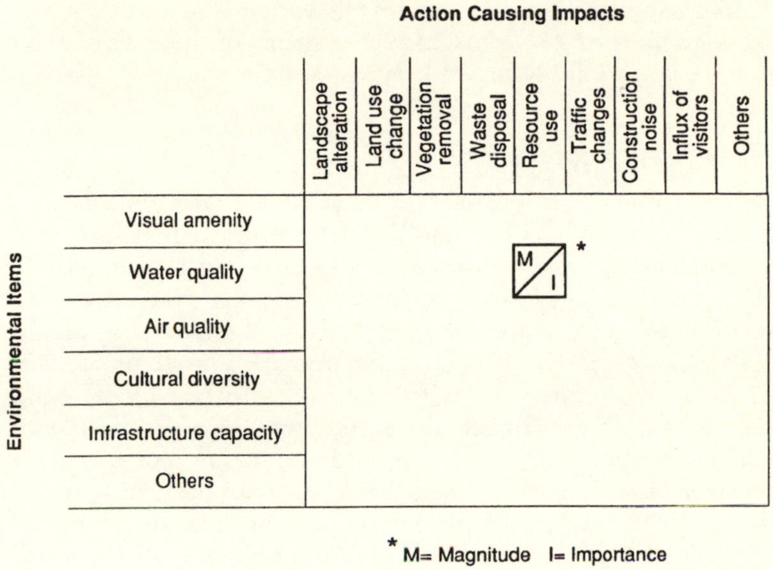

Action Causing Impacts

	Landscape alteration	Land use change	Vegetation removal	Waste disposal	Resource use	Traffic changes	Construction noise	Influx of visitors	Others
Visual amenity									
Water quality				M / I *					
Air quality									
Cultural diversity									
Infrastructure capacity									
Others									

Environmental Items (vertical label on left)

* M= Magnitude   I= Importance

Figure 5.1 An extract from a quantified and graded environmental impact matrix

Source: modified from Leopold (1971)

Although matrices offer the opportunity of describing major, first-order cause–effect interactions, both matrices and checklists focus on single and separated aspects of the environment, thereby excluding the possibility of considering further secondary and tertiary knock-on effects of development. In other words, matrices still do not offer an extension which caters for an appreciation of system-wide impact. Bisset (1992), for example, argues that:

> No matter how intricate and intellectually satisfying the mathematics involved, it is impossible to characterize "system-level" impacts by considering changes in specific components in isolation and then aggregating the results.
>
> (Bisset 1992: 53)

A full appreciation of impact generation and the inter-relationships between impacts and elements of the environment requires some kind of network or systems diagram.

Networks and systems diagrams

Basically, a network consists of a number of linked impacts such that the secondary, tertiary and higher-order impacts arising from an initial impact can be considered explicitly. The construction of an impact network means addressing a series of questions in relation to each major project activity (Lohani and Halim 1987). For example, what are the primary impact areas, and what are the primary impacts within these areas? Then, what are the secondary impact areas, and what are the secondary impacts within these areas? And so on. If one considers the construction of a marina development, for example, which entails dredging activity, then the primary impact might be an increase in water depth. This in turn may lead to the inhibition of the growth of aquatic plants as a secondary impact. This impact in turn might result in such tertiary impacts as the destruction of fish habitat and the loss of a recreational amenity (Sorenson 1971). These relationships are illustrated in Figure 5.2.

Networks have been developed for specific environments, based upon a knowledge of the actual impacts of various developments. Such networks can only be used for the environments for which they were constructed. However, once in existence they can be very useful in assessing the impacts of future developments. More usually, networks have been developed for specific projects and are speculative in nature rather than based on an existing knowledge of impact interactions. Irrespective of the way a network is constructed, it can become a complex and time-consuming task, and a large and detailed web of interactions can also be difficult to interpret. Thus, manually constructed networks may be restricted to a small number of environmental factors, e.g. the consideration of ecological impacts only. Some of these difficulties can be eased with the construction of a computerised network, which may act both as a data-base of impact interactions and as a decision-making tool for specific development proposals (e.g. the IMPACT network constructed by the Forest Service of the USA by Thor *et al.* 1978). Another potential difficulty with networks is that they normally do not provide any criteria for deciding on the

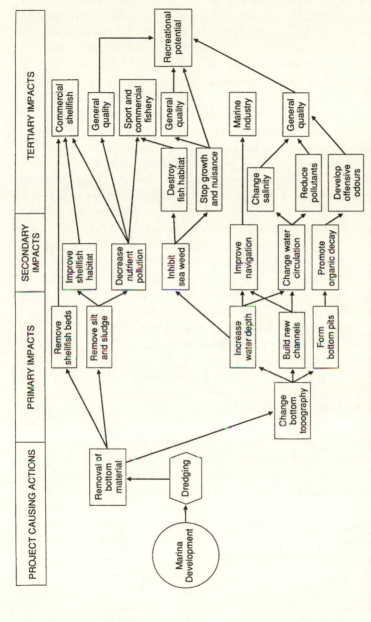

Figure 5.2 An extract from an impact network associated with dredging for a marina development
Source: modified from Sorensen (1971)

relative importance of impacts (Bisset 1987). However, unless very complex, they are useful for guiding EIA work to the indirect impacts which may arise from a project, and can provide concise visual summaries of project impacts easily understood by decision-makers and the general public.

Systems diagrams are conceptually very similar to networks in that they portray environmental systems as arrangements of inter-related components, and they can, therefore, deal with secondary and higher-order impacts. However, unlike networks which consider impact interactions, systems diagrams focus on the links between environmental components themselves, and are based on the assumption that energy flow through the environmental system can be used to measure the impacts of development at each component of the system. This method has its roots in the study of ecological energetics (Odum 1971), and has been most frequently employed in the consideration of ecological impacts alone (Bisset 1992). Typically, each project activity is assessed in terms of its effects on the amount of energy flow (e.g. in kilo-calories) between various components in the system. The result can be expressed as a percentage of the estimated gross primary production of the system (e.g. Gilliland and Risser 1977). Work has also been done on systems diagrams which attempt to integrate ecological and economic concerns. This can be done by converting all types of energy flow into a common energy 'currency', such as coal equivalents (see, for example, Lavine *et al.* 1978). Systems diagrams can be attractive because they utilise a common (and scientifically measurable) unit of measurement for all impacts, allowing information to be given on the relative importance of different project activities and impacts. However, they generally require the collection and synthesis of much data and tend, therefore, to be time-consuming and expensive to construct. Additionally, they are best suited to the consideration of ecological impacts and specifically the energy relationships between ecosystem components. This latter aspect tends to give energy flow a priority over other ecological considerations. For example, the destruction of a particular vegetation regime used as a breeding ground for a rare bird species, may have little consequence in terms of the utilisation of energy within the total system, but may have profound significance for the preservation of species diversity (Bisset 1987).

Overlay mapping

The use of overlays has a long history in the field of land use planning and landscape architecture. Even before the legal requirement of EIA in the USA the potential of overlay maps to portray the spatial distribution of impacts had been recognised (McHarg 1968). The method allows a composite picture of project impacts to be seen in the context of environmentally-sensitive locations in the vicinity. Typically, a base map transparency is prepared showing the location of the project, the boundaries of the area to be considered in the assessment and a summary of the environmental characteristics of the area likely to be affected by the project. For each characteristic or feature of the local environment (e.g. visual amenity, human population, valuable ecological habitats, etc.), a transparent over-lay sheet is prepared showing the degree of impact on the feature using a standard black-to-white shading code, for example. Usually, the darker the shade the more serious the impact. Once all the individual transparencies associated with each environmental feature have been prepared and are overlain on the base map, the result is an aggregate impact map with spatial variations of total impact indicated by the relative intensity of shading.

The use of overlay maps is an excellent means of showing the spatial distribution of impacts which is easily interpreted by decision-makers and members of the local community. However, the use of manually produced overlays is restricted since it is difficult to interpret more than about twelve overlays at one time (Bisset 1987). This constraint effectively limits the number of potential impacts that can be considered. The use of computerised overlays can overcome this difficulty. A computer can produce a composite map capable of showing much more information than is possible with manual overlays. Additionally, a weighting system for the impacts can be built-in to the shading routine, allowing decision-makers to view the composite impact under varying assumptions of individual impact importance. According to Bisset (1987), experience with the use of the overlay method indicates that it is most suited to the consideration of linear development proposals (such as roads, pipelines, ski-runs and transmission lines), particularly as a means of searching for the most appropriate route. Bisset also suggests that much detailed information concerning the nature of environmental characteristics on the ground may be lost in the process of simplification in the preparation of maps. Additionally, overlays are not conducive to the consideration of impact characteristics such as reversibility and the length of time over which an impact is significant. This said, overlays have been used in a tourism context. The method has been successfully employed to identify key tourism development areas in strategic planning exercises (Gunn 1979; Laventhol and Horwath 1982).

Simulation modelling

This method was developed in Canada (Holling 1978) in response to a number of perceived weaknesses in the operation of EIA at that time, including a deficiency in impact prediction, a lack of communication and consultation between developers and decision-makers, a reduction in the influence of EIA in decision-making, and the 'measure everything' syndrome of those responsible for producing the EIS in an attempt to avoid possible litigation on the grounds of inadequacy in the coverage of poten- tial impacts (Bisset 1992). Simulation modelling, alternatively known as Adaptive Environmental Assessment and Management (AEAM), functions through the operation of intensive, short-term workshops, involving an inter-disciplinary team of scientists, decision-makers and computer modelling experts who have to reach consensus on the important features and relationships which characterise the particular system being studied (Bisset 1987). The small core group may interact with a wider set of relevant experts to aid in the workshop sessions (Lohani and Halim 1987). The important features and relationships in the system being studied can then be formalised into a computer model using, as far as possible, quantitative relationships between the chosen parameters. The model can then be operated under different assumptions to allow the impacts of different projects or policies to be portrayed. Research work can be targeted on areas where the data in the model are deficient, and periodic workshops allow the model to be refined.

   On the positive side, simulation modelling is capable of considering environmental interactions and the knock-on impacts of development. It is also capable of considering a wide range of impacts, including social and economic concerns. The consensus required for model development also encourages an early focus on key issues, thus potentially speeding up the EIA process (Lohani and Halim 1987), and facilitates co-operation between developers and decision-makers. However, skilled computer personnel are required and the method can be costly. Furthermore, the method can be criticised for perhaps limiting the scope for public participation and understanding, and for a common tendency to quantify relationships on the basis of uncertain data (Bisset 1992).

Comments on EIA methods

The methods outlined above do not constitute a comprehensive review of all those available. They are, however, commonly encountered and still being developed for use in EIA. It is tempting at this stage to make a recommendation on the most appropriate method for the assessment of tourism projects. However, this is a difficult task and would, in any case, be undesirable given the current knowledge of the efficacy of different methods. As pointed out by Bisset (1992), much of the discussion on the relative merits of EIA methods is hypothetical since there exists very little information on the actual operational performance of different methods. Bisset argues that a large study comparing the costs, resource requirements and predictive abilities of various methods should be a feature of research over the next few years. However, given the great variety of situations in which EIA is, or could be, applied, it is unlikely that a single, universally applicable method will ever be developed (Canter 1983; Bisset 1987). Consequently, it is important that those involved in EIA appreciate the advantages and disadvantages of each method, outlined above, so that the most appropriate can be selected according to the circumstances surrounding any particular project.

In the general literature on EIA, opinions have been expressed on the relative utility of different EIA methods. These do have a bearing on the use of EIA for the appraisal of tourism projects. With reference to the use of EIA in Developing Countries, Lohani and Halim (1987), for example, suggest that checklists and matrices are the most suitable methods, due to their broad applicability and relatively low resource demands. They argue that faced with the constraints of time, assessment expertise and monetary costs, perhaps more acute in Developing Countries than elsewhere, these methods provide the means to rapidly identify project impacts without the (expensive) collection of a large amount of baseline environmental data. They are also suitable for allowing public participation in the decision-making process. There is some evidence from Developed Countries that the 'simpler' EIA methods are also regarded as useful frameworks for directing the thinking of those involved in EIA. Bisset (1987), for example, presents the findings of a survey into the use of EIA methods in the USA. This survey appears to confirm the finding that older methods are still more widely used than newer, more 'advanced' methods such as simulation modelling. The survey indicates that checklists, matrices, manual overlays and networks have been very widely utilised. Certainly, with specific reference to tourism projects, Williams (1987) focuses attention on these methods.

Finally, it is important to note that any tendency to force EIA practitioners to choose between methods may be inappropriate. There is no reason why different methods, or parts of methods, should not be used together in the assessment of a project, programme or policy. Indeed, distinct methods have been used in conjunction to assess a single project. Bisset (1987) argues that a combination of simple interaction matrices and networks can be a very effective means of guiding the assessment process, identifying impacts and presenting results. For example, a simple interaction matrix can be used in the first instance to identify potential first-order impacts. This done, a network approach would then allow the range of indirect impacts to be identified. In an EIA study of a tourism-related railway development in Norfolk, England, for example, both a checklist and a matrix were employed in the identification of potential impacts (Farrinton and Ord 1988).

Predictive techniques

The aim of this section is to provide a brief overview of the types of techniques which can be employed in EIA to predict the magnitude of potentially significant environmental impacts. Despite the central importance of impact prediction in EIA, it is an area in which very many EIA studies have been found to be deficient. This may be because impact prediction is an inherently difficult task, and one which frequently relies on the contributions of specialists, perhaps to the exclusion of others. Many EIA studies have been criticised for rather too much emphasis on the description of a project's characteristics and the baseline environmental conditions, to the neglect of impact prediction. This may be especially true of the treatment of secondary and other higher-order impacts, which are generally even more difficult to predict than primary impacts. Frequently, higher-order impacts are ignored or very poorly covered in EIA studies.

The potential number of predictive techniques which might be employed in EIAs for tourism projects probably runs to several hundred. It is important, therefore, to be aware of criteria which might aid in the selection of suitable techniques for any given tourism project. Lee (1989) suggests that the task of choosing between different techniques can be based on four criteria, namely, appropriateness, replicability, consistency and economy.

Any predictive technique must be appropriate to the specific task being undertaken. For example, does the output from the technique need to be quantitative or qualitative? Is information needed on the spatial and temporal distribution of the impact? Are the necessary data inputs (e.g. baseline information) for the technique to operate properly actually available or obtainable? What degree of accuracy is required from the prediction? Replicability is also important. In other words, a technique should, ideally, be sufficiently free from assessor bias that different assessors using the same technique would obtain similar results. In evaluating the likely replicability of a predictive technique, Lee (1989) suggests that the following questions might prove helpful.

- Does the technique provide a clearly expressed and precise measure of impact?
- Is an explicit declaration of the nature and extent of any uncertainty associated with the prediction from the technique available?
- Are the essential features of the technique which are used to derive the prediction clearly stated?
- Are the sources and quality of data used when applying the technique clearly stated?
- Are any assumptions made in the use of the technique (including those related to data deficiencies) clearly stated?

It is also important that a technique should have the capability of being applied to alternative forms of the same project, and/or to different projects within the same development initiative. In assessing the consistency of a technique in this respect, the following questions may be pertinent.

- Does the technique ensure that data inputs for evaluating alternatives are obtained on a consistent basis?
- Does it ensure that the output measures for the alternatives under consideration are strictly comparable?
- Does it provide sufficient guidance on the treatment of uncertainty to ensure that the assessments of alternatives are broadly comparable?

Finally, a technique should be cost-effective in the sense of enabling an EIA of sufficient quality to be completed as economically as possible, in terms of time, cost and other resource requirements.

In terms of the actual predictive techniques available for the appraisal of tourism-induced environmental change, these can generally be grouped into four categories:

1 formal mathematical or physical models;
2 laboratory or field experimental techniques;
3 inventory and survey techniques; and,
4 other approaches (e.g. prediction by analogy, indirect prediction through the use of environmental standards, and the use of expert opinion).

The reader is referred to Ortolano (1984) for a full description of these categories. The paragraphs below merely provide skeletal summaries. Examples of some commonly utilised techniques are given in Table 5.6.

Mathematical models utilise one or more mathematical functions to describe and formalise cause and effect relationships. Such models may be based on statistical estimates, or represent a deterministic simplification of environmental processes, based upon accepted scientific principles. Some models may utilise both statistical and process-based elements. A simple statistical model might be based on the observed relationship between two parameters of interest (e.g. sewage effluent load and an indicator of water quality) at some comparable site developed in a similar fashion to the project being considered. A more complicated process-based model might utilise a series of mathematical equations designed to simulate real-world mechanisms of pollutant storage and transfer in a river or estuary, for example.

A physical model provides a tangible illustration or working-scale replica of one or more aspects of the impact of the proposed

Table 5.6 Examples of impact magnitude prediction techniques used in EIA

Impact category	Predictive techniques
Air pollution (e.g. impact of single- or multiple-point emissions on ambient air quality)	Mathematical models of varying levels of complexity exist alongside other approaches: e.g. box models, rollback models, point source Gaussian models, multi-source models for chemically stable and chemically reactive substances.
Noise (e.g. impact of construction equipment, road traffic and aircraft on ambient noise levels)	Different models exist for each of the three types of noise source. Road traffic noise, for example, can be modelled as a function of: traffic volume, mix and speed; road elevation, slope and surface; distance of receptors from the roadside; intervening shielding effects etc.
Visual amenity (e.g. impact of a new road or building)	A variety of techniques exist to simulate post-project conditions: e.g. perspective drawings, computer-generated perspectives, photomontage and photo-retouching, three-dimensional models, video techniques.
Higher order impacts (e.g. impact of water pollution on aquatic plants and animals)	The use of expert judgement and surveys of receptors at risk are widely known techniques. Comparative analysis, monitoring approaches and small-scale experiments may also be used. Prediction based on the mathematical modelling of ecosystems has only been applied on a limited basis to date.

Source: modified from Lee (1989)

development on the environment. A physical model might be constructed to aid in the visualisation of a proposed tourism development within the physical context of the locality, for example. This would aid the assessment of the visual impact of the development. Similarly, wind tunnels and wave chambers can be employed to aid in the prediction of the impact of pollutant discharges on air and water quality, respectively. In trying to determine the number and types of receptors (humans, animals and plants) that might be damaged, disturbed or lost through a particular development, it may be necessary to conduct field and/or laboratory experiments. These may be particularly valuable where baseline information is lacking and other techniques, such as mathematical modelling, cannot be used reliably. In attempting to measure the nature and degree of disturbance to receptors, it may be necessary to utilise some existing inventory or conduct a special field survey (e.g. a habitat/species survey).

Less formalised predictive approaches can also be used. Although expert opinion through specialised technical assistance will normally be required in the use of any of the techniques outlined above, it is not uncommon for an expert to be asked to judge the magnitude and significance of an impact without using a formal predictive technique (see, for example, Newson 1991). To this end, the expert might use site visits to similar developments and/or literature searches to aid, by analogy, in the prediction of impact magnitude. The expert may also use environmental quality standards, combined with a knowledge of the operational characteristics of the project, to determine the likely degree of disturbance to receptors (e.g. the impact of increased noise on levels of human disturbance).

Surveys of the predictive techniques used in EIA suggest that it is the less formal approaches, most notably the use of expert opinion, which dominate. Where more formal approaches are employed, these tend to be the simpler versions of the techniques available. The use of complex mathematical models, for example, is still relatively rare. The reliance on relatively unsophisticated predictive techniques is not, necessarily, indicative of poor EIA practice. However, irrespective of the techniques employed, evidence does exist of the poor treatment of impact prediction in EIA. Lee (1989), for example, makes the following criticisms.

- The prediction of environmental impacts is infrequently treated as an explicit stage in the assessment process, for which the careful selection and application of clearly defined, predictive techniques is required.
- Explicitly defined techniques, of any kind, are only adopted in a minority of cases.
- Where predictive techniques are used, they are often not described in any detail in published EIA reports. Little reference is made to the appropriateness of the particular techniques chosen, or to the acceptability of the assumptions which underlie their use.
- In few cases are the quality and limitations of the predictions clearly indicated.

As a conclusion to this section, it is useful to provide an example of a tourism project for which an EIA was undertaken, and where a number of impact prediction techniques were used. Farrinton and Ord (1988) conducted an EIA for the Bure Valley tourist railway development in a predominately rural area of Norfolk in England. A selection of impacts with their associated predictive techniques is given below.

- Noise – use of a sound-level meter with measurements taken in the proposed area of the development and adjacent to an existing similar development.
- Smoke and smuts from the operation of steam locomotives – questionnaire survey of residents living close to a similar existing development; consultation with local authority experts; experiments conducted during the operation of a locomotive.
- Sparks and dust – assessed on the basis of experience at a similar, nearby operation.
- Visual impact – use of field visits and by examination of detailed plans of the proposed railway line. Photographs were included in the EIS as part of the information to accompany visual impact assessment.
- Vehicular traffic flows – assessed from traffic data supplied by the local public authority, together with data on the construction schedule and sites.
- Ecology – using data obtained during a 5-day survey along the existing track-bed, including an inventory of adjacent land uses. Information was obtained from the developer on proposed planting and selective clearance of vegetation for screening and operational purposes, respectively.

Clearly, relatively simple techniques were used by Farrinton and Ord (1988). Much of the predictive work appears to have been based on the informal views of experts, often using analogous developments. Some experimental and survey work was also conducted.

TOURISM AND COMMUNITY INVOLVEMENT THROUGH EIA

There are many unresolved or only partially resolved issues in EIA. Many aspects of EIA need to be improved to make it a more efficient environmental management tool. One could focus, for example, on a range of issues, including the post-monitoring of impacts and the auditing of EISs, training requirements for EIA, the use of EIA in the assessment of plans and policies, and the early integration of EIA into the project formulation process. Lack of space prevents a discussion of these, and other, important issues here. The reader is referred to Wathern (1992) for a comprehensive review of such issues. However, there is one area where a reading of the tourism and EIA literature forces one to recognise a common issue of substantial concern. This is the greater involvement of the local community in decision-making. The opportunity afforded by EIA, at least in theory, for early public involvement in the appraisal of development projects has long been recognised. While the lack of opportunity for public involvement in the EIA process still remains a valid criticism of many formal EIA systems (Kennedy 1984), significant advances have been made in recent years. Increasingly, it is being recognised that the use of public meetings or inquiries held after an EIS has been produced are inadequate mechanisms for the full participation of the local population in project decision-making (Wood and Jones 1991).

Relatedly, the tourism literature contains calls for early public consultation in decision-making on tourism developments. Miller and Auyong (1991), for example, suggest that local community participation in the planning of appropriate tourism development should be promoted. Similarly, Cronin (1990) argues that sustainable tourism planning means accepting a premise of careful consultation in the host area well in advance of the beginning of any development. Pawson *et al.* (1984) with reference to Nepal's Everest region, suggest that decisions affecting the future growth of tourist-related facilities in the region should continue to be made, where possible, at the local level because most Sherpas are fully conscious of the direct relationship between the preservation of the natural environment and continued tourist expenditure. Ahmad *et al.* (1990) contend that a detailed EIA should be carried out before opening up an area for tourism in the Himalayas, and that since women are the major workforce in the Himalayas, they should be consulted on all planning matters. According to Darbellay (1982), research work can also benefit from public input. In this paper, which describes the approach adopted in the management of research into the impacts of human activities in the Swiss Alps, much emphasis is placed on securing the involvement of local communities in order to make use of local knowledge in ecological research. It is argued that researchers need to come down from their 'ivory towers' if the maximum benefit of ecological research is to be realised. For Pigram (1990), public input to decision-making in the sphere of tourism development allows decision-makers to remain aware of changing attitudes and broadens the information base upon which action is taken. Pigram also argues that tourism developers who ignore the environmental concerns of locals risk delays, cost over-runs and even project cancellations. Some evidence for this latter view can be found in the early experience of delays and litigation in the USA, after the introduction of a formal EIA system, and from recent objections to tourism developments in Australia (Wathern 1992).

Community involvement in tourism planning and development can also facilitate the implementation of sustainable development policies and foster the growth of more environmentally compatible forms of development (Mader 1988; Pigram 1990). Omar and Ariffin (1992), for example, describe a strategic community participation approach in the formulation of a local plan in the Kampong Batu Feringghi, Penang, Malaysia. In this case, community participation through open meetings was used, successfully, to help in the formulation of the plan designed to promote an environmentally sustainable traditional village suitable for alternative tourism. Community involvement was sought in order to give the development more chance of long-term success. Similarly, Rauhe (1992) argues that community involvement in, and co-authorship of, local planning documents are a necessary and integral part of the success of any tourism project, and proposes a model for providing community input into the alternative tourism planning process.

Thus, in both the EIA literature and the tourism literature there is recognition of the need to involve local people early on in the decision-making process. This need arises for several reasons. The exclusion of the public at an early stage may foster anger and resentment, increase the likelihood of litigation and delay, and omits a potentially very valuable source of expert opinion and pressure regarding the quality of the local environment and the assessment of potential impacts. The last point recognises that the purpose of local community involvement in EIA for tourism should not be restricted to forestalling an adverse reaction to a particular development project, but rather that such participation can result in a positive and useful input to the EIA procedure. Specifically, the views of the local community can be critical both in the 'scoping' of potential impacts, and in assessing the relative importance of potential impacts. The concept of scoping is described below.

Social scoping

For the sake of the best use of time and resources in the operation of an EIA, and therefore the production of a high quality EIS, there is a great need to identify the important potential environmental impacts associated with a particular project at a very early stage in the EIA process. The EIS should consider in detail only those potential impacts thought to be significant. The identification of only those impacts judged to be significant (priority issues) is known as scoping and its importance in the more efficient use of EIA cannot be over-emphasised. In EIA systems, much emphasis is normally placed on the collection and interpretation of 'hard' environmental data, both to provide baseline information on existing environmental quality and to aid in the prediction of impacts. The collection of such data frequently accounts for a large proportion of the total cost of an EIA (Beanlands 1992). It is imperative, therefore, that before such environmental analysis begins, attention is focused on those issues of most concern. Otherwise, resources can be spread too thinly, resulting in the inadequate coverage, or even exclusion, of some important impacts and the unnecessary wasting of resources.

Scoping need not be an exercise confined to the experts or professionals involved in EIA. A so-called objective assessment of significant potential impacts is often, in reality, based upon the subjective value judgements of only one or two professionals (Wathern 1992). It has been argued that the involvement of local people at this stage, and also later on in the scaling and/or weighting of impacts, lends more credibility to the output of an EIA (e.g. Nelson 1987). While the surveying, monitoring and prediction of human-induced environmental change can (and should) be undertaken using objective scientific techniques, where possible, the identification of significant issues and the interpretation of results require and involve the incorporation of subjective, human value judgements. It is increasingly being recognised in EIA practice that the canvassing of the views of the local community is a valuable means of directing or aiding the scientific investigation of potentially significant impacts. Scoping which involves the local community in this way is often referred to as 'social scoping', and it could provide a platform for the early involvement of local people in decision-making about proposed tourism developments (Green and Hunter 1992). However, as pointed out by Pigram (1990) in relation to tourism development, questions arise over how community involvement might best be achieved, the degree of importance to be accorded to community input and how such input might need to be balanced against professional judgement.

In trying to mesh the views of EIA professionals and members of the local community to direct an EIA investigation some conflict of opinion is almost inevitable. Beanlands (1992), writing within the context of EIA research, illustrates such conflict by comparing the values of the general public with those of a scientifically trained ecologist engaged as an EIA professional. According to Beanlands, a number of themes appear to recur with reference to the priorities of the general public:

- the primary concern of the public with respect to environmental matters is human health and welfare;
- the public will have great concern for the potential loss of commercially important species or commercially available production;
- a high priority is placed on species of major recreational or aesthetic importance, regardless of their commercial importance;
- special interest groups will usually gain broad support in their concern for rare or endangered species on the basis of the custodial responsibility of humans to preserve other species; and,
- the public will normally be concerned over habitat losses which foreclose opportunities for future production.

The ecologist, however, may be primarily concerned with the more fundamental changes to the intrinsic structure and function of the natural system involved. Thus, it is suggested that with local community involvement, the ecological implications of a proposed development will usually get translated or shifted towards the effects on physical and biological resources valued by humans for commercial, recreational or aesthetic purposes, and that the ecologist will be required to extend the interpretation of impacts beyond the limits of professional interest. This can be frustrating for the scientist working as a consultant in EIA (see, for example, Newson 1991), especially since social concerns change with time and may be difficult to conceptualise scientifically, as with impacts on aesthetic value, for example.

The social scoping process itself can take a variety of forms. Irrespective of the approach adopted, a number of issues should be addressed (Beanlands 1992). These are:

- the target population must be clearly defined;
- adequate information about the project and its potential impacts should be given to the target population in a format which can be understood;
- the target group must be given sufficient time to organise its thoughts on the potential impacts; and,
- there should be a clearly understood mechanism by which the group can express its findings and concerns to the EIA professionals and decision-makers.

The target group may include local environmental experts and professionals without a direct involvement in the project (see, for example, Green and Hunter 1992). Representatives from local environmental special interest groups may also be included in the target population. Pigram (1990) reports on the 'experience survey' approach to obtaining public input to tourism planning initiatives, whereby a number of individuals in the local community are selected on the basis that they possess heightened awareness of the range of community views and attitudes due to their occupational experience and/or position in the community. In some cases, where communities are isolated or otherwise well-defined, it may be possible to assist the community itself (e.g. with financial support or organisational skills) to conduct its own scoping programme, thereby utilising existing community communication methods.

In social scoping for EIA both direct (public meetings) and indirect (questionnaires or surveys) approaches may be used to assess local community concerns. Beanlands (1992) argues that indirect techniques are less desirable than public meetings because of the normally low return rates of surveys which may then be biased towards the more vocal segments of the community. Also, proper survey design and execution require experts who may not be available when needed, and the analysis and interpretation of survey results may be prone to professional disagreements which may confuse, rather than clarify, the issues. Public scoping meetings, it is argued, allow an open dialogue between those responsible for the EIA and the community, which may lead to the resolution of perceived problems which are based on misunderstanding. Public meetings can, however, be time-consuming, requiring considerable financial and human resources, and to operate properly, require the co-operation of the developer. It could also be argued that public meetings may also be prone to bias, with the risk of domination by a vocal minority. Furthermore, by guaranteeing anonymity to the participants in a questionnaire survey, it is possible to gain the unqualified opinions of people (such as local government officers and those directly involved in the proposal) who might shun an open meeting or feel otherwise constrained in such a meeting (Green and Hunter 1992). This said, the use of direct scoping approaches appears to dominate current EIA practice. In Canada, for example, carefully mediated public meetings form the basis of project scoping. A similar system operates in the USA.

The use of EIA in the appraisal of individual tourism projects is still comparatively rare. Similarly, the methodical use of formal social scoping processes is uncommon outside a few countries, such as the USA, Canada and the Netherlands (Wathern 1992). There are examples in the tourism literature of community involvement in studies of tourism impact after the arrival of tourism, and examples have been given above of community involvement in the formulation of plans for alternative tourism. However, attempts to scope individual tourism projects with the involvement of the local community appear to be very rare indeed, at least as documented in the generally available tourism literature. In an attempt to ascertain the most important potential impacts of continued tourism development in the Mediterranean coastal areas of Acisu-Sorgun and Titreyengol in Turkey, Korca (1991) utilised the Delphi technique (see, for example Linstone and Turoff 1975) based on face-to-face interviews with a selected panel of 20 professionals and local residents. Despite doubts over the reliability of the technique, it was thought to be a useful mechanism for incorporating some views of the local residents on tourism impacts. A Delphi exercise incorporating local public opinion has also been used as a scoping mechanism in the assessment of the impacts of the redevelopment of a disused mill complex near Bradford in northern England (Green and Hunter 1992).

In the process of conducting a full EIA for a tourism railway development in Norfolk, England, Farrinton and Ord (1988) utilised scoping to identify the most significant potential impacts. Although not carried out in a formalised manner, the scoping involved discussions (by those responsible for producing the EIS) with statutory bodies and other agencies, and residents in the area through which the proposed line would pass. In addition, a postal questionnaire survey, which had a response rate of 56 per cent, was conducted of residents living adjacent to an existing, nearby and very similar line, to gain a better view of the potential impacts associated with the proposed development. In the EIS, some 28 recommendations designed to ameliorate or eliminate potential impacts identified in the study were made, and all of these were adopted by the local planning authority.

Scoping is now recognised as an important part of the EIA process, although formal implementation procedures are still under-developed in many countries. Local community involvement in decision-making over tourism plans and projects is similarly recognised as an important facet of sustainable tourism development. Although much remains to be learned about best practice in the scoping of projects and in finding the most efficient means of gaining local community involvement in decision-making, the use of social scoping has a potentially very valuable contribution to make to the use of EIA in the appraisal of tourism developments.

ISSUES IN THE USE OF EIA

It has been the central assumption of this chapter that many proposed tourism developments should be subject to EIA. A formal, comprehensive EIA system should aid in the better integration of tourism development with environmental protection. This view is increasingly being expressed in the tourism literature. However, EIA systems, procedures, methods and techniques are not fully developed or understood. Thus, any view of EIA as some kind of infallible and easily implemented environmental management tool which will ensure the easy operation of tourism developments on a sustainable basis must be regarded as overly optimistic. Even the most cursory reading of the EIA literature will reveal considerable uncertainty in the efficiency of EIA systems. A number of issues appear to be causing particular concern, and these are summarised briefly below.

At a general level, EIA systems can be criticised for being too narrow. Currently, there are no procedures in EIA for the systematic integration of natural environment concerns with social and economic aspects (Htun 1992). Thus, EIA can only provide a limited perspective in the appraisal of tourism projects. Also, in practice EIA has been used, almost exclusively, in the consideration of individual projects. Although in many ways more problematic, there is no reason why EIA cannot be used in theory for the appraisal of development policies, programmes or plans (Wood 1992). The potential contribution of EIA in the appraisal of tourism development plans has been recognised by Inskeep (1987), who suggests that the consideration of impacts should occur throughout the entire planning process, including the evaluation of alternative levels and types of tourism growth to determine the optimum pattern. However, it is difficult, if not impossible, for EIA to operate effectively at all unless it is part of a fully developed local planning and development control framework. The point has already been made that many Developing Countries lack such an institutional and legal infrastructure.

Such infrastructure enables rational, systematic decision-making on when and where tourism development projects should be subject to EIA. This said, the presence of an EIA system operating within a suitable institutional and legal infrastructure does nothing to guarantee, of itself, the appropriate consideration and appraisal of tourism development projects. EIA systems which incorporate explicit guidance on the treatment of tourism developments are very much the exception rather than the rule. Admittedly, there are difficulties in deciding which tourism projects should qualify for EIA. These complications may arise due to the great variability in the size, type and operational characteristics of tourism developments, for example, as discussed earlier in this chapter. Such variability, combined with the apparent ignorance of the potential environmental consequences of many major tourism development projects amongst policy-makers, may account for the exclusion of tourism developments from mandatory consideration in EIA systems such as that currently operated under the EC Directive on EIA. It is also important to recognise that there is no 'ideal' EIA system and, likewise, one cannot produce a universally applicable set of stringent guidelines as to when and where proposed tourism projects should be subject to EIA. Too much depends on specific national and local institutional arrangements, characteristics and priorities.

However, it is possible and valid to set out *general* guidance on the conditions under which proposed tourism projects should be subject to EIA, whether this is done on an *ad hoc* basis or via a formal EIA system operating within a suitable legal and institutional framework. The following list is an initial attempt to do this, produced with the aim of stimulating debate rather than as a concrete prescription. This said, it would appear prudent to subject a proposed tourism development project to EIA if it fulfils one, or more, of the following general criteria:

- if the project is to be located in an area of outstanding international, national or local importance/value in terms of its natural, built or cultural attributes (e.g. a nature reserve, a tribal homeland/reservation, close to an ancient monument);
- if the development can be considered as 'major', i.e. it is physically large or will substantially increase the number of people in a locality and/or will have a large sphere of influence generating many tourist trips into the surrounding area, which may contain important attributes such as those described above;
- if one or more specific characteristics of the proposed project or activities associated with it may prove particularly damaging (e.g. a project designed specifically and deliberately to generate tourist trips into fragile environments, such as 'wildlife' tourism to remote, previously 'undisturbed' locations);
- if the project will be novel to the location and there is no prior experience of tourism development; and,
- if the project is the first of its kind in an area earmarked for subsequent tourism development and/or the project is likely to stimulate further tourism-related development.

Such general guidance will (and should) always be subject to national and/or local interpretation (e.g. as to what constitutes a 'major' tourism development project, or the 'value' of the environmental attributes in a given area).

More specifically, for EIA to be fully effective, it must operate as part of the overall project formulation and planning process, rather than be seen as an 'add-on' to the procedure of gaining planning permission. The efficacy of EIA is also a function of the quality and availability of baseline environmental data. The lack of reliable baseline data, especially in Developing Countries, can make the objective evaluation of tourism-induced environmental change difficult, if not impossible. Paucity of adequate baseline data can have major cost implications, since the acquisition of information on the pre-development status of the environment is generally one of the most expensive and time-consuming activities in EIA (Htun 1992). Advances are, however, being made. In Peru, for example, government-sponsored research on natural resources may be used to provide baseline information for future EIAs (Moreira 1992).

Another area of specific concern is the use of methods and techniques in EIA. There is some evidence to suggest that the evaluation, prediction and assessment of potential environmental impacts is inadequate in a substantial proportion of EIA studies. The quality of EISs has come in for recent criticism in the UK, for example (Wood and Jones 1991), while in Australia, impact predictions are only 50 per cent accurate on average, and occasionally incorrect by over two orders of magnitude (Buckley 1991). Problems with the use of methods and techniques may be compounded by inadequate environmental baseline information, the lack of formal scoping procedures and the natural variability of different sites in terms of environmental processes, making it difficult to translate the information gained from one area to another (Newson 1991). With specific reference to tourism, these difficulties may be further compounded by an inadequate understanding of tourist behaviour (Pearce 1989). Some of these problems have recently been summarised by Bisset and Tomlinson (1992), who suggest that EIA often involves the:

> use of environmental information which is often characterized by scarcity and uncertainty, predictive techniques with unknown error margins and evaluation methods which assess and present information to decision makers in a variety of ways.

> (Bisset and Tomlinson 1992: 126)

Certainly, much more work is needed to refine the use of the various methods and techniques which can be applied in EIA. In this respect, post-development environmental monitoring and auditing of EIA studies are crucial. Only through monitoring and auditing can those involved in EIA learn through experience, and the use of methods and techniques be improved. Also, without post-development monitoring there can be no way of ensuring that any recommended mitigating measures have been implemented, or are working effectively. A recent survey of EISs in Australia found that only 3 per cent were suitable for the testing of predictive ability, because only this proportion had adequate monitoring schemes (Buckley 1991). With specific reference to tourism, Inskeep (1987) argues that as tourism development proceeds, the environmental and socio-economic impacts (at both regional and local levels) must be continuously monitored to reveal whether the impacts are predicted and acceptable.

Chapter 6

Conclusions

Colin Hunter

Tourism relies, directly and indirectly, on a range of resources, including aspects of the natural, built and cultural environments at destination areas and beyond. The development of a destination area may bring substantial economic and other benefits to the local community, and tourism is now a crucial component of many regional and national economies around the world. Undoubtedly, tourism can be a potent force for environmental 'good'. The fostering of appropriate tourism development in an area may allow or facilitate the protection and enhancement of natural, built and cultural features, providing an environmentally-conscious means of generating economic growth and enhancing the quality of life of local residents, whilst also giving the tourist a valuable set of experiences.

However, potentially there exists a paradox at the heart of all major tourism developments: that tourism will destroy or degrade the environmental resources which attract tourists in the first place, such that the tourism industry associated with a particular destination area will decline, or fail to fulfil its optimum potential, because it becomes environmentally unsustainable. In other words, the tourism industry should be in the business of trying to maintain what has been 'sold' to the tourist. The maintenance of environmental quality applies not just to features which attract tourists directly (such as sea, sand, ancient monuments and features of local culture), but also to a wide range of supporting resources which are not 'sold' directly to the tourist. For example, fresh-water supplies, sewage treatment facilities, other aspects of local infrastructure, and the attitudes of local residents towards tourism development.

Individual tourism developments will almost invariably be accompanied by a complex range and mix of (inter-related) positive and negative environmental impacts. The net impact of tourism development on an area's environmental quality will always be subject to personal opinion and interpretation. Certainly, one cannot generalise on the nature of the relationship between tourism development and environmental quality. Any such relationship is site-specific, according to characteristics of the local environment and of the local tourism industry. It is, however, becoming clearer that it is in the long-term best interests of decision-makers, local communities and those involved in the tourism industry to find principles, policies and management tools which both allow the development of tourism as an engine of economic growth (perhaps particularly relevant in Developing Countries) and the conservation and/or preservation of environmental resources. Striking such a balance is the aim at the heart of the concept of sustainable tourism development.

For those with an interest in finding an appropriate balance between tourism-generated economic growth and respect for the quality and quantity of environmental resources, there are guiding principles of sustainable development. If one accepts the interpretation of sustainable tourism development offered in Chapter 3, then existing and proposed tourism developments and operations should strive to fulfil the requirements of inter- and intra-generational equity of access to resources. In more detail, this implies that all private and public operators and agencies involved in the tourism industry should strive to achieve the following.

- The conservation, and where necessary preservation, of the quality and quantity of natural resources, i.e. the minimisation of the use of non-renewable resources such as fossil fuels; respect for the sustainable yields of renewable resources such as fresh-water, flora and fauna; respect for the tolerance of natural environmental components (atmosphere, waters, soils) to receive and assimilate wastes and other pressures.
- The conservation, and where necessary preservation, of the built environment, including such features as buildings, monuments, ancient sites and the components of infrastructure necessary to allow the smooth and non-degrading operation of tourism-related activities.
- Respect for the wishes of local communities at destination areas, such that their interests are protected and aspects of local culture valued by locals are not threatened.

• The equitable distribution of the socio-economic costs and benefits of development amongst locals, developers and tourists.

Sustainable tourism development, then, is about conserving, maintaining and enhancing environmental resources, the quality of life of local people and the quality of the tourist experience. These requirements present great challenges to all those involved in the tourism industry, including developers, operators, decision-makers, local communities and tourists. The nebulous nature of the tourism industry compounds these challenges, making co-ordination and co-operation between these various actors problematic, and the task of decision-makers in public development control and management authorities (if these exist) an unenviable one. Much can be achieved if tourism operations are planned and controlled, integrated with other economic activities, at the local, destination area level. However, it is also important to stress the potential role of tourism in protecting environmental quality on regional and global scales, because any area developed for tourism relies on operations, activities and resources outside of the immediate destination area (e.g. through air travel, power generation, water supply, etc.). A narrow geographical focus on the quality of the immediate environs of a destination area which ignores wider environmental interactions and dependencies, omits from consideration many potential contributions that tourism could make to sustainable development. It may also enable some operators, such as airlines which transport tourists to and from destination areas, to escape scrutiny and avoid upholding the obligations which they also have to contribute to sustainable development. The management of tourism activities, therefore, takes on regional, national and even international dimensions, and will require co-ordinated efforts from policy-makers and decision-takers at various tiers of government (e.g. the translation of national policies on environmental protection and tourism development to regional land use plans and down to development control decisions at the local level).

Having couched the concept of sustainable tourism development in terms of the need for tourism-related operations and activities to make a positive contribution to the general requirements of sustainable development, questions remain concerning the extent and degree to which tourism can or will make this positive contribution. In crude terms, this will depend, in part, on the relative weighting given to the words 'sustainable' and 'development' by those involved in the tourism industry. There is much scope for different interpretations of the meaning and implications of sustainable tourism development, and there can be little doubt that widely differing approaches will emerge. In practice, it is highly likely that particular aspects of the concept of sustainable tourism development will be emphasised, at the expense of others, according to different needs, priorities and attitudes. For example, under some circumstances attention might be focused on the conservation of natural resources without social equity concerns being considered. In this case, the issue is one of extent or coverage, i.e. the omission of some key aspects of sustainable development in favour of others. Relatedly, there is also the issue of degree, i.e. the amount of effort expended in trying to fulfil a particular requirement of sustainable tourism development. A new hotel complex, for example, might be based on an old design but have a few more trees planted around it, giving it a 'greener' appearance. Another developer, however, may take a more enlightened and responsible view, ensuring that the new hotel minimises its use of water and other resources, as well as contributing to the maintenance of tree cover. It could be argued that a positive contribution to sustainable development is being made by the tourism project in both of these cases, but the degree of positive action differs markedly.

In order to forestall and discourage such divergent interpretations of extent and degree, effective local control over development (perhaps guided by national policies and a national legislative framework) appears to be necessary so that minimum standards can be applied to similar proposals. Otherwise, a 'level playing field' cannot be created and the more enlightened developers may effectively penalise themselves by incurring extra expenses associated with resource conservation measures (especially if these measures are not apparent to the tourist, so that the tourist cannot easily identify developments which have truly sought to make the greatest contribution to sustainable development).

In theory, there is no logical impediment to the contention that sustainable tourism development requires every single tourism organisation, tourism operator, tourism activity and tourist around the world to behave (or be made to behave) in a manner which *maximises* their contribution to inter- and intra-generational equity of access to resources, where possible. It could be argued, therefore, that a tourism development cannot be said to be sustainable if it fails to achieve in full the requirements of sustainable tourism development listed above. While such a view might aid in resolving differing interpretations of the meaning and implications of sustainable tourism development in relation to issues of extent and degree, it represents a theoretical goal and a wholly unrealistic prospect over the foreseeable future. In reality, there will always exist a shortfall between what is theoretically possible and what is actually implemented in practice, according to the attitudes and actions of tourism operators, tourism agencies, local communities and national and local governmental authorities. It is to be hoped that with time, the shortfall between the theoretically possible and policy implementation in practice will diminish as understanding of tourism impacts and environmental protection implementation measures (such as Environmental Impact Assessment) improves.

While the fundamental principles of sustainable development may provide timeless guidance for tourism policy formulation, the tools adopted to translate these policies into practice should not be viewed as static. In this sense, sustainable tourism development is dynamic because those involved in the tourism industry should always be prepared to adopt measures, as they become widely understood and available, which will improve upon current environmental protection practice. New technologies for reducing the consumption of natural resources and the generation of waste, for example, are continually being developed. Similarly, our understanding of practical steps to improve the economic and other benefits of tourism development to local communities will also change through time. Moreover, tourism research has barely begun to consider, in any great detail, the application of economic and fiscal tools, for example, in fostering more environmentally-conscious forms of development, let alone the most appropriate use of combinations of legislative, economic, fiscal and management tools under different conditions (e.g. the early stages of tourism development in an area as compared to a mature destination area, the efficacy of different combinations of tools in different locations with different political structures, etc.).

Perhaps due to the assumption by many decision-makers for many years that tourism development is an essentially environmentally-friendly vehicle of economic growth, research into the broad range of environmental management tools which might be brought to bear on the tourism industry has apparently trailed behind other sectors. As the application of these, and other, tools becomes better understood, so those involved in the operation and management of tourism activities should be prepared to adapt their practices in order to progress towards the fulfilment of the requirements of sustainable tourism development, even if these requirements can never be achieved in full.

It could be argued that the recent focus on alternative tourism in the literature is symptomatic of a lack of knowledge of environmental management tools, since there frequently appears to be an underlying assumption that little can be done for existing mass tourism destinations and that (somehow) tourism will become environmentally sustainable on the basis of rather exclusive, small-scale operations in virgin, or only slightly tarnished, territories. If one adopts a strict 'eco-centric' view of the relationship between environmental quality and tourism-generated economic growth, it might be distinctly preferable to avoid alternative developments in remote areas and focus attention on making existing mass destinations more attractive to a wider variety of tourist and less demanding of environmental resources. However, such sentiments may well be regarded as a luxury in a country or region where poverty, unemployment, disease and a lack of infrastructure combine to make economic growth and an enhanced quality of life for citizens the imperative amongst politicians and other decision-makers. In some Developing Countries, the very choice of tourism-generated economic growth (whatever its environmental side-effects) over other, more overtly destructive, means of income generation (such as logging, minerals extraction or intensive livestock production) might be seen as a contribution to sustainable development in itself. Much more debate is needed on the extent and degree to which different countries (or regions) facing different problems and with different priorities can, or should, be expected to fulfil the requirements of sustainable tourism development.

It is in contrasting, at a very general and simplified level, the priorities of Developed and Developing Countries that differences of interpretation of the meaning and practical implications of sustainable tourism development may become most apparent. In crude terms, 'ethical' pontification on the importance of protecting ecosystems for future generations by those in Developed Countries may well be met with wry scepticism by governments of Developing Countries, given the scant regard paid to the utilisation of natural resources in the great majority of Developed Countries up until the last few decades. If those in the First World expect those in the Third World to protect environmental resources, then the former must ensure that the latter are not disadvantaged in the process. This implies that much more consideration should be given to the intra-generational aspect of sustainable development, and the contribution of tourism to current social justice concerns.

The World Commission on Environment and Development (WCED 1987), for example, suggest that overriding priority should be given to the role of development in meeting the needs of the world's poor. However, with a few exceptions, much of the tourism literature generated by those from Developed Countries focuses on aspects of sustainable development concerned with the status of the physical environment. Indeed, the attention given to land use planning and Environmental Impact Assessment (EIA) in this book, reflects not only the interests of the authors, but is also a tacit recognition of a general bias in the tourism literature towards physical environmental concerns. As suggested in Chapter 3, the conservation of natural resources may be of particular direct relevance to the peoples of Developing Countries. Certainly, tourism operators based in Developed Countries must embrace (or be forced to embrace) policies designed to protect the natural environment of host nations in the Developing World. However, they also have an obligation, along with the governments of Developing Countries, to ensure that their activities contribute, as far as is possible, to the social and economic well-being of host communities. The socio-economic characteristics of local, regional and global investments by the tourism industry need to be better understood and should be of enormous concern to those with an interest in sustainable tourism development. Sustainable development is a global endeavour, and a series of quotes from Rughani (1993), serves very well to illustrate the responsibilities of developers and governments of Developed Countries towards those in Developing Countries. Rughani writes:

In a world dividing rich and poor ever more starkly, the rich travel without boundaries and amuse ourselves with the 'discovery of the past'. But how can we value each other when our lives are unequal and our governments spend the rest of the year sucking the world's wealth behind fences like Fortress Europe? We arrive as representatives of wealth and opportunity, unwilling to see that Third World poverty is the price of our short-term success and distorts any contact we may have in the South.

(Rughani 1993: 9)

And:

Even with the objective of distributing income from tourism, most developing countries have limited room for manoeuvre. Many are now in a beauty contest to compete for tourism investment. They face a well-oiled coalition of multinational interests with practised negotiators who can afford to hold out for their terms, while asking the South to parade in its collective swimsuits ... results are often disappointing. Local jobs are generally unskilled. Many are seasonal and, contrary to the claims made for tourism, have the effect of reducing the diversity of the local economy. Expertise is brought in from outside and a large proportion of money spent in the South ends up being repatriated to the North in long-standing business relationships .... Yet the industry's window-dressers are busy promoting 'industry good practice' in Bangkok with projects such as landscaping around the Sukothai hotel .... Fine, reply local activists, but not exactly the point when faced with estimates of over half a million Thai children involved in prostitution.

(Rughani 1993: 11)

Large sections of the tourism industry would do well to heed the warning signals beginning to emerge from some countries in the Developing World where attitudes to tourism development are changing. Following the destruction of much of the tourism infrastructure on the island of Kauai, Hawaii in September of 1992 by hurricane Iniki, Patterson (1993) claims that many native Hawaiians actually welcomed the loss, given the systematic undermining of cultural values and the quality of natural resources that the tourism industry has brought. Indeed, large numbers of native Hawaiians supported the construction of a missile base on Kauai, in preference to another hotel before the hurricane struck.

According to Patterson, many native Hawaiians are now convinced that tourism development will never improve the quality of their lives; they remain the poorest and least educated of all those in Hawaii, while the benefits of tourism development have gone to local elites and transnational corporations.

Faced with such inequities, it should come as no surprise if Developing Countries begin to take drastic action to limit the involvement of foreign companies and/or the loss of earnings through leakage back to the Developed World. Greater co-operation and co-ordination between neighbouring countries may also become more of a feature in order to present potential foreign investors with an international 'level playing field' such that an investor cannot threaten to locate in an adjacent country on the basis of less stringent environmental controls and better financial terms. In a sense, one cannot blame multinational tourism companies from exploiting opportunities for quick financial returns. It appears to be an inescapable conclusion that the most beneficial development of tourism in Developing Countries (and indeed elsewhere) can only occur with strong, enlightened central and local governmental control, which fosters locally based community development initiatives. In the Seychelles, for example, legislative control by central government has long been a feature of tourism development, recently culminating in a ban on land sales to foreigners (Brittain 1993).

The issue of control brings to the fore the use of management tools such as land use planning and EIA which have been discussed in some detail in Chapters 4 and 5, respectively. It must be stressed again that these tools, although widely used in environmental management, represent a small proportion of those available. Neither are they set in stone. While it is necessary for land use planning and EIA systems to incorporate a number of desirable features (e.g. public participation, environmental monitoring, etc.), there are many variant forms in current use, and these systems are still evolving. There is no single 'correct' format for either land use planning or EIA and, indeed, caution should be employed in transferring a system developed in one country to another, as any system needs to be sensitive to particular political and administrative structures. This said, any management tool should be amenable to positive change, incorporating aspects of best practice from elsewhere.

It is also important to note that the efficacy of development control and management tools, such as land use planning and

EIA, depends on the extent and quality of available environmental information. The importance of continuous environmental monitoring cannot be over-stated. Wide-ranging, high-quality environmental information is a prerequisite for a meaningful land use plan or a successful EIA. The use of another management tool, environmental auditing, may be critical in this regard. Environmental audits can be conducted by tourism operators to appreciate their reliance on environmental resources and to minimise their negative impacts. Regular, area-based audits of environmental quality can also be carried out by local public authorities to inform development control decisions (perhaps paid for by a levy on tourists and/or tourism operators). In order to learn from experience it is also necessary to audit the performance of land use plans and specific EIAs in terms of actual, rather than predicted, environmental impacts. The gathering of environmental information requires the choice of specific indicators of environmental quality. Tourism both relies and impacts on many aspects of the environment, and this range should be reflected in monitoring programmes. The quality of the tourism resource base might be assessed (regularly) using parameters which reflect aspects such as air quality, water quality, habitat and species diversity, visual amenity, the status of buildings and monuments, pedestrian and traffic flows, infrastructure provision and the attitudes of residents to tourists and tourism developments.

Potentially, a statutory land use planning system can incorporate and perform a range of functions which will aid in translating some of the theoretical requirements of sustainable development into appropriate action on the ground. While a land use planning system can operate at various scales, it is at the local (including regional) level that attributes and functions such as development control, design guidance, community involvement, education, the zoning of activities, environmental monitoring and day-to-day decision-making normally have their fullest expression. Local plans and planning functions, however, may be informed by national (or even international) plans and policies. A land use planning system can accomplish an appropriate anticipatory juxtaposition of activities and associated infrastructure according to the characteristics of an area's environmental resource base and the characteristics and needs of particular activities. This is normally achieved through the formulation of land use plans which inform development control and decision-making.

Development control may itself incorporate a formal EIA system, thereby formalising EIA into the overall statutory land use planning system (as is the case in the UK, for example).

While tourism-related activities come in many forms, these will, generally, be so enmeshed with the other economic activities of an area as to require the integrated planning of tourism alongside other activities, and existing or proposed infrastructure (including transport links, water supply, waste disposal, etc.). In this sense, tourism planning should not, therefore, be regarded as separate from the planning of development generally or outside of the land use planning system which operates in any given country. Indeed, the efficacy of a land use planning system will depend, in part, on how successful it is in *integrating* a range of economic activities with community desires and physical resources, as well as on issues of actual operational performance. Furthermore, many development proposals may be multi-functional in nature such that tourism-related activities form only a part of the rationale for a particular development.

As with land use planning systems, EIA systems come in a variety of forms. Generally, however, EIA operates at the 'sharp end' of development control and management, considering the impacts, and the mitigation of impacts, associated with individual development proposals. Again as with land use planning, much faith appears to have been placed in EIA systems for the more environmentally-conscious development of tourism. This faith may be somewhat misplaced, given the scant regard paid to even major tourism proposals in many formal EIA systems, and the host of operational difficulties and limitations endemic to much current EIA practice. With respect to the appraisal of tourism developments, the latter are compounded by a lack of knowledge concerning tourist behaviour, the frequently large geographical sphere of influence of tourism projects and the wide variety of inter-related primary and secondary impacts which may be associated with tourism development. Additionally, it may be inappropriate to call for the immediate introduction of EIA systems in countries (including much of the Developing World) where the institutional, legal, administrative and technical bases necessary for the efficient operation of EIA are currently absent or poorly formed and implemented. On a more positive note, local community involvement in development planning (see Chapter 4) and decision-making is widely regarded as a crucial component of sustainable development policies. Through the process of social scoping, EIA, potentially, has much to offer as a vehicle of local community involvement and, through this, the promotion of developments which make a significant contribution to current social equity.

Given the focus in this book on land use planning and EIA as tools in the environmental management of tourism, it is perhaps appropriate to provide here a brief description of Strategic Environmental Assessment, which in attempting to marry land use planning (amongst other things) and EIA will surely become more of a feature of tourism research in the near future. Strategic Environmental Assessment (SEA) is the term used to describe the application of EIA to the appraisal of development policies, plans and programmes (PPPs) before the assessment of individual projects occurs. Currently, the use of EIA is largely restricted to the appraisal of individual development projects. This project-specific emphasis means that EIA is most frequently used to tackle 'end-of-pipe' technical issues like waste minimisation. Yet, it may be with reference to the appraisal of 'higher level' development proposals, in the form of PPPs, that EIA can best embrace the principles of sustainable development. Theoretically, there is no impediment to the extension of EIA to proposed PPPs (Wood 1992): EIA could be applied to assess a programme of projects (e.g. the construction of a series of hotels or tourist villages), a plan (e.g. the land use plan of a tourist destination area), or a policy (e.g. a national tourism policy).

As pointed out in Chapter 4, the mere presence of a land use plan does not necessarily protect environmental quality. EIA could be used to appraise alternative plans in order to find the most appropriate juxtaposition of activities, for example, prior to the consideration of individual development projects. Relatedly, as discussed in Chapter 5, project-level EIA is limited in its ability to tackle some issues such as the impacts which might arise through ancillary developments and the cumulative impacts of several projects. SEA may be much more appropriate for tackling such problems. Lee and Walsh (1992) explain the recent growth of interest in SEA amongst environmental management researchers with reference to the growing awareness of the limitations of traditional project-based EIA, and the need to better integrate environmental considerations into development planning in order to promote sustainable development. Many of the limitations of project-level EIA have been discussed in Chapter 5, but it is worth reiterating some of the major problems here, in the context of SEA. According to Lee and Walsh (1992), limitations of project-level EIA include the following.

The coverage of ancillary developments – a major project may give rise to significant impacts from induced and indirect activities which may not be properly assessed in the EIA for the initial project. Even if induced projects are subsequently subjected to EIA in sequence, this hampers investigation of cumulative impacts and, of necessity, provides for the consideration of fewer development options than is the case for simultaneous assessments through SEA.

Foreclosure of alternatives – by the time it becomes possible to apply EIA to an individual project, it is likely that a number of development options (with different environmental consequences) will have been eliminated from consideration at a previous point in the planning process. These options will not have been subject to EIA. Therefore, it seems appropriate to introduce some form of environmental assessment at an earlier stage in the planning process.

Cumulative impacts – these are unlikely to be handled in a satisfactory manner in the absence of previous sectoral and/or area-based environmental assessments where multiple developments or the expansion of activities associated with a particular sector are proposed.

Project exclusions from EIA – some projects may be excluded from EIA because they are individually too small, but may yet have significant impacts through cumulative effects.

The proper application of SEA could overcome many of these difficulties (see, for example, Therivel *et al.* 1992). However, for many commentators, SEA is actually seen as a practical requirement of sustainable development, in so far as it allows the 'integration of economic, social and environmental considerations when planning or guiding future development' (Lee and Walsh 1992: 130). Thus, it is possible to envisage the combined use of SEA and EIA to allow such integration at all development proposal levels. Recently, the European Commission, for example, stated that:

> Given the goal of achieving sustainable development it seems only logical, if not essential, to apply an assessment of the environmental implications of all relevant policies, plans and

programmes. The integration of environmental assessment within the macro-planning process would . . . enhance the protection of the environment and encourage optimisation of resource management.

(CEC 1992: para. 7.3)

Although formal provision for, and practical experience of, SEA is as yet very limited around the world, some countries (including Holland, France, Germany, the USA, New Zealand and Australia) have utilised SEA. Interestingly, the European Commission recently signalled its desire to formulate a new directive on SEA for certain policies, plans and programmes (CEC 1992). The potential importance of SEA has had (albeit very limited) recognition in a tourism context. Glasson (1993), for example, refers to the potential use of EIA in the evaluation of a tourism plan for the city of Oxford in England.

In summarising much of the detail of previous chapters, this chapter has sought to identify key conclusions and, in so doing, highlight areas where further research and debate are urgently needed. As a closing comment, it is appropriate to return to a point made early in Chapter 2; namely, the rather fragmented nature of much tourism research to date. The concept of sustainable tourism development, in seeking to integrate economic, social and ecological concerns, not only presents tremendous opportunities for the more environmentally-conscious development of tourism, but may also provide the conceptual framework necessary to encourage a more holistic and multi-disciplinary approach in tourism research.

Bibliography

CHAPTER 1

Chadwick, R.A. (1987) 'Concepts, definitions and measures used in travel and tourism research', in J.R.B. Ritchie and C.R. Gouldner (eds) *Travel, Tourism and Hospitality Research*, New York: Wiley.

Gilbert, D. (1990) 'Conceptual issues in the meaning of tourism', in C. Cooper (ed.) *Progress in Tourism, Recreation and Hospitality Management*, volume 2, London: Belhaven Press/University of Surrey.

Grahn, P. (1991) 'Using tourism to protect existing culture: a project in Swedish Lapland', *Leisure Studies* 10, 1: 33–47.

Jefferson, A. and Lickorish, L. (1988) *Marketing Tourism–A Practical Guide*, Harlow, Essex: Longman.

Krippendorf, J. (1987) 'Ecological approach to tourism marketing', *Tourism Management* 8, 2: 174–176.

Lascurain, H.C. (1991) 'Tourism, ecotourism and protected areas', *Parks* 2, 3: 31–35.

Latham, J. (1990) 'Statistical trends in tourism and hotel accommodation up to 1988', in C. Cooper (ed.) *Progress in Tourism, Recreation and Hospitality Management*, volume 2, London: Belhaven Press/University of Surrey.

Liu, J.C., Sheldon, P.J., and Var, T. (1987) 'Resident perception of the environmental impacts of tourism', *Annals of Tourism Research* 14, 1: 17–37.

Morrison, P. and Selman, P. (1991) 'Tourism and the environment: a case study from Turkey', *The Environmentalist* 11, 2: 113–129.

Poon, A. (1989) 'Competitive strategies for a new tourism', in C. Cooper (ed.) *Progress in Tourism, Recreation and Hospitality Management*, volume 1, London: Belhaven.

Romeril, M. (1985) 'Tourism and the environment: towards a symbiotic relationship', *International Journal of Environmental Studies* 25, 4: 215–218.

Smith, S. (1989) *Tourism Analysis: A Handbook*, Harlow, Essex: Longman.

Tyler, C. (1989) 'A phenomenal explosion', *Geographical Magazine* 61, 8: 18–21.

World Tourism Organisation (1991) *Tourism Trends Worldwide and in Europe*, Madrid: WTO.
World Tourism Organisation (1992) *Year Book of Tourism Statistics*, volume 144, Madrid: WTO.

CHAPTER 2

Ahmad, A., Rawat, J.S. and Rai, S.C. (1990) 'An analysis of the Himalayan environment and guidelines for its management and ecologically sustainable development', *The Environmentalist* 10, 4: 281–298.
Alleyne, G.A.O. (1990) 'Health and tourism in the Caribbean', *Bulletin of the Pan American Health Organisation* 24, 3: 291–300.
Andronikou, A. (1987) 'Cyprus: management of the tourist sector', *Tourism Management* 7, 2: 127–129.
Anon (1989) 'Visitors are good for you', *Economist* 310: 21–24.
Antunac, I. (1989) 'Economic aspects of tourist resources conservation and of development', *Acta Turistica* 1, 1: 95–107.
Archer, B.H. (1978) 'Domestic tourism as a development factor', *Annals of Tourism Research* 5: 126–141.
Ashworth, G. and Tunbridge, J. (1990) *The Tourist-Historic City*, London: Belhaven.
Bascom, W.W. (1976) 'Changing African art', in N.H. Graburn (ed.) *Ethnic and Tourist Arts: Cultural Expressions from the Fourth World*, Berkeley: University of California Press.
Battista, G. (1989) 'Architectural conservation in Genoa', in Architectural Heritage Reports and Studies, number 14, *Heritage and Successful Town Regeneration*, Strasbourg: Council of Europe.
Becheri, E. (1991) 'Rimini and Co: the end of a legend?', *Tourism Management* 12, 3: 229–235.
Bettum, O. (1989) 'The Aker River environmental park, Oslo', in Architectural Heritage Reports and Studies, number 14, *Heritage and Successful Town Regeneration*, Strasbourg: Council of Europe.
Bjonness, I.M. (1983) 'External economic dependency and changing human adjustment to marginal environment in the High Himalaya, Nepal', *Mountain Research and Development* 3, 3: 263–272.
Borgula, K. (1987) 'Fairness in sport: even with regard to nature', *Magglingen* 44, 12: 10–11.
Borys, T. and Prudzienica, J. (1987) 'Losses in the tourist economy owing to the threat to the environment as an element of the socio-economic accounts: the instance of Jelenia Gora basin', *Problemy Turystyki* 10, 4: 38–50.
Briand, F., Dubost, M., Pitt, D. and Rambaud, D. (1989) *The Alps: A System Under Pressure*, Gland, Switzerland: International Union for Conservation on Nature and Natural Resources.
Briassoulis, H. (1991) 'Tourism and the environment: planning issues and approaches', proceedings of an International Symposium on

Architecture of Tourism in the Mediterranean, Istanbul, Turkey: Yildiz University Press.

Briereton, U.A. (1991) 'Tourism and the environment', *Contours* 5, 4: 18–19.

Brockleman W.Y. and Dearden, P. (1990) 'The role of nature trekking in conservation: a case-study of Thailand', *Environmental Conservation* 17, 2: 141–148.

Brooke, J. (1990) 'A positive future for Broadland?', *Geography Review*, 3, 3: 31–36.

Buckley, P.J. and Witt, S.F. (1989) 'Tourism in difficult areas II: case studies of Calderdale, Leeds, Manchester and Scunthorpe', *Tourism Management* 10, 2: 138–152.

Butler, R.W. (1978) 'The impact of recreation on the life styles of rural communities', *Wiener Geographische Schriften* 51: 187–201.

Butler, R.W. (1991) 'Tourism, environment, and sustainable development', *Environmental Conservation* 18, 3: 201–209.

Bywater, M. (1991) 'Prospects for Mediterranean beach resorts: an Italian case study', *Travel and Tourism Analyst* 5: 75–89.

Cohen, E. (1978) 'Impact of tourism on the physical environment', *Annals of Tourism Research* 5, 2: 215–237.

Cohen, E. (1982) 'Thai girls and farang men: the edge of ambiguity', *Annals of Tourism Research* 9, 3: 403–428.

Copeland, E. (1992) 'The role of airlines in the tourism and environment debate', *Tourism Management*, March: 112–114.

de Groot, R.S. (1983) 'Tourism and conservation in the Galapagos Islands', *Biological Conservation* 26: 291–300.

Deitch, L.I. (1977) 'The impact of tourism upon the arts and crafts of the Indians of Southwestern United States', in V. Smith (ed.) *Hosts and Guests: An Anthropology of Tourism*, Philadelphia: University of Pennsylvania Press.

DoE (Department of the Environment) (1990) *Tourism and the Inner City: An Evaluation of the Impact of Grant Assisted Tourism Projects*, London: HMSO.

Dowling, R. (1991) 'Tourism and the natural environment: Shark bay, western Australia', *Tourism Recreation Research* 16, 2: 44–48.

Dupuy, A.R. (1987) 'Natural resources and African tourism. Senegal: souvenirs, souvenirs...', *Espaces* 87: 22–25.

Economic Intelligence Unit (1991) 'Managing tourism and the environment: a Kenyan case study', *Travel and Tourism Analyst* 2: 78–87.

ECTARC (1988a) *Study of the Social, Cultural and Linguistic Impact of Tourism in and upon Wales*, Cardiff, Wales: European Centre for Traditional and Regional Cultures/Wales Tourist Board.

ECTARC (1988b) *Contribution to the Drafting of a Charter for Cultural Tourism*, Llangollen, Wales: European Centre for Traditional and Regional Cultures.

ETB (English Tourist Board) (1991) *The Future of England's Smaller Seaside Resorts: Summary Report*, London: ETB.

ETB (English Tourist Board), Countryside Commission and Rural

Development Commission (1992) *The Green Light: A Guide to Sustainable Tourism*, London: ETB.

Erize, F. (1987) 'The impact of tourism on the Antarctic environment', *Environment International* 13, 1: 133–136.

Gasparavic, F. (1989) 'The interaction between tourism and resources', *Acta Turistica* 1, 2: 148–156.

Graburn, N.H. (ed.) (1976) *Ethnic and Tourist Arts: Cultural Expressions from the Fourth World*, Berkeley: University of California Press.

Grahn, P. (1991) 'Using tourism to protect existing culture: a project in Swedish Lapland', *Leisure Studies* 10, 1: 33–47.

Grant, R. (1990) 'Mallee tourism', in J.C. Noble (ed.) *The Mallee Lands*, Adelaide: CSIRO.

Gray, H.P. (1974) 'Towards an economic analysis of tourism policy', *Social and Economic Studies* 23: 386–397.

Green, H. and Hunter, C. (1992) 'The environmental impact assessment of tourism development', in P. Johnson and B. Thomas (eds) *Perspectives on Tourism Policy*, London: Mansell.

Green, M., Jenkins, M. and Madams, R. (1989) 'Conservation areas', in M. Norton-Griffiths and P. Ryden (eds) *The IUCN Sahel Studies* volume 1, Gland, Switzerland: International Union for Conservation of Nature and Natural Resources.

Greenwood, D. (1977) 'Tourism as an agent of change', *Annals of Tourism Research* 3: 128–142.

Grenon, M. and Batisse, M. (1989) *Futures for the Mediterranean Basin: The Blue Plan*, New York: Oxford University Press.

Greth, A. (1989) 'Mediterranean tourism and nature in Turkey', *Courrier de la Nature* 123: 32–36.

Hadjivassilis, I. (1990) 'Small sewage treatment plants and wastewater reuse in Cyprus', *Water Science and Technology* 22, 3/4: 9–16.

Hamele, H. (1988) 'Leisure in nature', *Naturopa* 59: 30ff.

Harris, C.M. (1991) 'Environmental effects of human activities on King George Island, South Shetland Islands, Antarctica', *Polar Record* 27, 162: 193–204.

Hassan, R. (1975) 'International tourism and intercultural communications', *Southeast Asia Journal of Social Science* 3, 2: 25–37.

Hazell, S.D. (1989) *Ecological Tourism: The Path to Sustainable Development*, Montreal: McGill University Management Graduate Department.

Henry, B. (1988) 'The environmental impact of tourism in Jamaica', *World Leisure and Recreation* 29, 1: 19–21.

Hills, T.G. and Rinke, R. (1989) *The Impact of Mass Tourism on the Bio-Physical and Socio-Cultural Environment of the Third World: A Corporate Responsibility*, Montreal: McGill University Management Graduate Department.

Holder, J.S. (1988) 'Pattern and impact of tourism on the environment of the Caribbean', *Tourism Management* 9, 2: 119–127.

International Chamber of Commerce (1989) *Environmental Auditing*, Paris: ICC.

Jackson I. (1984) 'Enhancing the positive impact of tourism on the built and natural environment', in OAS volume 5 *Reference Guidelines for*

Enhancing the Positive Socio-cultural and Environmental Impacts of Tourism, Washington D.C.: Organisation of American States, International Trade and Tourism Division, Department of Economic Affairs.

Jafari, J. (1974) 'The socio-economic cost of tourism to developing countries', Department of Habitational Tourism, University of Wisconsin.

Johnson, P.S. and Thomas, R.D. (1990) 'The development of Beamish: an assessment', *Journal of Museum Management and Curatorship* 9: 5–24.

Jones, R.J. (1985) 'Halifax town centre conservation study', *Landscape Design* 4: 22–25.

Kaur, J. and Singh, T.V. (1990) 'The tradition of Himalayan pilgrimages in Garhwal: an historico-geographical inquiry', in T.V. Singh (ed.) *Geography of the Mountains*, New Delhi, India: Heritage Publishers.

Klemm, M. (1992) 'Sustainable tourism development: Languedoc-Roussillon thirty years on', *Tourism Management*, June: 169–180.

Kocasoy, G. (1989) 'The relationship between coastal tourism, sea pollution and public health: a case study from Turkey', *Environmentalist* 9, 4: 245–251.

Koea, A. (1977) 'Polynesian migration to New Zealand', in B.R. Finney and A.A. Watson (eds) *A New Kind of Sugar: Tourism in the Pacific*, University of California, Santa Cruz: Centre for South Pacific Studies.

Lal, P.N. (1984) 'Environmental implications of coastal development in Fiji', *Ambio* 13: 5–6.

Liu, J.C., Sheldon, P.J. and Var, T. (1987) 'Resident perception of the environmental impacts of tourism', *Annals of Tourism Research* 14, 1: 17–37.

Luxmoore, R.A. (1989) 'Impact on conservation in wildlife production systems', in R.J. Hudson (ed.) *Impact on Conservation*, Cambridge: Cambridge University Press.

McKean, P.F. (1976) 'Tourism, culture change and cultural conservation in Bali', in D.J. Banks (ed.) *Changing Identities in Modern South East Asia and World Anthropology*, The Hague, Netherlands: Mouton.

McKean, P.F. (1977) 'From purity to pollution? In transition: the Balinese Ketjak', in A. Becker and A. Yengoyen (eds) *The World Imagination of Reality: Symbol Systems in Southeast Asia*, Tucson: University of Arizona Press.

McNulty, R. (1989) 'Lessons from North America', in Architectural Heritage Reports and Studies, number 14, *Heritage and Successful Town Regeneration*, Strasbourg: Council of Europe.

Marfurt, E. (1983) 'Tourism and the Third World: dream or nightmare?', *Swiss Review of World Affairs* 33, 4: 14–20.

Martinez-Taberner, A., Moya, G., Ramon, G. and Forteza, V. (1990) 'The limnological criteria for the rehabilitation of a coastal marsh: the Albufera of Majorca, Balearic Islands', *Ambio* 19, 1: 21–27.

Mathieson, A. and Wall, G. (1982) *Tourism: Economic, Physical and Social Impacts*, Harlow, Essex: Longman.

May, R.J. (1977) 'Tourism and the artifact in Papua New Guinea', in B.R. Finney and A.A. Watson (eds) *A New Kind of Sugar: Tourism in the*

Pacific, University of California, Santa Cruz: Center for South Pacific Studies.

May, V. (1991) 'Tourism, environment and development: values, sustainability and stewardship', *Tourism Management* 12, 2: 112–118.

Michael, P. (1991) 'Developing agrotourism in Cyprus', paper given at seminar on New Forms of Tourist Demand and New Products, Nicosia, Cyprus, May.

Miller, J. (1989) 'The European context: experience and lessons', in Architectural Heritage Reports and Studies, number 14, *Heritage and Successful Town Regeneration*, Strasbourg: Council of Europe.

Milne, S. (1990) 'The impact of tourism development in small Pacific Island States: an overview', *New Zealand Journal of Geography* 89: 16–21.

Monnier, Y. (1987) 'Tourist development and ecological upheaval in the small islands: the example of Saint-Martin', in J.P. Doumenge and M.F. Perrin (eds) *Iles Tropicales: Insularité, Insularisme*, Bordeaux: University of Bordeaux.

Morgan, M. (1991) 'Dressing up to survive: marketing Majorca anew', *Tourism Management* 12, 1: 15–20.

Morrison, P. and Selman, P. (1991) 'Tourism and the environment: a case study from Turkey', *The Environmentalist* 11, 2: 113–129.

Norton, D.A. and Roper-Lindsay, J. (1992) 'Conservation, tourism and commercial recreation: conflict or cooperation? – A New Zealand perspective', *Natural Areas Journal* 12, 1: 20–25.

O'Donnell, M. (1991) 'Rural tourism: the evolving Irish model', paper given at seminar on New Forms of Tourist Demand and New Products, Nicosia, Cyprus, May.

OECD (Organisation for Economic Co-operation and Development) (1981a) *The Impact of Tourism on the Environment*, Paris: OECD.

OECD (Organisation for Economic Co-operation and Development) (1981b) *Case Studies of the Impact of Tourism on the Environment*, Paris: OECD.

Olokesusi, F. (1990) 'Assessment of the Yankari game reserve, Nigeria: problems and prospects', *Tourism Management* 11, 2: 153–163.

Owens, S. and Owens, P.L. (1991) *Renewable Resource Management: The Norfolk Broads. Environment, Resources and Conservation*, Cambridge: Cambridge University Press.

Pacione, M. (1977) 'Tourism: its effects on the traditional landscape in Ibiza and Formentera', *Geography* 62: 43–47.

Page, S. (1989) 'Tourism planning in London', *Town and Country Planning*, December: 334–335.

Page, S. (1992) 'Managing tourism in a small historic city', *Town and Country Planning*, July/August: 208–211.

Papadopoulos, S.I. (1988) 'An examination of non-economic factors related to tourism in Greece', *Revue de Tourisme* 1: 29–30.

Pawson, I.G., Stanford, D.D., Adams, V.A. and Nurbu, M. (1984) 'Growth of tourism in Nepal's Everest region: impact on the physical environment and structure of human settlements', *Mountain Research and Development* 4, 3: 237–246.

Pearce, D. (1989) *Tourist Development*, second edition, Harlow, Essex: Longman Scientific & Technical.

Pizam, A. (1978) 'Tourism's impacts: the social costs to the destination as perceived by its residents', *Journal of Travel Research* 16, 4: 8–12.

Prechil, H. (1983) 'The impact of a tropical holiday resort on its environment; the example of Diawi Beach in Kenya', *Tourist Review* 38, 4: 16–18.

Pyrovetsi, M. (1989) 'Integrated Mediterranean Programmes and the natural environment: a case study from Greece', *Environmentalist* 9, 3: 201–211.

Romeril, M. (1989) 'Tourism and the environment: accord or discord?', *Tourism Management* 10, 3: 204–208.

Ronserray, D. (1989) 'The Avignon Acropolis: a large scale tourist project' in Architectural Heritage Reports and Studies, number 14, *Heritage and Successful Town Regeneration*, Strasbourg: Council of Europe.

Sindiyo, D.M. and Pertet, F.N. (1984) 'Tourism and its impact on wildlife in Kenya', *Industry and Environment* 7, 1: 14–19.

Smith, V. (1977) *Hosts and Guests: An Anthropology of Tourism*, Philadelphia: University of Pennsylvania Press.

Smith, C. and Jenner, P. (1989) 'Tourism and the environment', *Travel and Tourism Analyst* 5: 68–86.

Smith, K. (1990) 'Tourism and climate change', *Land Use Policy* 7, 2: 176–180.

Srisang, K. (1991) 'Alternative to tourism', *Contours* 5, 3: 6–12.

Stankovic, S.M. (1991) 'The protection of life environment and modern tourism', *Revue de Tourisme* 46, 2: 2–4.

Stark, J. (1990) 'Hawaii: tourism action network', *Contours* 4, 5: 19–21.

Tananone, B. (1991) 'International tourism in Thailand: environment and community development', *Contours* 5, 2: 7–9.

Thiele, K. (1987) '"Keep out": protected areas in a National Park', *National Park, Umwelt-Natur* 2: 11–12.

Thurot, J.M. (1980) *Capacité de chargé et production touristique*, Etudes et Memoires, 43, Centre de hautes etudes touristiques, Aix-en-Provence.

Tiard, M. (1987) 'Brotonne nature park: presenting its heritage', *Espaces* 85: 27–32.

Turner, L. and Ash, J. (1975) *The Golden Hordes: International Tourism and the Pleasure Periphery*, London: Constable.

Tyler, C. (1989) 'A phenomenal explosion', *Geographical Magazine* 61, 8: 18–21.

Urbanowicz, C.F. (1977) 'Tourism in Tonga: troubled times', in V. Smith (ed.) *Hosts and Guests: The Anthropology of Tourism*, Philadelphia: University of Pennsylvania Press.

Walker, T.A. (1991) 'Tourism development and environmental limitations at Heron Island, Great Barrier Reef', *Journal of Environmental Management* 33, 2: 117–122.

Watanabe, Y. (1990) 'Report of the 54th Conference of the Japanese Society of Limnology: present state of the lake environment in Shinshu', *Japanese Journal of Limnology* 51, 1: 15–23.

Westlake, T. and White, A. (1992) 'Venice: suffering city of tourist dreams', *Town and Country Planning*, July/August: 210–211.
Wheatcroft, S. (1991) 'Airlines, tourism and the environment', *Tourism Management* 12, 2: 119–124.
Wilson, D. (1979) 'The early effects of tourism in the Seychelles', in E. de Kadt (ed.) *Tourism – Passport to Development?*, New York: Oxford University Press.
Witt, S.F. (1991) *The Impact of Tourism on Wales*, University of Swansea, Wales: Centre for Development Studies.

CHAPTER 3

Ataby, S. (1992) 'Soft tourism and ecological planning', proceedings of an International Conference on Architecture of Soft Tourism, Trabzon, Turkey: Yildiz University Faculty of Architecture Press.
Butler, R.W. (1980) 'The concept of a tourist-area cycle of evolution and implications for management', *The Canadian Geographer* 24: 5–12.
Butler, R.W. (1989) 'Alternative tourism: pious hope or Trojan horse?', *World Leisure and Recreation* 31, 4: 9–17.
Butler, R.W. (1990) 'Alternative tourism: pious hope or Trojan horse?', *Journal of Travel Research* 28, 3: 40–45.
Butler, R.W. (1991) 'Tourism, environment, and sustainable development', *Environmental Conservation* 18, 3: 201–209.
Butler, R.W. (1993) 'Pre- and post-impact assessment of tourism development', in D.G. Pearce and R.W. Butler (eds) *Tourism Research: Critiques and Challenges*, London: Routledge.
Cronin, L. (1990) 'A strategy for tourism and sustainable developments', *World Leisure and Recreation* 32, 3: 12–18.
Duffield, B.S. and Walker, S.E. (1984) 'The assessment of tourism impacts', in B.D. Clarke *et al.* (eds) *Perspectives on Environmental Impact Assessment*, London: D. Reidel.
ETB (English Tourist Board), Countryside Commission and Rural Development Commission (1992) *The Green Light: A Guide to Sustainable Tourism*, London: ETB.
Fennell, D.A. and Eagles, P.F.J. (1990) 'Ecotourism in Costa Rica: a conceptual framework', *Journal of Park and Recreation Administration* 8, 1: 23–34.
Himmetoglu, B. (1992) 'What is soft tourism?', proceedings of an International Conference on Architecture of Soft Tourism, Trabzon, Turkey: Yildiz University Faculty of Architecture Press.
Klemm, M. (1992) 'Sustainable tourism development: Languedoc-Roussillon thirty years on', *Tourism Management*, June: 169–180.
Krippendorf, J. (1987) 'Ecological approach to tourism marketing', *Tourism Management* 8, 2: 174–176.
Laarman, J.G. and Durst, P.B. (1987) 'Nature travel and tropical forests', FPEI Working Paper 23, Research Triangle Park, NC: Southeastern Center for Forest Economics Research.

Mader, V. (1988) 'Tourism and environment', *Annals of Tourism Research* 15, 2: 274–276.

Martin, B.S. and Uysal, M. (1990) 'An examination of the relationship between the carrying capacity concept and the tourism lifecycle: management and policy implications', *Journal of Environmental Management* 31: 327–333.

Mathieson, A. and Wall, G. (1982) *Tourism: Economic, Physical and Social Impacts*, London: Longman.

Morgan, M. (1991) 'Dressing up to survive: marketing Majorca anew',*Tourism Management* 12, 1: 15–20.

Munt, I. (1992) 'A great escape?', *Town and Country Planning*, July/August: 212–214.

Nijkamp, P., Kiers, M. and Janssen, H. (1992) 'Strategies for sustainable tourism', proceedings of an International Conference on Architecture of Soft Tourism, Trabzon, Turkey: Yildiz University Faculty of Architecture Press.

O'Reilly, A.M. (1986) 'Tourism carrying capacity: concept and issues', *Tourism Management* 7, 4: 254–258.

O'Riordan, T. (1989) 'The challenge for environmentalism', in R. Peet and N. Thrift (eds) *New Models in Geography: Volume One*, London: Unwin Hyman.

OECD (Organisation for Economic Co-operation and Development) (1981a) *The Impact of Tourism on the Environment*, Paris: OECD.

OECD (Organisation for Economic Co-operation and Development) (1981b) *Case Studies of the Impact of Tourism on the Environment*, Paris: OECD.

OECD (Organisation for Economic Co-operation and Development) (1990) *Environmental Policies for Cities in the 1990s*, Paris: OECD.

Pearce, D. (1989) *Tourist Development*, 2nd edn., Harlow: Longman Scientific & Technical.

Pearce, D., Markandya, A. and Barbier, E.B. (1989) *Blueprint for a Green Economy*, London: Earthscan.

Pearce, D. (1991) 'Introduction: blueprint for a green economy', in D. Pearce (ed.) *Blueprint 2: Greening the World Economy*, London: Earthscan.

Pigram, J.J. (1990) 'Sustainable tourism: policy considerations', *Journal of Tourism Studies* 1, 2: 2–9.

Rauhe, W.J. (1992) 'Soft tourism: empowering citizens for community sustainability', proceedings of an International Conference on Architecture of Soft Tourism, Trabzon, Turkey: Yildiz University Faculty of Architecture Press.

Reime, M. and Hawkins, C. (1979) 'Tourism development: a model for growth', *Cornell Hotel and Restaurant Administration Quarterly* 20, 1: 67–74.

Romeril, M. (1985) 'Tourism and the environment: towards a symbiotic relationship', *International Journal of Environmental Studies* 25, 4: 215–218.

Romeril, M. (1989) 'Tourism and the environment: accord or discord?', *Tourism Management* 10, 3: 204–208.

Smith, C. and Jenner, P. (1989) 'Tourism and the environment', *Travel and Tourism Analyst* 5: 68–86.

Tananone, B. (1991) 'International tourism in Thailand: environment and community development', *Contours* 5, 2: 7–9.

Turner, R.K. (1991) 'Environment, economics and ethics', in D. Pearce (ed.) *Blueprint 2: Greening the World Economy,* London: Earthscan.

Wall, G. (1982) 'Cycles and capacity: incipient theory or conceptual contradiction', *Tourism Management* 3, 3: 188–192.

Wheatcroft, S. (1991) 'Airlines, tourism and the environment', *Tourism Management* 12, 2: 119–124.

WCED (World Commission on Environment and Development) (1987) *Our Common Future,* Oxford: Oxford University Press.

WTO (World Tourism Organisation) (1984) 'Tourist carrying capacity', *Industry and Environment* 7, 1: 30–36.

CHAPTER 4

Acerenza, M.A. (1985) 'Planificacion estrategica del turismo: esquema metodologoco', *Estudios Turisticos* 85: 47–70.

Aitchison, J.W. (1984) 'The national and regional parks of France', *Landscape Research* 1: 2–9.

Alcock, D. (1991) 'Education and extension: management's best strategy', *Parks and Recreation* 27, 1: 15–17.

Alipour, H. (1991) 'An alternative tourism policy: a case study of Turkey', proceedings of an International Symposium on Architecture of Tourism in the Mediterranean, Istanbul, Turkey: Yildiz University Press.

Ayala, H. (1991) 'Resort hotel landscape as an international megatrend', *Annals of Tourism Research* 18, 4: 568–587.

Baarse, C. and Rijsberman, F.A. (1986) 'Ecology and tourism: protecting the coast of the Dutch island of Texel', *Project Appraisal* 1, 2: 75–87.

Balbock, J. (1989) *Town Centre Management: Its Importance and Nature,* London: Hillier Parker.

Barrow, G. (1992) 'The British experience: interpretation, conservation and tourism', *Natour* 10: 34–37.

Beauchamps, P. (1983) 'Interpretation in parcs naturels and parcs nationaux', in R. Simpson (ed.) *Education and Interpretation For Conservation,* Losehill Hall.

Beddington, N. (1973) 'Mollycoddled into mediocrity', *Built Environment* 2, 12: 688–689.

Booth, P. and Beer, A.R. (1983) 'Development control and design quality', *Town Planning Review* 54: 265–284.

Booth, P. (1991) 'The theory and practice of French development control: rules, discretion and decision making in urban land use change', in J. Doak and V. Nadin (eds) *Town Planning Responses to City Change,* Aldershot: Avebury.

Booth, P. and Green, D.H. (1993) 'Urban policy in England and Wales and in France: a comparative assessment of recent policy initiatives', *Environment and Policy* 11: 381–393.

Braddon, C.J.H. (1982) *British Issues Paper: Approaches to Tourism Planning Abroad*, London: British Tourist Authority.

Bridge, N.J. and Hutchinson, P. (1988) 'Leisure, integration and community', *Journal of Leisurability* 15, 1: 3–16.

Chapman, D. and Larkham, P. (1992) 'Discovering the art of relationship, urban design, aesthetic control and design guidance', *Research Paper No. 9*, Birmingham: School of Planning, Birmingham Polytechnic.

Choy, D.J.L. (1992) 'Tourism planning: the case for market failure', *Tourism Management* 12: 313–330.

Countryside Commission (1992a) *Heritage Coasts in England: Policies and Priorities*, Cheltenham: Countryside Commission.

Countryside Commission (1992b) *Tourism in National Parks: A Guide to Good Practice*, Cheltenham: Countryside Commission.

Cronin, L. (1990) 'A strategy of tourism and sustainable developments', *World Leisure and Recreation* 32, 3: 12–18.

Cullen, P. (1981) *An Evaluation of the Heritage Coast Programme in England and Wales*, Cheltenham: Countryside Commission.

Cullingworth, J.B. (1988) *Town and Country Planning in Britain*, London: Unwin and Hyman.

Davies, H.W.E., Edwards, D., Hooper, A.J. and Punter, J.V. (1989) 'Comparative study', in *Planning Control in Western Europe*, Department of the Environment, London: HMSO.

Davies, H.E.W. and Healey, P. (1983) 'British planning practice and planning education in the 1970s and 1980s', *Working Paper 70*, Oxford: Department of Town Planning, Oxford Polytechnic.

Diatta, M., Corder, O.M., Yap, V. and Roy, S.K. (1986) 'Third world experts analyse third world tourism', in P. Holden, G.F. Pfaffin and J. Horlemann (eds) *Third World People and Tourism: Approaches to a Dialogue*, Third World Tourism Ecumenical European Network.

DoE (Department of the Environment) (1980) *Development Control: Policy and Practice*, DoE Circular 22/80, London: HMSO.

DoE (Department of the Environment) (1985) *Town and Country Planning (Use Classes) Order 1972*, DoE, London: HMSO.

DoE (Department of the Environment) (1987) *Change of Use of Buildings and Other Land: the Town and Country Planning (Use Classes) Order*, DoE Circular 13/87, London: HMSO.

DoE (Department of the Environment) (1988) *The Conduct of Local Authority Businesses: The Government Response to the Report of the Widdicombe Committee Inquiry*, DoE Cmnd. 433, London: HMSO.

DoE (Department of the Environment) (1990) *Tourism and the Inner City: An Evaluation of the Impact of Grant Assisted Tourism Projects*, DoE, London: HMSO.

DoE (Department of the Environment) (1992) *PPG21: Tourism*, DoE, London: HMSO.

Essex County Council (1966) *Thaxted, An Historical and Architectural Survey*, Chelmsford: Essex County Council.

Essex County Council (1973) *A Design Guide for Residential Areas*, Colchester: Essex County Council.

Fagence, M. (1990) 'Geographically-referenced planning strategies to resolve potential conflicts between environmental values and commercial interests in tourism development and environmentally sensitive areas', *Journal of Environmental Management* 31, 1: 1–18.

Foley, P. (1992) 'Local economic policy and job creation: a review of evaluation studies', *Urban Studies* 29, 3/4: 557–596.

Forestry Authority (1992) *Lowland Landscape Design: Guidelines*, London: HMSO.

French, C.N. (1991) 'How much tourism development is enough?', paper given at an International Conference on Tourism in Europe, University of Durham, England, December.

Getz, D. (1987) 'Tourism planning and research traditions, models and futures', paper presented at the Australian Travel Research Workshop, Bunbury, Australia.

Gloor, B. (1982) *Access to Nature in Mountain Regions*, Strasbourg: Council for Europe.

Green, D.H. and Hunter, C. (1992a) 'The environmental impact assessment of tourism development', in P. Johnson and B. Thomas, (eds) *Perspectives on Tourism Policy*, London: Mansell.

Green, D.H. and Hunter, C. (1992b) 'Tourism and the environment: the framework for protection in England and Wales', proceedings of an International Conference on The Architecture of Soft Tourism, Istanbul, Turkey: Yildiz University Press.

Green, D.H. and Foley, P. (1987) 'Planning control and the conversion of property for small business use', in R.A. Mordey and M.L. Harrison (eds) *Planning Control: Philosophies, Prospects and Practice*, London: Croom Helm.

Grenon, M. and Batisse, M. (1990) *Future for the Mediterranean Basin: the Blue Plan*, New York: Oxford University Press.

Gunn, A. (1988) *Environmental Design and Land Use*, New York: John Wiley and Sons.

Gurung, H.B. (1992) 'Environmental education in Nepal: a mechanism for resource conservation', *World Leisure and Recreation* 34, 2: 18–22.

Hall, C.M., Springett, D.V. and Springett, B.P. (1993) 'The development of an environmental education tourist product: a case study of the New Zealand Heritage Foundation's Nature of New Zealand programme', *Journal of Sustainable Tourism* 1, 2: 130–136.

Hall, P. (1970) *Theory and Practice of Regional Planning*, London: Pemberton Books.

Harrison, M.L. (1987) 'Introduction', in M.L. Harrison and R. Mordey (eds) *Planning Control: Philosophies, Prospects and Practice*, London: Croom Helm.

Haywood, K.M. (1988) 'Responsible and responsive tourism planning in the community', *Tourism Management* 9, 105–118.

Healey, P., McDougall, G. and Thomas, M.J. (1982) 'Theoretical debates in planning: towards a coherent dialogue', in P. Healey, G. McDougall and M.J. Thomas (eds) *Planning Theory: Prospects for the 1980s*, Oxford: Pergamon.

Healey, P. (1983) *Local Plans in British Land Use Planning*, Urban and Regional Planning Series 31, Oxford: Pergamon.

Healey, P., McNamara, P., Elson, M. and Doak, J. (1988) *Land Use Planning and the Mediation of Urban Change*, Cambridge, England: Cambridge University Press.

Healey, P. and Shaw, T. (1993) 'Planners, plans and sustainable development', *Regional Studies* 27, 8: 769–776.

Heeley, J. (1981) 'Planning for tourism in Britain', *Town Planning Review* 52: 61–79.

Henry, B. (1988) 'The environmental impact of tourism in Jamaica', *Revue de Tourisme* 43, 2: 24–27.

Hick, D. (1991) *Traffic in National Parks?*, Report to the Council for National Parks.

Hollaway, J.C. (1991) 'Cityscape: a comparative evaluation of the built environment and its influence on generating tourism', paper given at an International Conference on Tourism in Europe, University of Durham, England, December.

Inskeep, E. (1991) *Tourism Planning: An Integrated and Sustainable Approach*, The Hague: Van Nostrand Reinhold.

Jamieson, W. (1990) 'Creating historic districts: new challenges for historic preservation in western Canada', *Prairie Forum* 15, 2: 221–233.

Korca, P. (1991) 'Assessment of the environmental impacts of tourism', proceedings of an International Symposium on the Architecture of Tourism in the Mediterranean, Istanbul, Turkey: Yildiz University Press.

Leeds City Council (1990) 'Leisure and Tourism', *Unitary Development Plan Issues Paper No. 5*, Leeds: Planning Department, LCC.

Lewis, S. (ed.) (1986) 'Output and performance measurements in central government: progress in departments', *HM Treasury Working Paper 38*, London: HM Treasury.

MacEwen, A. and MacEwan, M. (1982) *National Parks: Conservation or Cosmetics?*, London: Allen and Unwin.

Manser, M. (1979) 'Barriers to design', *Royal Institute of British Architects Journal* 86, 9: 401–403.

Marsh, J. (1983) 'Canada's parks and tourism: a problematic relationship', in *Tourism in Canada: Selected Issues and Options*, Western Geographies Series 21, Victoria: University of Victoria.

Milne, S. (1990) 'The impact of tourism development in small Pacific Island States: an overview', *New Zealand Journal of Geography* 89, 1: 16–21.

Ministère de l'Intérieur et de l'Aménagement du Territoire (1993) *Les Sociétés d'Economie Mixte Locales*, La documentation Française, Paris.

MHLG (Ministry of Housing and Local Government) (1965) *People and Planning*, MHLG, London: HMSO.

MHLG (Ministry of Housing and Local Government) (1988) *The Future of Development Plans*, MHLG, London: HMSO.

Moore, B. and Townroe, P. (1990) *Urban Labour Markets: Review of Research*, Department of the Environment, London: HMSO.

Mordey, R. (1987) 'Development control, public participation and the need for planning aid', in M.L Harrison and R. Mordey (eds) *Planning Control: Philosophies, Prospects and Practice*, London: Croom Helm.

Murphy, P.E. (1985) *Tourism: A Community Approach*, London: Methuen.

Murphy, P.E. (1988) 'Community driven tourism planning', *Tourism Management* 9, 2: 96–104.

Ors, H. (1991) 'Tourism policies of national development plans and their approaches to tourism planning in Turkey', proceedings of an International Symposium on Architecture of Tourism in the Mediterranean, İstanbul, Turkey: Yildiz University Press.

Ostrowski, S. (1984) 'Tourism in protected areas: the case of Poland', *Tourism Management* 5, 2: 118–122.

Pearce, D. (1989) *Tourist Development*, second edition, Harlow, Essex: Longman Scientific & Technical.

Peltzer, R.H.M. (1989) 'The impact of recreation on nature in the Netherlands', in B.J.H. Brown (ed.) *Conference Papers and Reports 31*, Leisure Studies Association.

Pivert, M. (1987) 'The gorges of the Ardeche: nature reserve or leisure park', *Courrier de la Nature* 108: 24–31.

PPJPB (Peak Park Joint Planning Board) (1978) *Peak Park National Park: National Park Plan*, Bakewell, England: PPJPB.

PPJPB (Peak Park Joint Planning Board) (1988) *Peak National Park Plan*, Bakewell, England: PPJPB.

Punter, J.V. (1989) 'France', in *Planning Control in Western Europe*, Department of the Environment, London: HMSO.

Purton, R. (1992) 'Retailing and the street', *The Planner* 78: 19.

Robinson, F., Wren, C. and Goddard, J. (1987) *Economic Development Policies: An Evaluative Study of Newcastle Metropolitan Region*, Oxford: Clarendon Press.

Russell, A. (1989) 'Heritage and successful town regeneration', in *Architectural Heritage Reports and Studies*, Strasbourg: Council of Europe.

Salm, R.V. (1985) 'Integrating marine conservation and tourism', *International Journal of Environmental Studies* 25, 4: 229–238.

States Planning Department (1984) *Townscape Studies*, St. Helier, Jersey: States Planning Department.

Stroud, H.B. (1983) 'Environmental problems associated with large recreational subdivisions', *Professional Geographer* 35, 3: 303–13.

TDC (Tourism Development Corporation) (1975) *Tourism Development Plan: Malaysia*, Kuala Lumpur: TDC.

Thiele, K. (1987) 'Keep Out! Protected areas in a national park', *Natur* 2: 11–12.

Tiard, M. (1987) 'Brotonne nature park, presenting its heritage', *Espaces* 85: 27–32.

Tilden, F. (1977) *Interpreting Our Heritage*, Chapel Hill, Carolina: University of North Carolina Press.

Travis, A.S. (1988) 'New forms of tourism and ways of achieving compatibility between lifestyles and values of tourists and of their hosts', *Problemy Turystyki* 11, 4: 12–18.

Turok, I. and Wannup, U. (1990) *Targeting Urban Employment Initiatives*, Department of the Environment, London: HMSO.

Wahab, I., Che, M. and Che, O. (1992) 'Urban and regional planning strategies in promoting tourism in Malaysia', proceedings of an International Symposium on Architecture of Tourism in the Mediterranean, Istanbul, Turkey: Yildiz University Press.

Waite, C. (1982) 'Coastal management in England and Wales', *Ekisics* 49, 2: 124–127.

Whitney, D. (1993) 'Progress in Development Plan preparation in west Yorkshire', *The Regional Review* 3, 3: 7–8.

Whitney, D. and Haughton, G. (1990) 'Structures for development, partnerships in the 1990s', *The Planner*, June: 15–19.

Wieberdink, A. and van Ketel, A. (1988) 'Institutionalisation of an environmental programme for a Third World: the establishment of an environmental institute in Nicaragua', *Development and Change* 19, 1: 139–157.

Williams, P.W. (1992) 'Tourism and the environment: no place to hide', *World Leisure and Recreation* 34, 2: 13–17.

Witt, S.F., Brooke, M.Z. and Buckley, P.J. (1991) *The Management of International Tourism*, London: Routledge.

Wolman, H. (1993) 'Cross-national comparision of urban economic programmes: is policy transfer possible?', in D. Frasenfest (ed.) *Community Economic Development Policy Formulation in the US and UK*, London: Macmillan.

Wood, C. (1989) *Planning Pollution Prevention*, Oxford: Heinemann.

Woodley, S. (1989) 'Management of water quality in the Great Barrier Reef marine park', *Water Science and Technology* 21, 2: 31–38.

WTO (World Tourism Organisation) (1980) *Physical Planning and Area Development for Tourism in the Six WTO Regions*, Madrid: WTO.

Zube, E.H. and Busch, M.L. (1990) 'Park–people relationships: an international review', *Landscape and Urban Planning* 19, 2: 117–131.

CHAPTER 5

Ahmad, A., Rawat, J.S. and Rai, S.C. (1990) 'An analysis of the Himalayan environment and guidelines for its management and ecologically sustainable development', *The Environmentalist* 10, 4: 281–298.

Buckley, R.C. (1991) 'How accurate are environmental impact predictions?', *Ambio* 20, 3/4: 161–162.

Beanlands, G. (1992) 'Scoping methods and baseline studies in EIA', in P. Wathern (ed.) *Environmental Impact Assessment: Theory and Practice*, London: Routledge.

Bisset, R. (1978) 'Quantification, decision making and environmental impact assessment in the United Kingdom', *Journal of Environmental Management* 7: 43–58.

Bisset, R. (1987) 'Methods for environmental impact assessment', in A.K. Biswas and Q. Geping (eds) *Environmental Impact Assessment for Developing Countries*, London: Tycooly International.

Bisset, R. (1992) 'Developments in EIA methods', in P. Wathern (ed.) *Environmental Impact Assessment: Theory and Practice*, London: Routledge.

Bisset, R. and Tomlinson, P. (1992) 'Monitoring and auditing of impacts', in P. Wathern (ed.) *Environmental Impact Assessment: Theory and Practice*, London: Routledge.

Butler, R.W. (1991) 'Tourism, environment, and sustainable development', *Environmental Conservation* 18, 3: 201–209.

Canter, L. (1983) 'Methods for environmental impact assessment: theory and application', in PADC Environmental Impact Assessment and Planning Unit (ed.) *Environmental Impact Assessment*, The Hague: Martinus Nijhoff.

CEC (Council of the European Communities) (1985) 'On the assessment of the effects of certain public and private projects on the environment', *Official Journal* L175: 40–48.

Cook, P.L. (1979) 'Costs of environmental impact statements and the benefits they yield to improvements to projects and opportunities for public involvement', paper given to the Economic Commission for Europe Seminar on Environmental Impact Assessment, Villach, Austria.

Cronin, L. (1990) 'A strategy for tourism and sustainable developments', *World Leisure and Recreation* 32, 3: 12–18.

Darbellay, C. (1982) 'Ecological problems in the Swiss Alps: the Pays D'Enhaut project', *International Social Science Journal* 34: 427–439.

Davies, G.S. and Muller, F.G. (1983) *A Handbook on Environmental Impact Assessment for Use in Developing Countries*, Nairobi: United Nations Environment Programme.

Dean, F.E. (1979) 'The use of environmental impact analysis by the British gas industry', paper given at the Symposium on Practices in Environmental Impact Assessment, European Commission, Brussels.

Dee, N., Baker, J.K., Drobny, N.L., Duke, K.M., Whitman, I. and Fahringer, D.C. (1973) 'An environmental evaluation system for water resource planning', *Water Resources Research* 9: 523–535.

Duffield, B.S. and Walker, S.E. (1984) 'The assessment of tourism impacts', in B.D. Clarke *et al.* (eds) *Perspectives on Environmental Impact Assessment*, London: D. Reidel.

Farrington, J.H. and Ord, D.M. (1988) 'Bure Valley railway: an environmental impact assessment', *Project Appraisal* 3, 4: 210–218.

FEARO (Federal Environmental Assessment Review Office) (1978) *Guide for Environmental Screening*, Ottawa: FEARO.

Gilliland, M.W. and Risser, P.G. (1977) 'The use of systems diagrams for environmental impact assessment: procedures and an application', *Ecological Modeling* 3, 3: 188–209.

Green, H. and Hunter, C. (1992) 'The environmental impact assessment of tourism development', in P. Johnson and B. Thomas (eds) *Perspectives on Tourism Policy*, London: Mansell.

Gunn, C.A. (1979) 'Assessing community potential: land analysis for tourism planning', in *A Decade of Achievement: Tenth Annual Conference Proceedings*, Travel Research Association.

Haigh, N. (1984) *EEC Environmental Policy and Britain*, London: Environmental Data Services.

Holder, J.S. (1988) 'Pattern and impact of tourism on the environment of the Caribbean', *Tourism Management* 9, 2: 119–127.

Holling, C.A. (1978) *Adaptive Environmental Assessment and Management*, Chichester, UK: John Wiley.

Htun, N. (1992) 'The EIA process in Asia and the Pacific region', in P. Wathern (ed.) *Environmental Impact Assessment: Theory and Practice*, London: Routledge.

Inskeep. E. (1987) 'Environmental planning for tourism', *Annals of Tourism Research* 14, 1: 118–135.

Jones, C.E., Lee, N. and Wood, C. (1991) 'UK environmental statements 1988–1990: an analysis', *Occasional Paper 29*, Manchester: EIA Centre, University of Manchester.

Kennedy, W.V. (1984) 'US and Canadian experience with environmental impact assessment: relevance for the European Communities?', *Zeitschrift für Umweltpolitik* 7: 339–366.

Kennedy, W.V. (1992) 'Environmental impact assessment and bilateral development aid: an overview', in P. Wathern (ed.) *Environmental Impact Assessment: Theory and Practice*, London: Routledge.

Kirkpatrick, L.W. and Reeser, W.K. (1976) 'The air pollution carrying capacities of selected Colorado mountain valley ski communities', *Journal of the Air Pollution Control Association* 26, 10: 992–994.

Korca, P. (1991) 'Assessment of the environmental impacts of tourism', proceedings of an International Symposium on Architecture of Tourism in the Mediterranean, Istanbul, Turkey: Yildiz University Press.

Laventhol and Horwath (1982) 'Tourism development strategy for the Peterborough-Haliburton tourism zone', Ontario, Canada: Ministry of Industry and Tourism.

Lavine, M.J., Butler, T. and Meyburg, A.H. (1978) 'Bridging the gap between economic and environmental concerns in EIA', *EIA Review* 2: 28–32.

Lee, N. and Wood, C. (1980) 'Methods of environmental impact assessment for use in project appraisal and physical planning', *Occasional Paper 7*, Manchester: Department of Town and Country Planning, University of Manchester.

Lee, N. (1989) 'Environmental impact assessment: a training guide', *Occasional Paper 18*, second edition, Manchester: EIA Centre, University of Manchester.

Lee, N. (1992) 'Training requirements for environmental impact assessment', in P. Wathern (ed.) *Environmental Impact Assessment: Theory and Practice*, London: Routledge.

Leopold, L.B., Clark, F.E., Hanshaw, B.B. and Balsley, J.R. (1971) 'A procedure for evaluating environmental impact', *US Geological Survey Circular* 645, Washington D.C.: Department of the Interior.

Linstone, A.H. and Turoff, M. (1975) *The Delphi Method: Techniques and Applications*, Reading MA.: Addison-Wesley.

Lohani, B.N. and Halim, N. (1987) 'Recommended methodologies for rapid environmental impact assessment in Developing Countries: experiences derived from case studies in Thailand', in A.K. Biswas and Q. Geping (eds) *Environmental Impact Assessment for Developing Countries*, London: Tycooly International.

Lohani, B.N. and Thanh, N.C. (1980) 'Impacts of rural development and their assessment in southeastern Asia', *Environmental Conservation* 7, 3.

McHarg, I. (1968) 'A comprehensive highway route-selection method', *Highway Research Record* 246, Washington D.C.: Highway Research Board.

Mader, V. (1988) 'Tourism and environment', *Annals of Tourism Research* 15, 2: 274–276.

Martin, B.S. and Uysal, M. (1990) 'An examination of the relationship between the carrying capacity concept and the tourism lifecycle: management and policy implications', *Journal of Environmental Management* 31: 327–333.

Miller, M.L. and Auyong, J. (1991) 'Coastal zone tourism: a potent force affecting environment and society', *Marine Policy* 15, 2: 75–99.

Milne, S. (1990) 'The impact of tourism development in small Pacific Island States: an overview', *New Zealand Journal of Geography* 89: 16–21.

Moreira, I.V. (1992) 'EIA in Latin America', in P. Wathern (ed.) *Environmental Impact Assessment: Theory and Practice*, London: Routledge.

Morrison, P. and Selman, P. (1991) 'Tourism and the environment: a case study from Turkey', *The Environmentalist* 11, 2: 113–129.

Murphy, T. (1981) 'EIA and developing countries', *Planning Outlook* 24.

Nelson, P.J. (1987) 'Environmental impact assessment: physical impacts and hazard', paper given at Town and Country Planning Summer School, Bristol, September.

Newson, M. (1991) 'Environmental assessment and the academic environmentalist', *Planning Outlook* 34, 2: 72–74.

Nijkamp, P. (1980) *Environmental Policy Analysis: Operational Methods and Models*, Chichester: Wiley.

Odum, E.P (1971) *Optimum Pathway Matrix Analysis Approach to the Environmental Decision-Making Process*, Georgia: Institute of Ecology, University of Georgia.

Omar, C.M. and Ariffin, J. (1992) 'The development and conservation of traditional culture and meaning in the landscape in enhancing tourism through community participation in Malaysia: a case study of "Kampong" Batu Feringghi, Penang, Malaysia', proceedings of an International Conference on Architecture of Soft Tourism, Trabzon, Turkey: Yildiz University Faculty of Architecture Press.

Ortolano, L. (1984) *Environmental Planning and Decision-Making*, New York: John Wiley.

Pawson, I.G., Stanford, D.D., Adams, V.A. and Nurbu, M. (1984) 'Growth of tourism in Nepal's Everest region: impact on the physical environment and structure of human settlements', *Mountain Research and Development* 4, 3: 237–246.

Pearce, D. (1989) *Tourist Development*, second edition, Harlow, Essex: Longman Scientific & Technical.

Pigram, J.J. (1990) 'Sustainable tourism: policy considerations', *Journal of Tourism Studies* 1, 2: 2–9.

Rauhe, W.J. (1992) 'Soft tourism: empowering citizens for community sustainability', proceedings of an International Conference on Architecture of Soft Tourism, Trabzon, Turkey: Yildiz University Faculty of Architecture Press.

Ravenscroft, N. (1992) 'The environmental impact of recreation and tourism development: a review', *European Environment* 2, 2: 8–13.

Roberts, P. and Hunter, C. (1992) 'Environmental assessment: taking stock', *Working Paper 11*, Leeds: Centre for Urban Development and Environmental Management, Leeds Metropolitan University.

Romeril, M. (1985) 'Tourism and the environment: towards a symbiotic relationship', *International Journal of Environmental Studies* 25, 4: 215–218.

Solomon, R.C., Colbert, B.K., Hanson, W.J., Richardson, S.E., Canter, L.W. and Vlachos, E.C. (1977) 'Water resources assessment methodology (WRAM): impact assessment and alternative evaluation', *Technical Report Y–77–1*, Vicksburg, MI.: US Army Corps of Engineers.

Sondheim, M.W. (1978) 'A comprehensive methodology for assessing environmental impact', *Journal of Environmental Management* 6: 27–42.

Sorenson, J.C. (1971) 'A framework for identification and control of resource degradation and conflict in the multiple use of the coastal zone', unpublished Masters thesis, University of California.

Starzewska, A. (1992) 'The legislative framework for EIA in centrally planned economies', in P. Wathern (ed.) *Environmental Impact Assessment: Theory and Practice*, London: Routledge.

Thor, E.C. *et al.* (1978) 'Forest environmental impact analysis: a new approach', *Journal of Forestry* November: 723–725.

UNEP (United Nations Environment Programme) (1988) *Environmental Impact Assessment: Basic Procedures for Developing Countries*, Bangkok: UNEP.

United States Government (1969) *National Environmental Policy Act*, Washington D.C.: United States Government Printing Office.

Wathern, P. (1992) 'An introductory guide to EIA', in P. Wathern (ed.) *Environmental Impact Assessment: Theory and Practice*, London: Routledge.

Wheatcroft, S. (1991) 'Airlines, tourism and the environment', *Tourism Management* 12, 2: 119–124.

Williams, P.W. (1987) 'Evaluating environmental impact and physical carrying capacity in tourism', in J.R.B. Richtie and C.R. Goeldner (eds) *Travel, Tourism and Hospitality Research: A Handbook for Managers and Researchers'*, New York: John Wiley & Sons.

Wood, C. and Jones, C. (1991) *Monitoring Environmental Assessment and Planning*, London: HMSO.

Wood, C. (1992) 'EIA in plan making',in P. Wathern (ed.) *Environmental Impact Assessment: Theory and Practice*, London: Routledge.

World Commission on Environment and Development (1987) *Our Common Future*, Oxford: Oxford University Press.

CHAPTER 6

Brittain, V. (1993) 'The canny key to paradise', article in the *Guardian* newspaper (London), 10th September 1993: 14–15.

CEC (Commission of the European Communities) (1992) *Towards Sustainability*, Brussels: CEC.

Glasson, J. (1993) 'Environmental Impact Assessment: only the tip of the iceberg yet?', lecture in the professional lecture series, School of Planning, Oxford Brookes University, 24th November 1993.

Lee, N. and Walsh, F. (1992) 'Strategic environmental assessment: an overview', *Project Appraisal* 7, 3: 126–136.

Patterson, K. (1993) 'Hawaii. Aloha! Welcome to paradise', *New Internationalist* 245: 13–15.

Rughani, P. (1993) 'From tourist to target!', *New Internationalist* 245: 7–12.

Therivel, R., Wilson, E., Thompson, S., Heaney, D. and Pritchard, D. (1992) *Strategic Environmental Assessment*, London: Earthscan.

WCED (World Commission on Environment and Development) (1987) *Our Common Future*, Oxford: Oxford University Press.

Wood, C. (1992) 'EIA in plan making', in P. Wathern (ed.) *Environmental Impact Assessment: Theory and Practice*, London: Routledge.

Index

Note: Towns, cities, topographical features and institutions are indexed by country (e.g. *Leeds* will be found under *England*; *Ayres Rock* under *Australia*)

acculturation 39
Acerenza, M.A. 98
acid deposition 21–2, 33, 44
Adams, V.A. 20, 25, 26, 158
Adaptive Environmental Assessment and Management (AEAM) 150
agreements 88–9
Ahmad, A. 25, 29, 158
air pollution: built environment 33; Environmental Impact Assessment 135; natural environment 21–2; *see also* pollution
Aitchison, J.W. 105
Alcock, D. 117
algal blooms 19, 26, 75
Alipour, H. 121
Alleyne, G.A.O. 40
alternative tourism 47, 78–86; adverse consequences 83–5; attributes 80; benefits 82–3; compared with mass tourism 85–6; planning model 81–2; tourist characteristics 82
ancient monuments 105
Andes route 99
Andronikou, A. 15, 20, 42
Antarctica 17, 20, 22
Antunac, I. 44

Archer, B.H. 40
architectural pollution 26–7
areas of outstanding natural beauty 105
Ariffin, J. 159
Ash, J. 40
Ashworth, G. 30
Ataby, S. 84
Australia: Ayres Rock 23; Great Barrier Reef 17, 117; impact predictions 167; mallee shrublands 43; Shark Bay 22, 25; Snowy Mountains 45
Austria 15
Auyong, J. 158
avalanches 15
aviation 21, 77
Ayala, H. 108

Baarse, C. 106
Baker, J.K. 139
Balbock, J. 114
Bali 34
Balsley, J.R. 142
Barbier, E.B. 53, 60, 61, 72
Barrow, G. 117
Bascom, W.W. 37
Batisse, M. 15, 99
Battista, G. 32

Beanlands, G. 160, 161, 162
Beauchamps, P. 117
Becheri, E. 19, 22
Beddington, N. 110
Beer, A.R. 108, 109
Bettum, O. 31
Bisset, R. 138–40, 145,
    148–52, 167
Bjonness, I.M. 39
Booth, P. 106–9, 120
Borgula, K. 15
Borys, T. 44
Braddon, C.J.H. 95
breeding grounds 16–17
Briand, F. 21
Briassoulis, H. 12–13
Bridge, N.J. 111
Briereton, U.A. 18
Brittain, V. 177
Brockleman, W.Y. 43
Brooke, J. 22–3
Brooke, M.Z. 111
Buckley, P.J. 37, 111
Buckley, R.C. 167, 168
built environment 11;
    erosion/pollution 32–3;
    infrastructure 29–32;
    restoration 32; tourism
    impacts 27–33; urban form
    27–9
Busch, M.L. 111
Butler, R.W. 47–8, 63–6, 75,
    80, 85, 89–91, 122
Butler, T. 148
Bywater, M. 19

Canada: British Columbia 119;
    climate change 45; design
    108; Environmental Impact
    Assessments 129; evaluation
    process 115; zoning 106
Canter, L. 132, 139, 151
carbon dioxide 21
Caribbean: negative tourism
    impacts 29, 30, 40;
    overfishing 25; restoration
    32; rural preservation 18;
    Tourism Research and
    Development Centre

(CTRC) 46; vegetation
    removal 15; water pollution
    20; water use 24
carrying capacity 48, 63–9
Chadwick, R.A. 2
Chapman, D. 109
Che, M. 102
Che, O. 102
Chernobyl nuclear accident 44
chlorofluorocarbons (CFCs) 23
Choy, D.J.L. 98
Clark, F.E. 142
climate change 45, 51
coastal resorts: England 20, 44;
    heritage coasts 113, 116,
    119; zoning 105, 106
Cohen, E. 34, 40, 41
Colbert, B.K. 139
conservation areas 105
Cook, P.L. 132
Copeland, E. 21
coral reefs 16, 19
Corder, O.M. 111
cost-benefit analysis (CBA):
    Environmental Impact
    Assessment 126; and
    sustainable development
    58–9, 62
Countryside Commission 105,
    108, 116, 119
crime 40
Cronin, L. 70–71, 94, 115,
    117, 122, 127, 158
Cullen, P. 113, 116
Cullingworth, J.B. 100
cultural environment 11–12;
    history 36–7; language/
    literature 37–8; religion 38;
    tourism impacts 33–40;
    traditional arts 37; values/
    norms 39–40
Cyprus: flora and fauna 15;
    restoration 32; sewage
    pollution 20, 22, 24–5

Darbellay, C. 158
Davies, G.S. 126
Davies, H.W.E. 100, 103, 107
de Groot, R.S. 16, 20

Dean, F.E. 132
Dearden, P. 43
decision-making 106–8,
    124–5
Dee, N. 139
definitions 1–6
deforestation 15, 25
Deitch, L.I. 37
Delphi technique 163
design 108–11
developers 132–4
development control 103–4
development evolution 63–9
Diatta, M. 111
Doak, J. 93
Dowling, R. 22, 25
Drobny, N.L. 139Dubost, M.
    21
Duffield, B.S. 68, 69, 127
Duke, K.M. 139
Dupuy, A.R. 16
Durst, P.B. 80, 82

Eagles, P.F.J. 85
ecological balance 13–18
economic development 4–5,
    53–7; versus sustainable
    development 57–63
economic effects of tourism
    38–9
education, environmental 48,
    83, 87; land use planning
    116–18
Edwards, D. 100, 103
Egypt 33
Elson, M. 93
employment opportunities
    38–9
energy conservation 76–7
England: Bradford 164;
    Canterbury 30, 33; coastal
    resorts 20, 44; Countryside
    Commission 105, 108, 116,
    119; Department of
    Environment Planning Policy
    Guidance notes 101–2; Essex
    Design Guide 109; Halifax
    27, 32; heritage coasts 113,
    116, 119; Leeds 101; London

30, 33; national parks 119;
    Norfolk 152, 157, 164;
    Norfolk Broads 20, 23;
    protection/designation
    104–6; regional policies 97;
    Thaxted 110; Town and
    Country Planning Acts
    105–6; Town Planning Acts
    100; Unitary Development
    Plan 101
English Tourist Board 77–8
environment: classification
    (natural/built/cultural)
    10–11; land use planning see
    land use planning;
    management 112–15;
    protection/designation
    104–6; resource base 6–9,
    10–12; resource base,
    modifying 47–8; rural
    112–14; tourism impacts see
    tourism impacts; see also built
    environment; cultural
    environment; natural
    environment
environmental audit 49–50,
    178
Environmental Evaluation
    System 139 Environmental
    Impact Assessment (EIA)
    122–68, 179–80; air
    pollution 135; background
    123–30; checklists 138–42;
    classification by task 137;
    community involvement
    157–64; cost-benefit analysis
    126; decision-making 124–5;
    definitions 125–6; European
    Community 127, 129–30;
    issues 164–8; matrices 142–6;
    methods 136–52; networks
    146–8; overlay mapping
    149–50; predictive
    techniques 152–7; principles
    125; selection criteria 127–8;
    simulation modelling
    150–51; social scoping
    160–64; and sustainable
    development 58–9, 62;

system features 130–36;
systems diagrams 148;
United States 126
Environmental Impact
Statements 124, 132–6
Erize, F. 17
erosion: built environment
32–3; and land use planning
113; natural
environment 22–3; soil erosion
15
Eskimo communities 39
European Alps 15, 21, 45
European Community 127,
129–30
expenditure on tourism 4–5

Fagence, M. 113
Fahringer, D.C. 139
Farrington, J.H. 152, 157, 164
Fennell, D.A. 85
Fiji 19
flora and fauna 13–18
Foley, P. 107, 115, 120
Forteza, V. 18
fossil fuels 76–7
France: Ardeche region 106;
Avignon 27; Brotonne
Nature park 43, 117;
Délégation d'Aménagement
de Territoire et de l'Action
Régional (DATAR) 97; land
use planning 100;
Mercantour National Park
117; Plan d'Occupation des
Sols 100; Pyrenees 20;
regional policies 97; Sociétés
de Dévelopment Mixte 118
free market 89
French, C.N. 113

Galapagos Islands 16, 20
Gasparavic, F. 39
Germany: Bavarian National
Park 15; Black Forest 21–2;
regional policies 97
Getz, D. 95
Gilbert, D. 2, 3–4
Gilliland, M.W. 148

global warming 21, 44–5
Gloor, B. 117
Goddard, J. 115, 116
golf courses 24, 25, 74
Graburn, N.H. 37
Grahn, P. 7, 34, 36
Grant, R. 43
Gray, H.P. 36
Greece: breeding grounds 17;
erosion 33; infrastructure 31;
Prespa National Park 46;
restoration 32
Green, D.H. 107, 110, 111,
120, 161–4
Green, M. 18
greenhouse effect 21
Greenwood, D. 38
Grenon, M. 15, 99
Greth, A. 17
Guatemala 99
Gunn, A. 99, 120
Gunn, C.A. 150
Gurung, H.B. 118

Hadjivassilis, I. 22, 25
Haigh, N. 123
Halim, N. 145, 146, 150–51
Hall, C.M. 118
Hall, P. 95
Hamele, H. 15, 16, 17, 21, 22,
24
Hanshaw, B.B. 142
Hanson, W.J. 139
hardwood trees 23
Harris, C.M. 17, 20, 22, 26
Harrison, M.L. 103
Hassan, R. 36
Haughton, G. 118
Hawaii: attitudes to tourism
176–7; environmental
protection 7; Visitor
Destination Areas 98; water
pollution 20
Hawkins, C. 64
Haywood, K.M. 96
Hazell, S.D. 43
Healey, P. 93, 96, 102, 106, 107
Heaney, D. 181
Heeley, J. 95

Henry, B. 19, 31, 108
Hick, D. 113
Hills, T.G. 42
Himalayas 25, 29, 38, 39
Himmetoglu, B. 80
history 36–7
Holder, J.S. 15, 20, 24, 29, 30, 32, 40, 46, 122
Holling, C.A. 150
Holloway, J.C. 108
Honduras 99
Hooper, A.J. 100, 103
Horwath, 150
housing stock 28–9
Htun, N. 123, 124, 130, 136, 165, 167
human needs/aspirations 53–7
Hunter, C. 110, 111, 125, 161–4
Hutchinson, P. 111

India: Goa 24; Taj Mahal 33
infrastructure 29–32; provision 88; tourism impacts 95
Inskeep, E. 96, 165, 168
inter-generational equity 54, 60–62
international tourism 5–6
interpretation 117–18
intra-generational equity 54, 60–62, 71–2
investments 89
Ireland 18
Isle of Skye 37–8
Italy: Adriatic coast 19; Florence 29; Genoa 32; Rimini 19; Venice 20, 26, 29, 33, 75

Jackson, I. 16, 23, 24, 25, 30
Jafari, J. 39
Jamaica 19, 31, 108
Jamieson, W. 108
Janssen, H. 87
Japan: Honshu Island 20; pollution 21
Jefferson, A. 3
Jenkins, M. 18

Jenner, P. 15, 17, 20–22, 24–6, 33, 44, 75
Jersey 110
Johnson, P.S. 37
Jones, C. 158, 167
Jones, R.J. 27, 32

Kaur, J. 34, 38
Kennedy, W.V. 124, 158
Kenya: pollution 25; tourism benefits 18; tourism dependency 36; traditions 39; vegetation 15
Kiers, M. 87
Kirkpatrick, L.W. 135
Klemm, M. 50, 86
Kocasoy, G. 20
Koea, A. 38
Korca, P. 121, 163
Korea 130
Krippendorf, J. 7, 82

Laarman, J.G. 80, 82
Lal, P.N. 19
land use planning 93–4, 96–8, 178–9; accountability 115; decision-making 106–8; design issues 108–11; development control 103–4; education 116–18; and erosion 113; international comparison 119–21; key elements 100; local authorities 106–8; local communities 111–12; local level 99–119; monitoring/evaluation 115–16; partnership 118–19; regulations 106–8; structure plans 99–103; zoning 106
language/literature 37–8
Lapland 34, 36
Larkham, P. 109
Lascurain, H.C. 4
Latham, J. 4–5, 6
Laventhol, 150
Lavine, M.J. 148
Lee, N. 127, 128, 132, 134, 137–8, 153, 156, 180–81

legal instruments 88
Leopold, L.B. 142
Lewis, S. 115
Lickorish, L. 3
Linstone, A.H. 163
listed buildings 105
litter 26
Liu, J.C. 7, 22
local communities 29, 34–6,
    111–12; Environment
    Impact Assessment 157–64;
    and sustainable tourism
    development 71–2
Lohani, B.N. 145, 146, 150–51
Luxmoore, R.A. 18

McDougall, G. 96
McEwen, A. and M. 105, 116
McHarg, I. 149
McKean, P.F. 34, 37
McNamara, P. 93
McNulty, R. 31
Madams, R. 18
Mader, V. 80, 159
Majorca: coastal ecosystem 18;
    coral reefs 15; pollution 22;
    re-vitalising mass tourism
    73–4
Malaysia: land use planning 96,
    159; Tourism Development
    Corporation 98, 102–3
Manser, M. 110
Marfurt, E. 34
Markandya, A. 53, 60, 61, 72
Marsh, J. 106
Martin, B.S. 63, 68, 69, 122
Martinez-Taberner, A. 18
mass tourism: attributes 80;
    compared with alternative
    tourism 85–6
Mathieson, A. 34, 66
May, R.J. 37
May, V. 48
Maya route 99
Mediterranean: Blue Plan 99;
    Integrated Mediterranean
    Programmes (IMP) project
    46–7
Mexico 99

Meyburg, A.H. 148
Michael, P. 32
Miller, J. 29
Miller, M.L. 158
Milne, S. 16, 20, 24, 25, 28, 32,
    112, 122, 133
ministries 96–7
Monnier, Y. 17
Moore, B. 116
moral values 39–40
Mordey, R. 112
Moreira, I.V. 124–5, 130, 167
Morgan, M. 15, 22, 73
Morrison, P. 4, 6, 17
Moya, G. 18
Muller, F.G. 126
Munt, I. 54, 60, 85
Murphy, P.E. 95, 119
Murphy, T. 125

national parks 105–6, 110, 113,
    119
national policies 96–7, 98–9,
    124–5
natural environment 11;
    erosion 22–3; flora and fauna
    13–18; natural resources
    23–6; pollution 18–22;
    tourism impacts 13–27;
    visual impact 26–7
natural resources 23–6;
    conservation 54–5;
    conservation versus economic
    development 57–63; equity
    of access 54; and inter-
    generational equity 61;
    preservation 62; resource
    base 6–9, 10–12; resource
    base, modifying 47–8
Nelson, P.J. 160
Nepal: cultural tourism 34;
    decision-making 158;
    deforestation 25;
    interpretation 118; litter 26;
    water pollution 20
New Zealand 118, 136
Newson, M. 156, 162, 167
niches 89
Nigeria 43

Nijkamp, P. 87, 126
nitrogen oxides 21, 22
noise pollution 22
North America; Eskimo
  communities 39; Great Lakes
  45; see also Canada; United
  States of America
Norton, D.A. 43
Norway 31
Nurbu, M. 20, 25, 26, 158

O'Donnell, M. 18
O'Reilly, A.M. 66–9
O'Riordan, T. 57, 59
Odum, E.P. 148
Olokesusi, F. 43
Omar, C.M. 159
Ord, D.M. 152, 157, 164
Ors, H. 98
Ortolano, L. 154
Ostrowski, S. 106
Owens, S. and P.L. 20

Pacific Islands: Cook Island 25;
  coral reefs 16; housing 28;
  restoration 32; tourism
  management 112; vegetation
  resources 25; water pollution
  20; water use 24
Pacione, M. 38
Page, S. 27, 28, 30, 33
Papadopoulos, S.I. 31, 32, 40
Patterson, K. 176–7
Pawson, I.G. 20, 25, 26, 158
Pearce, D. 13, 50, 53, 60, 61,
  63, 68–9, 72, 95, 123, 135,
  136, 167
Peltzer, R.H.M. 113
permissions (quotas) 89
Pertet, F.N. 15, 16, 18, 25
Peru 167
Pigram, J.J. 59, 72, 85, 90, 91,
  159, 161, 162
Pitt, D. 21
Pivert, M. 106
Pizam, A. 40
planning: Environmental
  Impact Assessments see
  Environmental Impact

Assessments; land use
  planning see land use
  planning; national policies
  96–7, 98–9; and tourism 94–6
Poland: environmental
  protection 106; pollution 33,
  44
pollution 44–5; air see air
  pollution; architectural 26–7;
  built environment 32–3;
  natural environment 18–22;
  noise 22; Poland 33, 44;
  sewage 19–20, 26; water
  19–21, 26
Poon, A. 5
Prechil, H. 36, 39
Pritchard, D. 181
prostitution 40
Prudzienica, J. 44
Punter, J.V. 97, 100, 103
Purton, R. 115
Pyrovetsi, M. 46

quotas 89

Rai, S.C. 25, 29, 158
Rambaud, D. 21
Ramon, G. 18
Rauhe, W.J. 81, 159
Rawat, J.S. 25, 29, 158
Reeser, W.K. 135
regional policies 97
Reime, M. 64
religion 38
restoration 32
Richardson, S.E. 139
Rijsberman, F.A. 106
Rinke, R. 42
Risser, P.G. 148
Roberts, P. 125
Robinson, F. 115, 116
Romeril, M. 6, 7, 11, 15, 18,
  23, 24, 29, 32, 33, 68, 74,
  134
Ronsseray, D. 27
Roper-Lindsay, J. 43
Roy, S.K. 111
Rughani, P. 175–6
rural environment 112–14

Russell, A. 113

Sahel states 18
Saint Martin Island, West
   Indies 17
Salm, R.V. 106
scoping 160–64
Scotland: Gaelic language
   37–8; land use planning 100
seasonal patterns 135
Selman, P. 4, 6, 17
Senegal 16, 111
sewage pollution 19–20, 26
sex industry 40
Seychelles 40, 177
Shaw, T. 93
Sheldon, P.J. 7, 22
Sindiyo, D.M. 15, 16, 18, 25
Singapore 36
Singh, T.V. 34, 38
Skeffington Report 111–12
Smith, C. 15, 17, 20–22, 24–6,
   33, 44, 75
Smith, K. 45, 51
Smith, S. 2
Smith, V. 39
social scoping 160–64
socio-economic change 127
soil erosion 15; see also erosion
Solomon, R.C. 139
Sondheim, M.W. 139
Sorenson, J.C. 146
South America: Andes route
   99; Peru 167
South Shetland Islands,
   Antarctica 17, 20, 22
souvenir trade 16
Springett, D.V. and B.P. 118
Srisang, K. 36, 40, 42
Stanford, D.D. 20, 25, 26, 158
Stankovic, S.M. 42
Stark, J. 20
Starzewska, A. 124
Strategic Environmental
   Assessment (SEA) 180–82
street furnishings 27
Stroud, H.B. 99
subsidies 88
sulphur oxides 21

sustainable development:
   concept of 52–63;
   cost-benefit analysis 58–9,
   62; Environmental Impact
   Assessments 58–9, 62;
   extreme resource-
   preservationist view 58–9;
   inter-generational equity 54,
   60–62; intra-generational
   equity 54, 60–62, 71–2;
   resource-conservationist view
   60–61; resource-exploitative
   view 57–8; sustainable
   tourism development see
   sustainable tourism
   development; and tourism
   carrying capacity 63–9; and
   tourism impacts 76–8; versus
   enconomic development
   57–63
sustainable tourism
   development 69–78; English
   Tourist Board guide 77–8;
   implementation 86–92; local
   communities 71–2; planning
   93–121; policy instruments
   86–9
Switzerland: acid deposition
   22; avalanches 15; cultural
   tourism 34; development 49,
   134; ecological research 158

Tananone, B. 20, 24, 25, 42, 91
Tanzania 17
taxation 88
Tenerife, Canary Islands 17–18
Thailand: cultural tourism 34;
   Environmental Impact
   Assessments 130; golf courses
   24, 25; health impacts 40;
   natural environment 43, 128;
   water pollution 20–21
Therivel, R. 181
Thiele, K. 15, 113
Thomas, M.J. 96
Thomas, R.D. 37
Thompson, S. 181
Thor, E.C. 146
Thurot, J.M. 50

Tiard, M. 43, 117
Tilden, F. 117
Tomlinson, P. 167
Tonga 38–9
tourism: activities 2; benefits 42–3; decisions 51; definitions 1–6; development control 103–4; development evolution 63–9; environmental impacts *see* tourism impacts; environmentally-conscious policies 42–7; as industry 2–5; planning 94–6
tourism impacts 10–51; amelioration measures 47–51; assessment 12–13; assessment *see* Environmental Impact Assessment; built environment 27–33; cultural environment 33–40; infrastructure 95; minimising 77–8; on natural environment 13–27; prediction 152–7; and sustainable development 76–8; and tourists 90–91
tourist environment management 112–15
tourist ghettos 34–6
town centre management 114–15
Townroe, P. 116
traditional arts 37
traffic congestion 30
Travis, A.S. 111
trees: deforestation 15, 25; hardwood 23; protection 105
Tunbridge, J. 30
Turkey: Black Sea region 84; breeding grounds 17; five-year development plan 98; Istanbul 7; land use planning 96; sewage pollution 20; tourism impacts 163; tourism planning 121
Turner, L. 40
Turner, R.K. 57, 60, 61
Turoff, M. 163

Turok, I. 115
turtles 17Tyler, C. 7, 15, 20, 24, 26, 42, 44

United Kingdom: Forestry Authority 111; *see also* England; Scotland; Wales
United States of America 31; Cape Cod 40; Colorado 135; Environmental Impact Assessments 126; Geological Survey 142; National Environmental Policy Act (1969) 126
urban environment management 114–15
urban form 27–9
Urbanowicz, C.F. 40
Uruguay 130
Uysal, M. 63, 68, 69, 122

values/norms 39–40
van Ketel, A. 120
Var, T. 7, 22
vegetation 15–16
visual impact 26–7
Vlachos, E.C. 139

Wahab, I. 102
Waite, C. 106
Wales 34; heritage coast programme 113, 116; language 37; North Wales 7; Town and Country Planning Acts 105–6; Town Planning Acts 100; Unitary Development Plan 101
Walker, S.E. 68, 69, 127
Walker, T.A. 17
Wall, G. 34, 66, 69
Walsh, F. 180–81
Wannup, U. 115
Watanabe, Y. 20
water: fresh-water supplies 23–5; pollution 19–21, 26
Water Resources Assessment Methodology 139
Wathern, P. 126, 128–9, 133–4, 158–60, 163

Westlake, T. 20, 29
Wheatcroft, S. 21, 77, 122
White, A. 20, 29
Whitman, I. 139
Whitney, D. 101, 102, 118
Wieberdink, A. 120
wildlife 13–18
Williams, P.W. 100, 152
Wilson, D. 38
Wilson, E. 181
Witt, S.F. 34, 37, 111
Wolman, H. 119, 120
Wood, C. 96, 124, 137, 158, 165, 167, 180
woodland protection 105

Woodley, S. 113
World Commission on Environment and Development 122, 175; report (1987) 53–7, 60, 61
World Travel and Tourism Council 122
Wren, C. 115, 116

Yap, V. 111

zoning 106; coastal resorts 105, 106
Zube, E.H. 111